The
EVERYTHING
Wedding Book
THIRD EDITION

Dear Reader:

You're engaged! Good for you—you found a winner! So . . . where and when do you start planning the wedding?

The answer is *now*. No matter how long your engagement, it's never too soon to start planning. I've seen various friends throw together beautiful weddings in a matter of months, and I've seen others plan events over the course of years. If you have a lot of time, take advantage of it—but if you're short on time, don't panic. There's a perfect wedding out there for every bride who's willing to do the work.

When I got married, my mom almost literally held my hand and took me through the process of planning my wedding. If you don't have the advantage of a personal (and free!) wedding consultant, this book will be a great help to you. It covers every aspect of the planning. The information is here at your fingertips—the rest is up to you.

Congratulations!

Shelly Hagen

The EVERYTHING® Series

Editorial

Publishing Director	Gary M. Krebs
Managing Editor	Kate McBride
Copy Chief	Laura MacLaughlin
Acquisitions Editor	Kate Burgo
Development Editor	Karen Johnson Jacot
Production Editor	Jamie Wielgus

Production

Production Director	Susan Beale
Production Manager	Michelle Roy Kelly
Series Designers	Daria Perreault
	Colleen Cunningham
Cover Design	Paul Beatrice
	Frank Rivera
Layout and Graphics	Colleen Cunningham
	Rachael Eiben
	Michelle Roy Kelly
	John Paulhus
	Daria Perreault
	Erin Ring
Series Cover Artist	Barry Littmann

Visit the entire Everything® Series at www.everything.com

THE
EVERYTHING®
WEDDING
BOOK
THIRD EDITION

The ultimate guide to planning
the wedding of your dreams

Shelly Hagen

A
Adams Media
Avon, Massachusetts

This book is for the women out there with the shiny new engagement rings on their fingers, the incessant grins on their faces, and the big dreams in their heads. Good luck, girls.

An Everything® Series Book.
Everything® and everything.com® are registered trademarks of F+W Publications, Inc.

Published by Adams Media, an F+W Publications Company
57 Littlefield Street, Avon, MA 02322 U.S.A.
www.adamsmedia.com

ISBN: 1-59337-126-8
Printed in the United States of America.

J I H G F E D C B

Library of Congress Cataloging-in-Publication Data
Hagen, Shelly.
The everything wedding book / Shelly Hagen.—3rd ed.
p.   cm.
(An everything series book)
Rev. ed. of: The everything wedding book / Janet Anastasio, Michelle Bevilacqua, and Stephanie Peters.
Rev. and expanded 2nd ed. c2000.
ISBN 1-59337-126-8
1. Wedding etiquette. 2. Weddings–Planning. I. Anastasio, Janet. Everything wedding book.
II. Title. III. Series: Everything series.
BJ2051.H34 2004
395.2'2–dc22
2004001788

This book is available at quantity discounts for bulk purchases.
For information, call 1-800-872-5627.

Contents

Acknowledgments

The following people made it possible for me to work on this book, and for that, I am in their debt: Jessica Faust, my agent at Bookends, who feeds me my work; Bethany Brown at Adams, for keeping me in mind for this project; and my husband, Mike, who is (almost) always ready with offers of encouragement and another cup of coffee.

Top Ten Utterances of the Bride
Who Didn't Consult This Book

1. "What do you mean I should have registered at a store? I registered to *vote*!"

2. "Thanks for coming to my shower. Sorry I can't invite you to my wedding. Great gift, though!"

3. "Gee, you know what? There's just no way to save money when you're planning a wedding."

4. "Sure, I invited my ex and his whole family. We're all friends!"

5. "Why *should* I ask my fiancé's parents what they want?"

6. "Wedding planners do the same thing that I could do . . . and I *will* do, after I'm done working eighty hours this week."

7. "I'll just go ahead and bake my own wedding cake. I'll make it from brownie mix and just pile it all up like a big tower."

8. "Even though my fiancé has wild tastes and we're having a traditional wedding, I trust him to pick out his own tux."

9. "Our honeymoon is going to be absolutely perfect, or it will mean that we made a big mistake getting married."

10. "Adjusting to married life? Piece of cake!"

Introduction

▶ DING DONG! Are those wedding bells you hear? Congratulations on your engagement and on finding the man of your dreams! Though you've been busy showing off your ring (and cleaning it and admiring it on your hand), you need to get yourself in gear. Time's a-wasting! You have an event to plan, and you can't start soon enough.

Whatever kind of wedding you have in mind, chances are you'll run the bridal gamut through the dress shops, through the reception halls, through the caterer's office, through the baker's shop . . . and you'll be exhausted long before the big day arrives. Maybe you'll enlist the help of a wedding planner, or maybe you'll just start going to bed a lot earlier so that you can deal with the long days ahead.

The funny thing about planning the various aspects of a wedding is that each little part of the planning takes on a life of its own once you get into it. Who knew that your wedding cake could come in any flavor under the sun, and almost any shape? No one ever told you that a limo isn't the only option for transporting you and your wedding party around town. And the honeymoon—narrowing down *those* choices is practically a job unto itself, an exercise in which you and your future husband will become adept negotiators.

Since you've probably never taken on the planning of a wedding, you may be feeling overwhelmed. But don't brides plan weddings every day? They make it look so easy! Don't be fooled. The brides who went before you were just as nervous and as unsure as you might be feeling right now. They educated themselves on the finer points of planning a wedding, which is how they pulled off their own successful ceremonies and receptions. All you have to do is find the information you need, and your wedding will be a hit, too.

Remember what you learned in school—there are no silly questions. If you don't know something, ask. If, for example, you're interviewing a photographer and you have no idea what he's talking about when he mentions candid shots, stop him right there and make him explain. You can't make an educated decision without all the information.

The Everything® Wedding Book also provides you with lots of helpful information about whom you'll be hunting down and what to ask them when you find them. It takes you through your engagement season straight through to your walk down the aisle, answering many of the questions you run into along the way. The appendices are filled with worksheets that will help you to get organized and stay that way, so that nothing (and no one) gets lost in the process of planning the big day.

Above everything else, take the time to enjoy this time in your life. You may not believe it now, but your wedding will be a memory one day—you want the days leading up to it to be as special as your marriage is.

Congratulations, best wishes . . . now get crackin'!

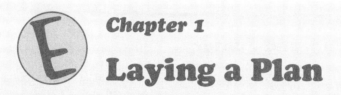

Chapter 1

Laying a Plan

Congrats! You're engaged! You've got a lot of things to consider before you reach the state of wedded bliss. You have to figure out how to announce the news, pick a date, plan the finances, find a consultant, and last—but by no means least—adapting to the diplomacy upon which every successful wedding depends. This is the beginning of a long road—whether the trip turns out to be a smooth or jarring and bumpy one depends largely on the initial planning.

Hear Ye, Hear Ye!

Once you've made the big decision, you'll probably want to tell everyone you know—and even people you don't. But wait! As hard as it may be in all the excitement, calm down. Collect yourself, and think about who should be told first. There is a certain protocol that should be followed, and you don't want to offend anyone.

Telling Mom, Pop, and Junior

Announce your engagement in person to both sets of parents first. If either set lives too far away for you to do so, call them to pass on the good news. If possible, try to arrange a visit soon so that everyone can start getting acquainted (if they haven't already). Discuss the possibility of getting all the future in-laws together before the wedding.

If your or your fiancé's parents are divorced and/or remarried, think long and hard about which parent to inform first. You know your family better than anyone else does. Do what you feel most comfortable with.

If either you or your groom has children from a previous marriage, make sure you tell them of the impending new marriage right away. Don't let them hear it from someone else! A parent's new marriage can be a delicate and stressful event for children. Give them all the reassurance they need, try to sense and quell their fears, and make them as much a part of the wedding as the situation allows.

FACT

Bowing to protocol is something you're going to have to get used to. Unless you truly feel comfortable throwing courtesy and tradition to the wind, protocol is usually as big a part of planning and having a wedding as your budget, your gown, and your guest list.

Your Ex Carries an Ax (?!)

You should also inform your own former spouse (if you have one) of your new marriage plans. Don't send the word through someone else, and avoid using a child to send this message. If things are still tense between the two of you, send a note. Issues of alimony and child support may come up; try to resolve them calmly and rationally. You don't want any old problems resurfacing as you start your new life.

Of course, if you feel your former spouse is the type to try to disrupt your wedding, you will want to keep all wedding details quiet. Ultimately, it would be best if he or she did not know of the impending nuptials; you can drop the bomb later. If the problematic former spouse lives out of state, hiding a wedding is a great deal easier, but if he or she resides in the same city, it's important to keep the festivities as private as possible. Make sure family and mutual friends don't spill the beans, and refrain from newspaper and other public announcements.

If you don't have custody of your children but you want them to attend the wedding without the knowledge of your former spouse, get ready for some fancy footwork. Schedule the nuptials for one of your times of scheduled visitation.

ALERT!

The issue of a former spouse can be a source of great difficulty for a couple planning to get married. The best course to take is to be open and honest with your fiancé and both of your families; together, you should be able to decide what's best for all.

Your Late Spouse's Family

If either you or your groom were married before to a person who is now deceased, news of the remarriage may be painful to the late spouse's parents. Depending on how close you are to them, you may choose to tell them about your marriage in person or with a tactful note. Whatever the mode, make sure it's *you* who tells them; don't let them hear it through the grapevine.

Formal Announcements

After all the delicate family matters have been taken care of, it's time to start yelling the news from the rooftops. Tell your friends. Tell your coworkers. Tell the paperboy. Tell the grocery clerk. Tell until you don't want to tell anymore or until someone sticks a sock in your mouth— whichever comes first.

See You in the Funny Pages!

One easy and time-tested way to spread the word of your impending nuptials is through a newspaper announcement. This announcement is usually made by the parents of the bride; typically, it gives general information about her and the groom, their schooling, careers, and so on. Many couples include an official engagement photo along with the announcement.

The announcement information is usually sent to the lifestyle or society editor, but you should call the paper's offices just to make sure. You should also inquire about any fees associated with placing an announcement.

If the groom's family lives in another city or state, send them a copy of your engagement photo so that they can announce the good news in their local paper, too.

Timing It Right

If you're planning a very long engagement (one year or more), you may want to wait a while before sending an announcement to the news-paper, as they are usually printed no earlier than a year before the wedding. Many papers will advise you on this matter, but generally speaking, it's a good idea to announce your impending nuptials during a particular window of time—not too early, and not too close to the wedding itself. (Three to four months before the wedding is appropriate.)

Pick a Date, Any Date

When people learn of your engagement, the first thing you're likely to hear after "Congratulations!" is "When's the date?" Until you set a date, you will have no good answer to this question, and what's worse, you will be unable to go ahead with any of your other planning.

Picking the date is absolutely crucial. Without it, you have no accurate idea of when you will need the ceremony and reception sites. You won't know how long you have to find a dress; when you will need a photographer, a caterer, a florist, or any of the other professionals whose time you will be paying for; or even what colors or kinds of flowers would look best in that season.

Seasons' Reasons

What season do you prefer? Do you want a garden wedding in the spring? A seaport wedding in the summer? A fall celebration at a refurbished farmhouse? Does the season matter to you at all? If not, is there a time of year that your family or the groom's family finds particularly meaningful? Once you settle the issue of the season (if there *is* an issue, that is), you can start working on the details.

How much time do you have to plan the wedding? Does the availability of a ceremony and reception site coincide with your desired date? Are there conflicts that might complicate matters for you, your family, or attendants (such as another wedding, a vacation, a graduation, or a pregnancy/birth)? It's doubtful your matron of honor is going to enjoy standing beside you in her eighth month, wearing a dress that could double for a tent. By the same token, your parents are unlikely to appreciate having to choose between attending your wedding and your brother's high school graduation.

FACT

The peak season for weddings is between April and October, so there may be a lot of competition for everything from flowers to frosting if you plan a wedding in those months. In comparison, off-peak weddings are often much easier to plan.

Are there military commitments to consider? If either you or your fiancé is in the military, you must work out an appropriate time to take leave. The same is to be considered if there is a close relative or special friend in the military who wishes to be there for your big day.

The most popular months for weddings are August, June, and

September. December is also popular, most likely because of the festive air and beautiful decorations of the Christmas season.

Happy Holidays?

Should you have your wedding on a holiday weekend, such as Memorial Day, Labor Day, or Columbus Day? There are pros and cons to this idea. On the plus side, people may appreciate a wedding on a long weekend; it gives them an extra day to recuperate from the festivities or to travel, if they are coming from another city or state.

For you and your fiancé, taking your honeymoon during a holiday week may give you an extra day away (or allow you to save a vacation day for a later time).

But what if your guests have some long-weekend vacation plans of their own? This is where problems may arise. Some people, for instance, may not be able to attend a wedding scheduled for the Friday after Thanksgiving because of obligations to visit family who live out of town. On the other hand, your own out-of-town relatives might appreciate the convenience of a single trip combining both the holiday and the wedding.

ALERT!

If you have friends who are Jewish (especially friends you want to include in the wedding party), you may want to schedule around Jewish holidays so they aren't faced with a tough decision—their religious observance or your wedding.

A wedding during the Christmas season can be a beautiful and spiritual experience, but it can also be very hectic for you, your attendants, and your guests. You will need to plan for a wedding and get your shopping, wrapping, cooking, and similar projects done in time for the holiday, and that can be quite a chore.

If you and/or your spouse is Jewish, there are certain religious restrictions placed on dates you should be aware of. Weddings are not permitted on the Sabbath (Friday evening to Saturday one half hour after sundown) or the major holidays (Rosh Hashanah, Yom Kippur, Passover, Shavuot, and Sukkot).

Setting a Budget

You say money is no object when it comes to your wedding? You say you're one of the very few (and very lucky) people with an unlimited supply of funds just waiting to be spent on the wedding of a lifetime? Great! Go all out, and make your wedding an extravaganza filled with all you've ever dreamed of.

If you're like most people these days, though, you'll need to set up a budget. If money is especially tight, it's best to prioritize so that your wedding can have the things that are most important to you. Where to begin?

What Kind of Wedding?

First, decide on the type of wedding you want. Your job is to try to construct a budget based on your desires, using the resources available. Perhaps you and your fiancé don't even want a "big" formal (or semi-formal) wedding. You may both shy away from frills and thrills, preferring to avoid much of the headache and expense by holding a small, simple affair. If this is how you want to go, there are plenty of options: a back-yard wedding, a wedding in a home, a civil ceremony—it's up to the two of you.

You may decide, though, that you want as much of the grand, traditional wedding that your budget will allow. In either case, planning expenses becomes particularly important. You'll want to make every dollar go as far as it possibly can.

Run the Numbers

After you decide on the type of wedding you'd like to have, you'll need to figure out exactly how you're going to afford it. The amounts you allocate yourself will help you to determine the number of guests you can invite, the location of your reception, the food you will serve, the number of photographs you will have taken, the flowers on display, and just about every other element of the celebration.

There are two ways of going about setting a budget. The first is to determine the amount of money that's available right now. This will include any money that you and your fiancé may have squirreled away for the event, as well as any contributions that you're aware of. For instance, you might know exactly how much your parents have saved in your wedding fund. The total of these resources is your total budget—assuming that you're planning on paying cash for the bulk of your wedding expenses.

If there's no wedding fund, but you're pretty sure your parents will want to chip in and help defray the cost of the whole shindig, try tallying up the cost of your ideal wedding before asking for financial assistance. You may find that you'll get a better response if you have a ballpark figure to present (rather than asking for a vague contribution). The worksheet in Appendix A will be a valuable resource to you in this regard, as it will give you a good idea of the amount of services and items many weddings include.

You'll need to do your homework. If you have friends who have recently been married, don't be shy about asking them how much they paid for what. Most newlyweds are happy to pass on the wisdom they gained from going through the wedding-planning experience themselves.

FACT

Though your figures may differ from your friends' in the end—you may want to spend more on photography than they did, or decide to have a DJ instead of a band—at least you'll have a idea of what certain services might cost.

Once you've consulted your friends, pick up the phone. Call a variety of reception sites and caterers and ask for their wedding menus to get an idea of how much the per-person charges can run. Be sure to ask for any additional fees you may be charged (such as rental fees, setup fees, gratuity, corkage, or cake-cutting fees). Do the same with photographers, limousine services, videographers, and any other service you might want.

Once you have the paperwork in hand, you can insert cost ranges into the budget to give you a "cheapest to costliest" scenario. You can also find the average price of each item for an overall approximate picture.

Then it's off to the parents to ask the big money question . . .

Traditional Expenses

It is customary for the bride's family to bear the majority of the wedding expenses, but circumstances can dictate other arrangements. These days it is not uncommon for the bride and groom to bear the brunt of the wedding expenses themselves. If the idea of paying for your own wedding sends your head spinning (especially after you start finding out how much things can cost!), keep in mind that your own opinions carry more weight if *you* are the one writing the check.

The opposite holds true if you accept contributions from your parents. If you're spending their money, you'll want (or will be encouraged—by them) to carefully consider all their suggestions.

The bride and her family traditionally pay for the following:

- The groom's wedding ring and gift
- Invitations, reception cards, and announcements
- Bride's wedding gown and accessories
- Fee for ceremony location
- Flowers for ceremony and reception (including flowers for attendants)
- Photography
- Music for ceremony and reception
- All reception costs (location rental, food, decorations, and so on)

Other expenses include rented transportation, such as limousines; accommodations for bridesmaids; and gifts for bridesmaids.

ALERT!

Remember: These are *traditional* guidelines. If circumstances require that you do things differently for your own wedding, don't be afraid to throw out tradition. Be aware though, that other traditions will go out the window, too. (You can't be too choosy about the food if your future in-laws are paying for it.)

The groom and his family are traditionally held responsible for these expenses:

- The bride's wedding and engagement rings
- Gift for the bride
- Marriage license
- Officiant's fee
- Bride's bouquet, mothers' and grandmothers' corsages, boutonnieres for groom's wedding party
- Rehearsal dinner
- Honeymoon

His family may also opt to pay for the groomsmen's lodging.

Cash, Check, or Charge?

You will have to start tapping into your wedding funds the minute you begin hiring people and renting places for your wedding because most will require a deposit of some sort. There are three ways to handle payments: cash, check, or charge. Most people don't carry around wads of hundred-dollar bills, so for the sake of argument, the discussion will center on checks and credit cards.

Where's That Money?

If your parents have set aside a lump sum for your wedding, you can do one of three things. Ask for the sum to be deposited into your or your fiancé's checking account so you can write checks as you need to; have your parents send the checks directly to the person or place being hired (keep in mind, however, that if someone else's check gets there first, they may beat you to the band or reception site you wanted); or set up a separate checking account just for the wedding money.

This last option might prove the easiest all around. You know that the money you take from the account was set aside solely for wedding expenses and that you're not accidentally tapping into your rent money.

You have the option of adding to the account, should extra money come your way. You'll also have your cancelled checks as proof positive that your deposits and payments were cashed—just in case a question ever comes up.

Credit Caution

Using a credit card can also be a handy way of keeping track of your deposits and payments, but be careful to remember how much you've charged each month so you're not surprised when your statement arrives—and be sure to pay off each bill as it comes in so your credit rating doesn't suffer. Remember, weddings can cost thousands of dollars. You don't want to begin your life together with that kind of credit-card debt hanging over your head!

Wedding Consultants

Professional wedding planners may not have quite the same recognition as professional athletes and entertainers, but to many harried brides, they are truly superstars. Otherwise known as wedding consultants, these walking wedding encyclopedias will either have the answers to all your questions or know where to find them. You'll pay for the expertise, of course—but if your schedule is a hectic one, you may come to the conclusion that it's worth it.

Since weddings are their business, consultants are experienced in every area of wedding planning. They have the knowledge, ideas, and contacts you might not otherwise be able to take advantage of.

Why?

Not everyone needs or wants a consultant, and you shouldn't feel you have to hire one just because someone else does. Some brides enjoy planning their own weddings and have plenty of time to do so. For them, the process is as important and exciting as the result. Others—who have at their disposal the past experience of their mother, aunts, sisters, friends, cousins, and so on—ask why they should pay for the advice when they can get it for free.

But there are also brides out there who don't have the help of anyone with experience, or who don't have the time or energy required to plan the wedding they want. It can be very difficult for a woman who works sixty hours a week and/or happens to live across the country from her mother (or sister, or friends) to plan a wedding entirely by herself.

Sounds like your life? You may find that a consultant can relieve a great deal of the planning pressure you find yourself facing.

Types of Consultants

There are two types of wedding consultants: independent and store-affiliated. Independent consultants can help you with all phases of the wedding and may even act as the master or mistress of ceremonies at the reception. A consultant like this can sit down with you and plan your wedding from A to Z. She can act as the go-between for you and the florist, baker, caterer, DJ/band, and photographer. In fact, she can do just about everything for you except show up in a white dress on your wedding day.

If you decide to go this route, make sure you're honest about your budget from the beginning. Because of her extended contacts and experience, your consultant should be able to help you stick to your budget and still include most of the things you really want.

Store-affiliated consultants are those people employed by the bridal salons, reception sites, and other businesses that cater to weddings. Their knowledge may not be as broad as the independent's, but they will be able to help you with any questions you have that fall within their areas of expertise.

It's essential to communicate your desires and to double-check that the consultant understands them. If you tell her you'd like the reception band to specialize in harmonies, you may not be thrilled to find out later that she'd booked a barbershop quartet.

Stealing the Show?

Remember that hiring a wedding consultant does not mean you have to stand in a corner while someone else makes all the decisions.

With an independent consultant, you will want to select someone who listens to your needs and ideas and who you feel is capable of handling the job. Ask friends, family, and coworkers for referrals. If they all come up empty, consult the local phone book and ask people in the industry, such as florists, photographers, and bridal shops.

Once you find someone you think you might be interested in working with, you'll schedule an appointment with her. What will you ask her?

- How long has she been in business?
- Is she a full-time or part-time consultant?
- Does she have any references?
- How many weddings does she plan in a typical month? On a typical weekend?
- What is the cost, and how will you be charged? (Hourly? Flat fee? Percentage?)
- What is included in her quoted price?

The consultant you choose may offer different levels of service, giving you the option of either hiring her to help you plan the entire event down to the tiniest detail or simply using her services for scoping out reception locations and caterers.

ALERT!

You will want to avoid any consultant who seems likely to disregard your wishes and run away with the show. You should also keep an eye out for overall compatibility. Look for someone who seems likely to work well with you and who specializes in the areas where you require assistance.

Don't forget to check references. She may seem wonderful, but she could also be using your money to book herself a cruise around the world instead of a reception site for your wedding.

The cost of a wedding consultant will vary, depending upon the type and extent of service you require. Some will bill for 10 to 20 percent of the total cost of the wedding, while others will charge a flat fee. Store-affiliated consultants, on the other hand, are usually at your service at no extra charge, provided you are already doing business with their shop.

If you think you might want to work with an independent consultant but doubt that you can afford one, don't be afraid to ask around. Some consultants receive commissions from the companies they refer business to, a practice that allows them to offer their services at a lower rate than they otherwise would. And although it may not feel quite as luxurious as working with a private consultant, this book can do much the same job when it comes to providing help in planning your wedding—and at a much cheaper rate!

Tick Tick Tick . . .

You may think you have all the time in the world, but beware: The last thing you want is to suddenly discover that it's three months before your wedding and you don't have a dress yet.

Draw up a schedule, and stick to it. Though your tendency may be to procrastinate in the early months, don't! If it can be done months before the wedding, do it months before the wedding. Don't worry—you won't be bored later. There will be *plenty* to do as the wedding draws near. Wouldn't you rather be free to deal with last-minute details in the weeks prior to the ceremony instead of being bogged down by tasks that could have (and should have) been done much earlier?

Plan to secure the key items in your wedding (ceremony site, reception site, caterer, photographer, flowers, gown, rings, music) as far in advance as possible. Starting early gives you the breathing room to take your time and make unrushed choices.

The Diplomacy of Planning

Planning a wedding can be a hectic and stressful experience. Quite often tempers will flare, particularly when nerves act up—you may end up wanting to choke your parents, your fiancé, your friends, and anyone else who gets in the way. What you don't need in this already explosive atmosphere is any unexpected sticks of dynamite, issues such as family feuding, friends fighting, and relationship politics in general.

The In-Laws and the Outlaws

The bride's family traditionally plans the majority of the wedding details. This can sometimes make the groom's family feel left out or as if they are being ordered around without consideration. If you're concerned there may be some competition between families, take some steps toward achieving a warm, cooperative environment.

If possible, get the families acquainted a bit before the formal engagement is announced. With luck, the families will get along, and some rapport can develop between the parents. When it comes time to work together, everybody will feel comfortable with one another and you'll all be free to focus on the wedding— instead of on each other's peculiar personality traits.

Keep the lines of communication open for all the wedding details, and consult with both families on all major decisions. Encourage both mothers to consult with one another on any major events that each is planning. For example, if your mother is hosting an engagement party for you and the future groom, your future mother-in-law would probably appreciate feeling like more than an invited guest. She may be more than happy to help out with the menu or the decorations.

The groom's family may offer to take on other responsibilities in addition to the rehearsal dinner, or they may offer financial assistance. If the bride's family decides to accept, make sure everyone behaves graciously. It wouldn't be wise for the bride's parents to take money from the groom's parents and then refuse to let them make suggestions.

If the bride's family declines the money (for whatever reason), they should be gracious and friendly. Make sure they let the groom's family know that even if their money is not needed, their suggestions and input are welcome.

There are other ways to make the groom's family an active part of the wedding. Include them in the ceremony, perhaps by asking them to do a reading or light a candle; have the groom's father walk the groom's mother down the aisle as part of the procession; put both sets of parents' names on the invitation (and anything else you can think of).

For your part, be patient and, most of all, diplomatic; you want to step into the biggest day of your life with your best foot forward.

Chapter 2

The Meaning Behind the Traditions

Have you ever wondered why a bride wears a veil? Why people throw rice at the newlyweds? Why certain ethnic groups do certain things at their weddings? These traditions (and many others) have been a part of weddings for centuries. It's a pretty good bet you'll include some of them at yours and that you'll see many of them in other weddings that you attend. If you really just have to know what's good luck, what's bad luck, and what's just plain silly, read on.

Pre-Wedding Customs

Before you walk down the aisle, you'll find yourself involved in many activities that seem commonplace. Every engaged woman does these things, right? Once you discover the origin of many of these customs, you may have a whole new outlook on them.

Do you ever wonder why your fiancé proposed with a diamond engagement ring? In medieval Italy, precious stones were seen as part of the groom's payment for the bride. The groom would give a gift of such stones, which symbolized his intent to marry.

Though the traditional engagement ring holds a diamond at its center, you may have your heart set on another stone. Speak up and let your feelings be known! There's nothing more romantic than an engagement ring with individual flair.

The custom of gifting the bride-to-be is believed to have started in Holland, where legend has it that a disapproving father would not provide his daughter with a dowry so that she might marry a less-than-wealthy miller. Her friends provided her with the then-essential dowry by "showering" her with gifts. (If only you knew who this mysterious Dutch girl's friends were . . . so that you could thank them for starting this tradition!).

When French brides went to their new homes with their new husbands, they brought their clothes and other meager possessions with them in a small bundle. The French word for this bundle was *trousseau*. When the standard dowry became more than what you could carry in a small bundle, the name was no longer adequate, but it stuck just the same. Today, the gifts a bride-to-be receives at her wedding shower could be considered a modern-day version of the trousseau.

Ceremony Customs

Why do people wear rings on that one finger that's also impossible to hold up on its own? (Well, they just do, and that's all the reason *you* need.) Dig deeper, and you'll find that the true reason is really due to an incorrect physiological assumption from centuries past. (Suddenly intrigued, are you? Keep reading.)

The Ring Finger

The third finger on the left hand is considered the ring finger. All engagement and wedding rings are worn there because centuries ago that finger was believed to be connected by a vein directly to the heart. The idea of the wedding ring itself dates back to ancient times, when a caveman-husband would wrap circles of braided grass around his bride's wrists and ankles, believing it would keep her spirit from leaving her body. The bands evolved into leather, carved stone, metal, and later silver and gold. (Luckily, you only have to wear them on your finger nowadays—and the groom usually reciprocates.)

Keep in mind that your wedding bands don't need to match. If you're only comfortable wearing gold but your future husband prefers platinum, it's perfectly acceptable to pick out rings that will suit each of your tastes.

FACT

Back when a daughter was considered her father's possession, some formal transfer was necessary during the wedding ritual. Today, the custom of giving the bride away symbolizes the parents' acceptance of the bride's passage from child to adult, and a sign of their blessing of her marriage to her chosen groom.

The Wedding Cake

Wedding cakes originated in ancient Rome, where a loaf of wheat bread was broken over the bride's head to symbolize hope for a fertile and fulfilling life. The guests ate the crumbs, which were believed to be good luck.

The custom found its way to England in the Middle Ages. Guests brought small cakes to a wedding; the cakes were put in a pile, which the bride and groom later stood over while they kissed. Apparently, someone came up with the idea of piling all the cakes together and frosting them, creating an early ancestor of the multitiered wedding cakes of today.

(And apparently someone *else* came up with the idea that newlyweds should humiliate each other by smashing the confection into one another's faces at the reception. Whether you choose to follow this part of the tradition should be based on how fast you can run away from your groom before he returns the favor by ruining your hair and makeup with icing.)

The Bride's Must-Have Accessories

Brides are fairly particular about their wedding-day wear. Many brides will simply not leave the house until every last tradition has been followed. Most brides do this without knowing why. When your friends ask you why you're insisting on wearing blue underpants under your wedding dress, you'll be able to tell them. And don't forget—no bride's ensemble is complete without a friend or two to stand by her as she takes her vows.

"Something Old, Something New . . . "

The odds are pretty good that you'll be wearing all of the above on your wedding day. But do you know why? The *old* is to stand for a bride's ties to her past; the *new* represents her hope for the future; the *borrowed* item is something that's dear to a close friend or family member—and must be returned to ensure good luck; and the *blue* is thought to come from an Israeli tradition, when brides wore blue ribbons to symbolize fidelity.

In a traditional English poem, the custom is as follows:

Something old, something new
Something borrowed, something blue,
And a lucky sixpence in your shoe.

The coin in the shoe is to symbolize wealth in the coming years, and many brides still slip a coin into their shoe before they walk down the aisle. In the United States, the dime is the currency of choice.

The Veil

The symbolism of the veil, like many other wedding traditions, has many theories behind it. One theory suggests that the veil was used as a disguise to foil any evil spirits. (In this same theory, the bridesmaids are also used as decoys.) In other legends, veils were originally meant to symbolize the virgin bride's innocence and modesty.

These days, our society considers the veil a purely romantic custom. But in parts of the Middle East and Asia, the veil is still used to hide the bride's face completely.

The first lace veil is said to have been worn by Nelly Curtis, George Washington's adopted daughter, who married one of his aides. Apparently, the first time the aide ever saw her, she was behind a lace curtain. He was mesmerized by her beauty. Nelly, the story goes, made herself a lace veil for the ceremony in an effort to duplicate the effect.

The Attendants

What's the point of having all those attendants standing up for you? Aside from the help they offer with all the wedding planning and pre-wedding craziness, they have had other purposes in the past.

The Best Man and Ushers

Your groom proposed in the most romantic way. Consider yourself lucky. The groom from way back when used to take a group of his friends with him while in pursuit of the bride to help him capture her.

Often as not, young brides were "kidnapped" from a protective family—which typically included a few big brothers. Sometimes there would even be a battle between competing suitors. If a potential groom wanted to show that he meant business, he took along the "best men" for the job of helping him fight for his love. Aren't you glad you live in *this* century?

The Maid of Honor and Bridesmaids

These were the women who helped the bride get away from her overprotective family and other suitors so that she could be captured by the groom she wanted. (Kind of like when your best friend would wait with her car while you snuck out your bedroom window to go clubbing and meet your beau.) Even after such difficult methods of getting the bride and groom together faded in popularity, the honor roles survived.

After "I Do"

You don't want to end up spitting out rice or having to show your garter off to the whole world? Knowing the reasons behind these traditions might just help you to eliminate the ones you find unnecessary.

Throwing Rice—and *Shoes?*

The tradition of throwing rice began in the Orient. Rice (which symbolizes fertility) was thrown at the couple in the hope that this would bring a marriage yielding many children.

ALERT!

Many churches and wedding locations no longer permit the throwing of rice after weddings, as it's a fatal snack for most birds. Birdseed is sometimes offered as an option, but check with your location first. Depending on where the seeds are thrown, they may cause some guests to slip.

Throwing shoes at the newlyweds' carriage in Tudor times was also a way to wish the couple luck, and this is the reason why shoes are sometimes tied to the back of the newlyweds' getaway vehicle. The bride's father would also sometimes give the groom a pair of the bride's shoes as a symbolic passing of the responsibility for this woman. The well-known tradition of tossing the bouquet was originated by the custom of brides throwing a shoe over their shoulder.

Tossing the Garter and Bouquet

This custom may have begun in fourteenth-century France, where guests used to chase the bride and tear off her garter because they believed it was good luck. To save herself, her leg, and her dress, the bride began removing the garter voluntarily and tossing it into the eager crowd. Later, the bouquet was added to this toss. The lucky recipient of the bouquet is now believed to be the next woman in the group to get married. The man who catches the garter is supposed to be the next groom.

Another theory holds that guests used to follow the newlyweds to their bed. Some of these guests got a little touchy-feely with the bride (probably after drinking too many pints of mead), and so, in an effort to save his bride from being assaulted, the groom would throw her garter into the crowd gathered in his bedroom.

And yet another story has it that the garter was a token of affection in times gone by, and that in a move symbolizing loyalty and faithfulness, a young maiden would have her initials sewn into her garter before giving it to her true love.

QUESTION?

Where does the word *honeymoon* come from?
In ancient times, Teutonic couples would marry beneath a full moon, and then drink honey wine for thirty days after; hence the name. (Too bad today's honeymoons rarely last for thirty days!)

The garter is seen weekend after weekend at weddings nowadays—with the added scene of the garter catcher slipping the garter up, up, up the leg of the woman who was fortunate enough to catch the bouquet. The higher he goes, the better your luck in the future. Feeling averse to this practice because you can't for the life of you imagine subjecting your (rather reserved) female friends to such torture? You can still throw the bouquet and/or the garter—and leave it at that.

The Threshold

This wedding custom originated in Italy—Rome, to be exact. The bride had to be carried across the threshold because she was (or pretended to be) reluctant to enter the bridal chamber.

Of course, where traditions are concerned, there's usually more than one theory. Another explanation for carrying the bride over the threshold holds that the practice prevents the bride from tripping over the threshold, which is considered a bad omen. (And if the groom trips while carrying the bride over the threshold, it's a *really* bad omen . . . in the form of an expensive emergency room visit—for two.)

Wedding Verses

Roses are red . . . and wearing a green dress on your wedding day means that you're a harlot! Pure poetry! Hopefully, no one will write such things about you, but if they do, and you want to know what the heck they mean by it, everything you need to know is here.

Your Wedding Dress

Most brides wear white, or some variation of white (such as off-white, eggshell, or ivory). It wasn't always so easy to decide on a color, however. Brides used to wear their best dress for their wedding, whatever color it happened to be. Legend has it that Queen Victoria herself set the trend for marrying in a white gown, defying the royal tradition of marrying in a silver number.

If you prefer not to walk down the aisle in a white (or off-white) gown, here's a little time-honored poem to help you decide on an appropriate hue:

Married in white, you'll have chosen right;
Married in blue, your love will always be true;
Married in pearl, you will live in a whirl;
Married in brown, you will live in town;
Married in red, you will wish yourself dead;

Married in yellow, ashamed of your fellow;
Married in green, ashamed to be seen;
Married in pink, your spirit will sink.
Married in grey, you will go far away;
Married in black, you will wish yourself back.

FACT

Interestingly enough, legend has it that the explanation for a bride's shame in her green wedding dress is due to the fact that the dress is actually grass-stained—from her amorous outings in the fields. (If you're an Irish bride, however, you have the go-ahead to wear a green gown.)

Your Wedding Day

Well, if brides adhered to the advice of the following poem, the wedding industry would have a major shift on its hands:

Monday for wealth,
Tuesday for health,
Wednesday the best of all,
Thursday for losses,
Friday for crosses,
Saturday for no luck at all.

And if you're wondering about the month you've chosen . . .

Married when the year is new, he'll be loving, kind and true.
When February birds do mate, you wed nor dread your fate.
If you wed when March winds blow, joy and sorrow both you'll
*   know.*
Marry in April when you can, Joy for Maiden and for Man.
Marry in the month of May, and you'll surely rue the day.
Marry when June roses grow, over land and sea you'll go.
Those who in July do wed, must labor for their daily bread.
Whoever wed in August be, many a change is sure to see.

Marry in September's shrine, your living will be rich and fine.
If in October you do marry, love will come but riches tarry.
If you wed in bleak November, only joys will come, remember.
When December snows fall fast, marry and true love will last.

Why is May an unsuitable month for marriage? Back in Pagan times, May was the month of the orgiastic outdoor festivals that marked the beginning of summer. Someone thought that this was, therefore, an inappropriate time for newlyweds to be starting their lives together. You're a modern woman. If you want to walk down that aisle in May, go for it.

June was considered to be the luckiest wedding month because it takes its name from Juno, the goddess of love and marriage.

Signs and Omens

Many brides are so busy these days that they wouldn't know an omen if it hit them in the head (which, hopefully, will not happen to you). If you're interested in knowing whether the fates are conjoining to offer you good luck—or bad tidings—this section will be of special interest to you.

Lizards and Pigs and Spiders

It's considered bad luck to see a lizard, a pig, an open grave, a monk, or a nun on your wedding day. So it might be best for you to stay out of the reptile house of the zoo, off the farm, out of the cemetery, and away from the monastery and/or convent on the morning of your wedding. Just a thought.

Now, seeing a chimney sweep on your way to your wedding is good luck. (Your luck will be better still if you manage to somehow get a kiss from him.) And if you manage to catch a glimpse of a spider (especially in your wedding dress), a lamb (not in your wedding dress), or a black cat, you can also breathe a sigh of relief. Apparently you were born under a lucky sign.

Mirror, Mirror

Taking one last look at your gorgeous reflection in the mirror once you're fully dressed and before you leave for the wedding will bring you good luck—as long as it's the *last* look. If you're pondering your image all the way to the church, you're just asking for trouble. (And don't try to say that studying your image in the limo on the way to the church *is* actually your last peek in the mirror—you can't fool fate, you know.)

ALERT!

Legend has it that saying your wedding vows in the first thirty minutes of any given hour (while the minute hand is going down) is bad luck. Saying "I do" when the minute hand is on the rise is supposed to be symbolic of the two of you working together successfully in your marriage.

Very Odd Odds and Ends

Here are some other superstitions:

- It's good luck to have a cat eat out of your shoe a week before the wedding.
- The bride shouldn't make her own wedding dress—it's bad luck.
- Lit candles that sputter and go out are indicative of evil spirits hovering nearby.
- Marrying a man with a surname that begins with the same letter as your maiden name is unlucky.
- Your right foot should be the first one over the threshold of the church for good luck.
- Red and white flowers are bad luck—they symbolize blood and bandages.

So should you change your plans because your fiancé's last name is Smith and your maiden name is Sullivan? No. Take these admonitions with a grain of salt. You might simply want to be aware of these things just so you aren't caught off guard when someone else brings them to your attention when you're highly emotional. For example, if your aunt tells you at your rehearsal dinner that she can't believe that you made your own wedding dress because it's bad luck, you can tell her that you're planning on having your chimney swept on the morning of the wedding. She'll feel much better, even if you don't have a fireplace.

African Customs

Some of the most beautiful and exotic wedding customs (think belly dancers) come from Africa. Of course, if you're not into sword brandishing, there are also some low-key and lovely traditions you can incorporate into your wedding.

Though many women might not consider the sentiment an example of well wishing, the common greeting to a new bride in some tribes is, "May thou bear twelve children with him." Some African ceremonies include the binding of the couples' wrists with plaited grass ("tying the knot"). Another tradition has the newly married couple jumping over a broomstick for good luck. Today the broomstick is often a keepsake memento made especially for the occasion. At one time, African weddings also included pouring wine on the ground, as an invitation for the gods to join the festivities.

For the rowdiest wedding procession you're likely to see, head to Egypt. Belly dancers, men brandishing swords, and people blowing loud horns all accompany the wedding party and guests as they troop from the ceremony to the reception. In an interesting twist, the guests wear traditional Egyptian clothing, but the bride dresses in a Western-style wedding gown.

European Roots

Got a touch of French blood? You're a wee bit Irish? This section includes a brief look at how your European relations might celebrate their nuptials. Most of these rituals can easily be shifted overseas to include in your own wedding.

En Français, S'il Vous Plaît!

French couples drink a toast from a "coupe de marriage," a two-handled silver cup. The cup is passed down through the family to future generations. In some French towns, the groom calls for the bride at her home and the couple walks together to the church. Kids run alongside them, throwing white ribbons.

The coupe stands under a silk canopy during the ceremony, which is used to ward off evil spirits. (It's for this same reason that the traditional French wedding uses extremely fragrant flowers.) This same canopy, called a "carre," is then used when the couple baptize their children. In southern France, guests leaving the church throw coins to children.

The French wedding cake is comprised of many small crème-filled pastry puffs, which are shaped into a pyramid.

Polish Weddings

Polish weddings are all about the food. Beet soup, dumplings, pierogi, roasted meats and veggies, macaroons . . . you name it, it's there in some form or another.

At the reception, the parents of the bride and groom may offer the newlyweds the bread and salt blessing. The couple is given lightly salted bread and a glass of wine. The bread symbolizes the parents' hope that their children will never know hunger; the salt is to remind the newly married couple that life is full of difficulties and that they will have to work hard when faced with tough times. The wine symbolizes the parents' hope that the newlyweds never know thirst and is also a wish for health and happiness.

The dollar dance is also a popular mainstay at many Polish weddings, where the guests pay for the honor of dancing with the bride. Many brides wear an apron with pockets to collect all the cash, but it's also not unusual to see the maid of honor wearing the apron or for the guests to pin the money on the bride's dress. The money is traditionally spent on the honeymoon.

When the Polish bride enters the reception hall, her veil is removed during the *oczepiny* ceremony as a symbol of her exit from the single world and her entrance into marriage. The groom, meanwhile, is sometimes asked to don a strange hat, as a wish for happiness and levity in the marriage.

That's *Italiano!*

The Italian groom will sometimes carry a piece of iron in his pocket for luck. If the bride's veil is torn, that's also good luck—as long as the bride hasn't worn any gold before her wedding band is placed on her finger.

The best man at an Italian wedding offers a toast of *"Per cent'anni"*— "for one hundred years." Confetti (candy-coated almonds tied up in little mesh bags), are traditionally given at Italian weddings and are a symbol of fertility. The meal at the reception is often simply unbelievable—course after course after course, followed by desserts to die for. These feasts often include a pastry table during the Venetian Hour (an Italian tradition during which cakes and pastries are served in large quantities, displayed in beautiful style), or in some cases, an entire room set aside for the purpose.

FACT

At the reception of an Italian wedding, the bride and groom often break a glass. The number of shards will be equal to the number of happy years the couple will have—so if you're Italian (or you're marrying an Italian man), don't be shy about stomping.

Other European Customs

In Belgium, the bride takes a family handkerchief with her name newly embroidered on it with her to the wedding. After the ceremony, it is framed and displayed in the family house until another daughter gets married. Then this daughter adds her name and carries it to her wedding.

In the English countryside, the bride and her attendants walk to the church on a floor strewn with flower petals, meant to guarantee a smooth and joyous path through life. As the couple enters the church, the bells chime; when they exit as husband and wife, they chime again, only to a different tune. (Bells were once believed to ward off evil spirits.)

Many Irish believe there is a lucky day for weddings, one that comes but once a year: New Year's Day. For good luck, a swatch of Irish lace may be sewn into the bride's gown and then be used later for a baby bonnet. The couple also receives a horseshoe to put up in their new home.

Although they are now popular in America simply as friendship rings, claddagh rings remain the standard Irish wedding ring. The heart, crown, and hands found on the claddagh symbolize love, loyalty, and friendship.

Asian Traditions

While many of the Asian wedding customs aren't usually seen in traditional American weddings, maybe they should be. (Drinking sake during the ceremony? It's just the thing many nervous brides and grooms would welcome.) In the Philippines, the groom's family pays for the wedding. They also give the bride old coins, which stand for prosperity. In return, the bride's family gives the new couple a cash dowry.

Part of the Japanese wedding ceremony requires both the bride and groom to take nine sips of sake. They may be a little tipsy after the nine sips, but they are considered married after the first. During the ceremony, the bride leaves to change clothes three to four times. (And you thought finding one wedding gown was tough!) As usual, the groom has it easy, wearing only one black kimono. Guests at a Japanese wedding are very lucky—not only are they fed and entertained, but the wedding favors they receive from the couple's families sometimes equal up to half the price of the gifts given to the couple.

In India, the families of both the bride and groom prepare puffed rice for the ceremony as a symbol of fertility and good luck. The groom's brother douses the new husband and wife with flower petals at the ceremony's end. Henna dye is used to paint designs on the couple's hands, and the couple usually leaves their handprints on the outside door of their new home for good luck.

In the Chinese wedding ceremony, a goblet of honey and a goblet of wine are tied together with a red ribbon. Red is the color of love, and the ribbon stands for unity. The bride and groom take a drink to symbolize a union of love. After a wedding dinner that might feature delicacies like bear nose, the guests receive fortune cookies for good luck.

Latino Traditions

The bride and groom in Latino families may be blessed by their parents at home before the ceremony. During the ceremony, the couple is often joined by the *lazo,* a long rosary that symbolizes their union, and then blessed by the priest. The groom presents the bride with the *arras,* thirteen gold coins, which are a symbol of prosperity.

During the reception, the dollar dance is customary, with the proceeds going toward the honeymoon. Mariachi bands also make the rounds, and piñatas are popular entertainment. The wedding cakes are used as favors—each is a small round confection made of almonds, flour, and butter. The cakes are wrapped in colored tissue paper and sent home with the guests.

If you like the sound of any of these ethnic traditions, by all means, incorporate them into your own wedding ceremony. It's all about creating an event that is meaningful to you, your fiancé, and your families. Ⓔ

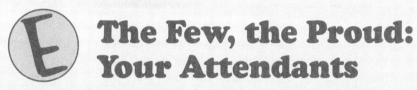

Chapter 3

The Few, the Proud: Your Attendants

Having the right group of people in your wedding party can provide comfort and laughter during an occasionally trying time. You don't want to worry about the best man losing the rings or a bridesmaid complaining that she doesn't like her dress. (You need your attendants to help you *out* of minor disasters, not into them!) You'll also be hunting for the perfect bridesmaid dresses and tuxedos and showering your wedding party with gifts.

Picking and Choosing

Yikes! You have too many people in your life to choose from. You can't possibly offend your five best friends—or your sisters, or your extended family—by not including them in the wedding party . . . can you? You're going to have to make some choices. No one said it would be easy, but you really can't have twenty bridesmaids parading down the aisle. (No, really. You can't.)

Since your attendants will have certain duties to perform, however, you'll be able to eliminate from the get-go anyone you wouldn't want to tax with the burden.

How Many? And Who?

Your wedding party can be as big—or as small—as you like. Formal weddings usually have a larger number of attendants than informal ones, but you can feel free to bend tradition here if you think it's appropriate.

Think about which of your close friends and family members you and your groom would really like to have in the wedding. Brides often feel obligated to have certain people in the wedding, even if they're not that close. But surrounding yourself with close friends and with family members you can depend on may lead you to discover that those pre-wedding parties, fittings, and rehearsals are going more smoothly than you expected—and are even fun!

Don't bow to your mother's pressure to include your cousin as a bridesmaid if you really don't like her. However, if not asking her promises to cause family strife, you may want to consider including the cousin in some other way—by asking her to do a reading, for example.

The Final Cut

Once you have a list in mind, write it all down. Traditionally there are an equal number of bridesmaids and ushers, but there is no reason why you have to adhere to this "rule." The general guideline is one usher for every fifty guests. One concern is that all the bridesmaids have a partner to walk them down the aisle and to dance with them during scheduled dances at the reception. But having a couple of extra ushers is no crime. They can walk with each other down the aisle, and they probably won't shed a tear over not dancing in the traditional wedding party dance at the reception.

As soon as you figure out the people you want to include in your wedding party, get out there and ask them. Sometimes, due to monetary problems or other conflicts, one of your first choices may have to decline. You want to make sure you have enough time to dig up a replacement.

Above all else, try to select attendants who are comfortable working with people, who don't get flustered easily, and who have known you or your groom for a while. This is no time for surprises. If you're up front about what you expect all attendants to do, you shouldn't run into any complications. (The low-down on their duties is included later in this chapter.)

ALERT!

Being part of a wedding is a big and often expensive responsibility. You want to give everyone ample time to plan and save. Six months is the absolute minimum amount of notice you need to give everyone involved.

Special Circumstances

Planning a wedding isn't a walk in the park, obviously. You need help, and that's one reason you're tapping certain people as your attendants. What if your best friend lives overseas, though? Or what if your closest friend is a man? What if your sister, your matron of honor, is going to be very pregnant on your wedding day? How can you include these people, and what should you expect of them?

Distant Maid of Honor

Should distance stop you from having your best friend beside you on your special day? The maid of honor has considerable responsibility before the wedding. You should keep in mind that an out-of-town maid of honor can't be expected to help you with as much of the pre-wedding planning as someone who lives locally. Just establish as early as possible what it is you would like her to help with that she can do from afar. Spell out your expectations for her so she knows how she can be helpful even without being in the same time zone.

Maid or Matron or Mommy?

The word "maid" suggests a single woman, but there's nothing wrong with having married attendants. They're still called bridesmaids, but a married maid of honor is called a *matron* of honor.

What if you have pregnant bridesmaids? Many designers now offer maternity-style bridesmaid dresses. Bear in mind that if any of your attendants (particularly the maid or matron of honor) will be eight and a half months pregnant at the time of your wedding, you may need a standby.

If you're having a hard time deciding between two women for the role of your honor attendant, dual titles may make your life easier. If you have two sisters, for example, and one of them is married and one isn't, *voila*! You have a maid of honor *and* a matron of honor. Divide the duties equally between them.

My Best Friend, Bill

What if your best friend is a guy? There's no reason why he shouldn't be included in your wedding party. Just don't make him wear a dress, dance with an usher, or do any of the traditionally "feminine" duties, such as helping you get into your wedding gown or arranging your train and veil.

If he's taking the place of your maid of honor, he's called the honor attendant; if not, he's simply another attendant. He stands on your side, and in the processional and recessional he can walk in before the rest of the bride's attendants. Or, if there are more bridesmaids than ushers, he can escort one of the bridesmaids.

It's also perfectly acceptable to have a female usher (or two) at your wedding, providing the female in question is comfortable with the idea. While she certainly doesn't have to wear a tux, and she shouldn't wear a bridesmaid's dress, she should wear something that coordinates with the rest of the wedding party.

Attendants' Duties

Here's the good stuff—the duties that your attendants typically take on when they agree to be in your wedding. Don't just assume, though, that this is automatic. You still have to spell out for your friends and family the duties you hope they will take on. This way, you don't get left resenting a bridesmaid for something that she didn't even realize you wanted her to do. Herewith, the list of who does what.

Maid/Matron of Honor

The maid or matron of honor typically helps the bride address envelopes, record wedding gifts, shop, and take care of other important pre-wedding duties. She is charged with arranging a bridal shower, with the help of your bridesmaids.

The maid of honor helps the bride dress for the ceremony. At the altar, she arranges the bride's dress and veil, holds the bride's bouquet during the vows, and holds the groom's ring until the appropriate moment. She signs the wedding certificate (with the best man) as a witness.

After the ceremony, the maid of honor stands in the receiving line. She helps the bride change clothes after the reception and takes charge of the bridal gown.

ALERT!

Read through this list carefully, and you will realize that this is not a job for the faint of heart (or for the lazy). There's quite a bit involved with being the maid of honor. Unless you want to end up taking care of *all* the details—the big ones and the small ones—choose this attendant wisely.

Best Man

The best man organizes the bachelor party, which may be the thing your groom is most interested in. After that, he pays for his own formal-wear, drives the groom to the ceremony, and holds the bride's ring until it's needed during the ceremony.

The best man is also charged with handing over the checks to the officiant just before or after the ceremony. He may also be asked to take care of paying other service providers, such as the chauffeur or the reception coordinator. If this is to be part of his duties, your groom (or the groom's family) will give the best man the payments ahead of time, which he'll then pass on to the appropriate parties.

Bridesmaids and Ushers

You're asking a lot of the girls who become your bridesmaids, so make sure they're up to the task. Bridesmaids pay for their own wedding attire and help run and organize the bridal shower. One of the bridesmaids will keep a record of the gifts you receive at the shower and who gave what. The bridesmaids will assist you and/or the maid of honor with pre-wedding shopping or tasks and will also help you prepare for the ceremony.

After the ceremony, they will stand in the receiving line. If you choose to have birdseed thrown or bubbles blown as you exit the church, the bridesmaids will provide the guests with the necessary projectiles.

Ushers are sometimes overlooked, but they are given a significant amount of responsibility, too. For starters, they'll rent (or purchase) their own formalwear. Ushers are asked to arrive at the wedding location early to assist with the setup and important finishing touches, such as lighting candles or tying bows on reserved seating. They'll escort guests to their seats and meet, welcome, and seat guests of honor (such as grand-parents). Just before the processional, one or two of your ushers will roll out the aisle runner.

After the ceremony, the ushers stand in the receiving line. They'll oversee the transfer of the gifts to a secure location after the reception, and, of course, they'll likely decorate your getaway vehicle.

Kids' Stuff

If you or your fiancé has younger relatives (or children of your own), you might want to let them play a part in your ceremony. Junior bridesmaids are usually between ten and fourteen, while flower girls are younger. Little boys, usually under ten, can be ring bearers. Other little boys and girls, called trainbearers or pages, can walk behind the bride, carrying the train of her dress as she walks down the aisle.

FACT

You may want to avoid having children under five in your wedding. Their behavior can be unpredictable. If you have just too many nieces or nephews to choose from, you might want to forget altogether about having kids in the ceremony. Choosing one child over another could cause family strife.

The flower girl is the last person down the aisle before the bride. Traditionally, she sprinkles fresh flower petals for the bride to walk on, but brides have been known to slip on the petals (get a visual on this right now—you, feet up in the air, flat on your back in the middle of the aisle), so you may want to think twice about this. As an alternative, you could have her toss paper petals or carry a pretty basket of fresh flowers.

The ring bearer precedes the flower girl in the procession (or, in the case of a shy ring bearer or flower girl, the kids can totter down the aisle side by side). He carries rings, which are displayed on a satin pillow and tied with a ribbon. For those of you who are worried about the ring bearer losing or eating your wedding bands, don't worry. The rings he carries are fake and, to be doubly safe, perhaps sewn or otherwise secured to the pillow. The best man and/or maid of honor has the real rings.

The page/trainbearer's only duty is to carry the bride's train and help to arrange it neatly. Strictly speaking, this job is only necessary if the bride has a very long train, but you may wish to have one or two even if your train is short (as one more way to include cute kids in the wedding). Although most people assume that pages are always boys, there's nothing wrong with them being girls, too.

The Parents' Role

You're not done yet. Your parents do much more than simply sign the checks. This is a special day in their lives, too, and they get to dress the part and even offer their opinions once in a while.

Your Parents

On the surface, your father's duty is to accompany you to the church, walk you down the aisle, and give you away. In reality, his more important (and unspoken) responsibilities are usually (a) to be a little sad that his daughter has grown up and no longer considers him the most important man in her life, and (b) to wonder how he's going to pay for all this.

Though you may not realize it, the mother of the bride is considered part of the wedding party. And why not? After all, your father gets his moment in the sun. Shouldn't the woman who endured hours of labor to give you life be included as well? At the onset of the ceremony, the mother is the last person seated before the processional begins. But, like your attendants, she has plenty to do before the wedding, both officially and unofficially.

Your mother does all of the following:

- Helps you in choosing your gown and accessories, and helps you find the perfect bridesmaid gowns.
- Works with you and the groom's family to assemble a guest list and a seating plan.
- Helps your attendants coordinate the bridal shower.
- Helps address and mail invitations.
- Stands at the beginning of the receiving line.
- May act as hostess during the reception.

She will, of course, occupy a place of honor at the ceremony and at the parents' table during the reception. Her biggest official duty is to assist you with any of the hundreds of details you need to handle before the ceremony.

Her *unofficial* duties also include these:

- Listening to you complain about not being able to find the "right" gown.
- Arguing with you when you feel the need to argue with her.
- Providing the emotional support you won't find anywhere else.
- Persuading your dad that he shouldn't declare bankruptcy because of this wedding.

The Groom's Parents

These people have a fairly easy job, in comparison to the duties that are laid on your mom and dad. Your new in-laws will sit at the parents' table during the reception, have their picture taken, and remark to each other, "Aren't you glad we have a *son*? We just saved ourselves a ton of money!"—*unless*, of course, you choose to blaze a trail of your own and divide the wedding duties (and/or finances) equally between the parents.

If there are any special family members or friends that you couldn't fit into the wedding party but would still like to be part of the ceremony, don't despair. There are ways to fit them in. You might have them do a Scripture reading, light candles, or hand out ceremony programs. Is a close friend musically talented? Perhaps she could sing a song or play an instrument. Be creative!

The Bridesmaids' Dresses (Eek!)

Now you've got your wedding party. All participants should have a good idea of what they're supposed to be doing and when they're supposed to do it. All that's left to decide is what they're going to be wearing when they do it.

Deciding whether the party should dress formally or casually is the easy part—the type of wedding you're planning will tell you that. Finding something everybody likes and looks great in, however, is a whole *other* can of worms. (Warning: you may end up concluding it would be easier to dress the worms.)

Color Your Wedding

First, decide on your wedding colors. These should be colors you *really* like, as you'll be seeing them on your bridesmaids, your flowers, your wedding favors, your decorations, and even your cake. If you have a couple of favorites that go well together, choose both of them. If your favorites happen to clash, however, you might consider picking only one—a purple and orange wedding is not something that anyone wants to bear witness to.

In a quandary as to what colors to pick? There are some guidelines that can help you decide. If your wedding will be in one of the warmer months, cool pastel shades like ice blue and pale pink work very well. In cooler months, forest green, midnight blue, burgundy, or other warm tones can give the wedding a cozy feel.

Start looking for your bridesmaids' dresses as soon as you finalize the wedding party. The women need to begin the process early because their dresses have to be made (or ordered) and altered. The men can afford to wait awhile because, as usual, finding the right attire for them is much easier. A few stitches here and there to some rented tuxedos and they'll be ready to go.

The Search

When searching for bridesmaids' gowns, check the formal dress section of a quality department store in your area before you go to a bridal salon. You may find appropriate dresses your attendants can wear again in the future—and at a cheaper price than salon dresses.

Whether you buy from a department store or a bridal salon, avoid outfits that look great on one or two people but lousy on everyone else. Try to find something everyone finds acceptable. It's not fair to make your bridesmaids wear a style that is wrong for them just because you like it. Even if something is unflattering on only one bridesmaid, it's wise to forget that style and find something else. You don't want anyone to feel awkward or unattractive.

FACT

Don't be afraid to choose bridesmaids' dresses in your favorite color just because someone told you it wasn't right for the season. Just be sure the dresses are of a fabric and style appropriate for the time of year. Don't dress your bridesmaids in velvet if you're getting married in July, and don't have them wear sleeveless dresses in January.

Traditionally, the members of the bridal party wear the same style dress, but you shouldn't be afraid of a little variety. Consider having everyone wear the same style but with each in a different color, creating a rainbow effect.

If you really want to make your bridesmaids happy, allow each one to pick out whatever dress looks best on her (as long as it meets your basic color and style guidelines). This approach works especially well in a black-and-white wedding, with each woman wearing a different style of black-and-white gown. Another option is to dress the bridesmaids uniformly, but to have the maid of honor wear a dress of a different style or of a slightly different shade from the rest.

Can't find what you're looking for in any bridal shop? Consider working with a seamstress to have the dresses custom made. The upside is that you can choose the exact fabric and style you want; the downside is that it can be a bit more expensive, and a bit more time consuming than simply ordering dresses from a store.

Attendants do not have to troop to the bridal shop as a group for fittings. Once dresses have been ordered, they can go for alterations at their own convenience; just be sure to give them a deadline for getting it all done. If one of your bridesmaids lives far away and can't make it to town for the fittings, ask your salon about alternate arrangements. If you can, send her a photo of the dress you have in mind, and make sure it's something she will feel comfortable wearing. Then ask her for her measurements so that you can order her dress along with the others.

Once the dress comes in, send it to her so she can have alterations done at a bridal salon in her city.

ALERT!

Don't ask your bridesmaid to order a dress at her own bridal salon. All of the dresses should be ordered together so that they come from the same dye lot; otherwise, the shades of fabric color may vary. The same rule applies to shoes. It is best to have them dyed together to ensure an exact color match.

The Other Women

A junior bridesmaid can wear the same dress as the other bridesmaids, or you might choose a different style for her that is appropriate to her age. In a black-and-white wedding, she should not wear solid black; a white dress with a black pattern or trimming is perfectly acceptable.

Flower girls wear either long or short dresses that match or complement the other dresses. If you have a hard time finding something appropriate, don't fret; a white dress trimmed with lace or fabric that matches the other dresses is a lovely option.

The mother of the bride usually has first choice when it comes to picking out a style and color for her gown. She then consults with the mother of the groom, who (you hope) picks out a dress color and style that complements, rather than copies, the bride's mother's dress. It's best if the mothers' dresses don't clash with the color scheme or style of the wedding. If your bridal party is in elegant long gowns, it's doubtful you'd appreciate your mother showing up in a beaded flapper dress.

Beware of Alterations

Alterations are one of the necessary evils in life, as far as wedding wear goes. You want the dresses to look perfect, after all, but the little nips and tucks can cost a fortune. Luckily, there are a few ways to protect your bridesmaids (and yourself) from paying an excessive amount for these repairs.

Use your best judgment instead of relying on the word of a saleswoman in the dress shop. There are salons out there, unfortunately, whose standard practices include advising women to order dresses in a size much larger than they normally would. Employees in these shops usually rely on the old line, "These dresses run so small! Why, I wear a size six myself and I would have to order a twelve!" Too often, the *real* reason you (or your bridesmaids, or your mother) are being encouraged to add inches to the dress is so that the shop can make a bundle off of the inevitable alterations.

If the dress you're considering has a tag in it, and the dress seems to fit the bridesmaid in front of you just fine (or, if it's a wedding dress, it feels perfect on you), order that size. If the tag has been removed, find another dress from the same maker and see for yourself if the sizes run true. And if there's any question about the honesty of the shop you're standing in, walk out. There are plenty of other bridal shops eager for your business.

On the other hand, if you have a bridesmaid who insists she's going to lose fifteen pounds before your wedding, try to convince her to order a dress that suits her present body. Weight loss is one of the many reasons that seamstresses make alterations, after all, but even the best seamstresses have their limitations. No one can make a dress that is three sizes too small that much larger.

Even though alterations will cost your dieting bridesmaid a pretty penny if she does lose the weight, ordering *another* dress in the size that she's actually wearing when your wedding rolls around will cost her much more.

Dressing the Men

As indicated earlier, the choices for men's attire are usually so simple that they're liable to drive any woman crazy. All the groomsmen dress the same, in a style and color that complements the groom's outfit. Most likely, the men will be wearing some form of tuxedo or suit, depending on the formality of the wedding.

Most men rent their formalwear. Your groom should start looking for his wedding wear at least three to four months before the wedding, and the groomsmen should reserve theirs as soon as your groom makes his decision. For a formal wedding, the fathers of the bride and groom should wear the same style and color as the attendants. Otherwise, they can wear nice suits.

Any male attendant who lives out of town should go to a reputable tuxedo shop in his area to be measured. Have him send the measurements to you so you can reserve his attire with the rest of the group's. Be sure to have him include shoe size. As hard on the feet as they may be, matching rented shoes that go with the tuxes will make your wedding party—and pictures of them—look much sharper.

Remember to ask your formalwear shop about exact prices, including alterations. Also inquire about their return policy and the time of return. Ring bearers and male pages can dress exactly as the other men in the party, or they can wear dress shorts or knickers to make them stand out— and look especially adorable.

Gifts for the Wedding Party

It's customary to show your gratitude to the wedding party by giving each member a little gift. Let them know you appreciate all the time, money, and aggravation they've spent helping to make your wedding day something you'll all enjoy.

For the Girls

After being on the receiving end of so much giving over the course of your engagement, you may be a little rusty on how to *give*—but you want to properly thank the gals who have stood by you, tried on countless bridesmaid dresses, listened to you prattle on about your new pots and pans, and have generally been patient, indispensable pals.

Possible gifts for your bridesmaids include these ideas:

- Jewelry (especially something that might complement their dresses for the wedding)
- Date book

- Stationery
- Perfume
- Jewelry box
- Handkerchiefs or silk scarves
- Gift certificates for a restaurant, spa, or boutique

It is most common to give all of the bridesmaids the same gift. If you want to do this but feel that it may seem less personal, you can individualize your gifts by monogramming them, or by giving each woman the same gift in a different color. (The same is true of the men's gifts.)

Because bridesmaids usually wind up doing the lion's share of pre-wedding work (compared to the groomsmen, at least), you may want to do a little *extra* to show your appreciation. Custom once called for the bride to take her attendants out for tea.

Since few people go out for tea anymore, many brides treat their bridesmaids to lunch or dinner several days before the wedding. If you're getting married in the late afternoon or evening and are feeling exceptionally calm, you can take your bridesmaids out for a nice brunch on the morning of the wedding.

Gifting the Groomsmen

The groom is really in charge of bestowing the gifts on his half of the wedding party, but it won't hurt to offer some suggestions, particularly if he's leaning toward buying each of them a case of beer.

Possible (tasteful) gifts include these:

- Money clip
- Date book
- Cologne
- Ties
- Travel or shaving kit

- Gift certificate to a sporting goods store or restaurant
- Something related to a favorite hobby of each man

You know your friends and family better than anyone else, so with a little thought you should be able to find something suitable for everyone. Don't forget to get a little something for the children in the wedding party—it's doubtful that a boy under fourteen would appreciate a shaving kit. Many kids love gift certificates to their favorite toy store.

Don't Forget Your Parents!

Parents (yours and your groom's) are often forgotten in this whole gift-giving frenzy, though heaven knows why. Whether they're providing most of the funds for the wedding, or are simply lending moral support, it's a nice touch to acknowledge the people who have given you so much already (you know, *life* and such).

A gift certificate for a weekend getaway (to relieve all the wedding stress) might be just the ticket; they might also enjoy a gift certificate for a nice dinner or a round of golf. Maybe they insist that they don't need thanks; they love you and they haven't for one moment thought twice about helping you plan the wedding you've always dreamed of. Thank them anyway. Everyone likes to feel appreciated.

Chapter 4

The (Gulp!) Guest List

Hammering out your guest list can be a smooth, effortlessly enjoyable process . . . for some brides, anyway. If you have a completely tension-free family life, an endless supply of wedding funds, unlimited reception space, and a magician who'll whip up a seating plan that pleases everyone, you're all set. Happy wedding. On the other hand, if you have family issues to deal with, and money and space are a concern as far as the guest list is concerned, you have your work cut out for you.

Making the List

Setting out to create your guest list sounds easy enough, at least until you sit down and try to do it. Then you realize that your mother thinks she's going to invite every last relative she can find, your coworkers think they're coming, and you don't have nearly enough room for everyone. The best strategy for addressing these problems is to hit them head on. Don't try to ignore them or push them aside until the last minute. You'll be surprised at how much easier things will seem when you are resolved not to let anything beat you.

Guessing the Guest List

If money is not an issue, you should be able to invite as many people as you want to your wedding, provided that your reception site will hold them all. But if, like most of us, you're on a budget, you'll have to do some fancy dancing.

Start out by listing everyone you'd ideally like to invite. It may turn out that the total number is not beyond your reach. (It's not that you're not as popular as you thought; you're just more selective than you give yourself credit for.) If you do end up having to cut people, don't throw everyone's name into a fishbowl and eliminate anyone whose name is picked out. Instead, set boundaries for your list and stick to them. In most cases the guest list is divided evenly between the two families, regardless of who is paying for what. Couples often split the list three ways: the bride's parents, the groom's parents, and the couple. Each invites one-third of the guests.

Don't forget to include your attendants and your officiant (and his or her spouse) in the final guest count. All of them should receive formal invitations even though they're all well aware that they're already invited.

The Kids Question

If you've decided not to invite children, you usually make this clear to parents by the fact that their children's names do not appear anywhere on the invitation. Just to be safe, however, make sure your mother (and anyone else who might be questioned) is aware of your policy.

Whatever you decide in the end—kids of a certain age and no

younger, or no kids at all—everyone has to play by the same rules. You can't make an exception for your favorite cousin, who happens to be under your determined age limit. If you do, it's a sure bet other parents will ask, "What's she doing here if my little sweetie couldn't come?"

QUESTION?

What is the cutoff point between children and young adults? It's up to you to pick an age. (Eighteen or sixteen are common cutoff points.) No matter what age you pick, make sure both families understand that they must adhere to that age—no exceptions.

If there are children who are very special to you, consider making them part of the wedding. That way they'll be present for your big day, and you won't be offending anyone else.

Coworkers and Distant Relations

If you were counting on talking to business contacts at your wedding to help strengthen business ties, it's not gonna happen. You'll be far too busy dancing the night away and mingling with your many other guests to talk shop. So if you do need to cut the guest list, and you feel comfortable excluding work acquaintances, this may be the way to go.

When you're deciding which coworkers you want to invite, *honestly* evaluate your business relationships. Many people feel burdened by an invitation to an acquaintance's wedding. You could end up straining a relationship instead of strengthening it.

Likewise, you may want to exclude your more distant relatives from the guest list. Again, be consistent. As long as your third cousins don't have to hear that your second cousins twice removed have been invited, they should understand your need to cut costs.

Invite Etiquette

Now that you've got a handle on the larger issues surrounding the guest list, you can start dealing with the details of it. Should your guests be allowed to bring guests? Do you have to invite everyone who has invited you to a wedding in the past? If you receive a lot of regrets, can you fill those spaces with other people?

The Guests' Guests

You will probably want to allow any "attached" guests to bring their significant others. It is also nice, but not necessary, to give unattached guests the opportunity to bring someone. This is especially appropriate for people who may not know many others at the wedding, as it will help them feel more comfortable.

ALERT!

If you simply can't afford to invite single guests with a date, don't be afraid to explain your position. It's hard for anyone to stay mad at a bride who is trying to be incredibly diplomatic.

Married guests are almost always invited with their spouses. There is one exception to this rule. If you are very friendly with some of your coworkers and would like to invite them, you can include them as a group without their spouses.

Always give your attendants the option to bring a date, even if they're not involved with anyone at the time. These people have worked hard (and taken on a hefty financial burden) to be part of your wedding. Do them the courtesy of allowing them to share the day with someone special to them.

Returning the Favor?

If a distant relative or acquaintance invited you to her wedding, this does not obligate you to invite her to yours. These people will understand if you make them aware that you're cutting costs and having a small affair. The best approach is to be honest right then and there. Tell them you'd love to have them, but you're having a small wedding and it is impossible to invite everyone. It may be a little awkward, but it beats dashing anyone's expectations later.

Last-Minute Invites

Because it's realistic to anticipate some regrets (on average, about 20 to 25 percent of invited guests will be unable to attend), you and your fiancé may decide to send a second mailing of invitations to people on a "wish list." If so, your first mailing should be sent ten to twelve weeks before the wedding date. The second should be sent no later than five weeks prior.

Be aware that if potential invitees become aware of the fact that they were not included in the first mailing, you may have some ruffled feathers to smooth. Some guests will be flattered that you thought of them at all, while others will assume that you're trying to fill seats after you received regrets. If you're cornered by an offended late invitee, all you can do is be gracious and honest. You may choose to explain your seating and/or financial limitations, which may be just the balm for this potential guest's wounded ego.

Sticky Situations

If a divorce between your parents or your groom's parents was amicable, be thankful. You won't have to plan around family tensions. If, however, the relationship between the ex-spouses—or the resulting mixed families— is comparable to the tensions in the Middle East, you'd better map out a battle plan of your own to deal with it.

Divorce

Do as much as you can before the wedding to prevent any "scenes" at the wedding. This is your big day, and you don't want anything to happen that will upset or embarrass you. Speak with the divorced set of parents openly and honestly. Request their cooperation and ask them to be on their best behavior.

With luck, they will be able to put aside their grievances for one day for your sake, but it's best to take precautions. Remind them of how much this day means to you. Divorced parents often think they're big enough to handle the situation but find that when the moment arrives, emotion and tension get the best of them.

To be on the safe side, don't require divorced parents to interact with each other. Seat them at separate tables, each with his or her own family and friends. If necessary, have their tables situated as far away from each other as you can without seating either of them in the next room.

Stepparents, Stepchildren, Steptension

In the same vein, if either one or both parents have remarried, consider yourself lucky if all the "exes" and "steps" get along. If there are tensions, they're your problem now—at least as far as your wedding is concerned.

If your natural mother and your stepmother are on the verge of ripping the earrings out of one another's ears whenever they're even in the same building, make it a priority to keep them separated. Don't seat them near each other in the church or at the reception, and don't ask them to pose for "one big happy family" picture. Take each woman aside before the wedding and lay down the law. There will be peace in the land on your wedding day or else. Beyond these steps, though, you must realize that your parents are adults. Expect them to act like adults. If they try to make a drama out of your wedding (threatening not to attend if the other ex-spouse attends, for instance), don't give in to the ploy.

If your mother or father has remarried someone you have grown close to, you may want him or her to hold a place of honor at the wedding. Just make sure you allow your natural parents their moment in the sun, too.

Doling Out the Spaces

In the case of divorces and remarriages, your guest list could easily turn into a roster of virtual unknowns, as far as you're concerned. Once you've determined how many guests to invite, you and the groom will most likely divide that number between your families and yourselves. Whatever number you're giving to your divorced parents will be divided equally between them (so that you aren't forced to hear that you're playing favorites).

What your parents choose to do with their part of the guest list is of great concern to you, especially if you're the one footing the bill for this affair. If your stepmother—a woman you don't know all that well to begin with—is insisting on inviting her mother—a woman you met once and found to be a lovely person, but not someone you were planning on hosting at your reception—maybe you can accept this *one* add-on guest. (After all, your stepmother may be worried about feeling out of place among your family at the wedding and reception.) However, if she also wants to invite her former stepchildren and her hairdresser, you'll have to speak up and tell her no.

FACT

If people approach you and assume they're being invited when they're not, be honest with them—right then and there. Don't go home and stew for weeks about how to break it to them. Waiting only makes things more awkward, and it also causes people to wonder whether something happened over that time to make you change your mind.

Remind your parents—and stepparents—when you give them a certain number of seats to fill that you expect them to fill them with appropriate guests. If your dad can't come up with twenty-five relatives, maybe you'd like those spaces back so that you can include some of the friends who had to be cut off of your original list.

The "Ex" Factor

There's no surprise here. One's ex-spouse and ex-in-laws are usually left off the guest list. Even if things are very amicable, the presence of your ex-spouse might be upsetting to your new groom (and vice versa). Former mates and family members are generally an unpleasant reminder of the past. Remember, this is a day dedicated to your future.

In all but the most special cases (where *everyone* feels comfortable with the situation), inviting an ex-husband, ex-wife, or ex-in-law usually turns out to be a bad idea. Weddings just dig up old emotions—and at exactly the wrong moments, as far as these guests are concerned.

The Paper Chase

Once you've finalized your guest list, be sure you have all the pertinent information correct. Names should be correctly spelled, titles used properly (such as doctors or religious and military personnel), and addresses should be current. You might also want to list phone numbers. They'll come in handy if you need to call someone late with an RSVP, or if any family members or friends want to contact guests to invite them to showers or other parties in your honor.

If you're not 100 percent sure that you've got the information right, don't hesitate to ask someone who would know or to ask the person in question. No one likes to receive a wedding invitation addressed to someone with a *similar* name. (And imagine *your* panic when you realize you sent an invitation to your mother-in-law's best friend, Joan . . . whose name is actually Joanne.) It's best to do the paperwork now and have all the correct information in front of you. This will help later, when you'll need to refer to your list for invitations and thank-you notes.

The Bride's Book

Consider using a three-ring binder to create your own bride's book. This is the ultimate organizational tool, one that every bride should have— unless she's depending on someone else to take care of every single task. Some brides call these their planners. Whatever name you prefer, no bride-to-be should be without her binder.

You can get as creative as you like, but bear in mind that the purpose of this book is to keep your information straight and to keep it handy. If covering the book in pink satin is going to keep you from handling it, it's probably best to forgo the frills. You'll need a large binder, alphabet tabs, and dividers. You might choose to type this information into your computer, or you might find that it's easier to write it longhand. You'll need paper either way, and lots of it.

You'll divide your book into sections (for example, the bride's family, the groom's family, the caterer, and so on). Here is where you'll keep track of all manner of information related to your wedding. To keep your guest list straight and accessible, start in the "Bride's Family" section of your planner. Start at the left side of the page and enter each name, address, and phone number. You can even specify what relation these people are to you (if you honestly don't think you'll remember when it comes time to write your thank-you notes).

Leave plenty of room for several columns across the page: Reception/ Dinner (R/D); Accept/Regret (A/R); Gift (the one you receive from them); and Note Sent (where you can either mark off your sent thank-you with a checkmark or with the actual date you mailed it).

Since planning a wedding is a huge job, make sure your binder is large enough to accommodate all of the information you need at your fingertips. Other sections you'll want to include will be devoted to your wedding vendors. (You'll have a section for your photographer, your caterer or reception hall, your band or your DJ, and so on.)

Out of Town? *Not Out of Mind!*

Since your out-of-town guests will be traveling some distance to be with you on the big day, you should try to make things as pleasant and convenient for them as possible. Start by helping them find a place to hang their hats over the course of their stay, either with family members, friends, or at local hotels.

Guests pay for their own lodging (unless either the bride's or groom's family can offer to pick up the tab), but it is customary for you to provide enough information to them that they can make their reservations.

The Low, Low Price

Some hotels will offer a lower rate for a group of rooms. Grouping your out-of-town guests in one hotel has several advantages:

- The group rates will lighten the burden to their pockets.
- They can mingle with the other guests during the downtime between wedding events.
- They can carpool to and from the festivities.

Though grouping everyone at the same hotel is preferable, some guests may not be able to afford the hotels you choose. (You can help avoid this by choosing a middle-of-the-road place.) Others may have specific preferences—or may simply want their privacy.

FACT

Don't assume anything about your guests' financial situation. Include a note with the invitation that lists several lodging options. Detail the prices and any special features of each place, and inform your guests about where you are trying to coordinate group rates. After that, the ball is in their court.

Little Niceties

Once you find out where your guests will be staying, you might go the extra mile and arrange to have a small gift awaiting them in their rooms (if your finances permit). A bottle of wine or a fruit basket would be a welcome sight to weary travelers, especially if they've just spent several hours on a plane crammed between a screaming baby and a high-strung first-time flyer.

If your guests are flying into town and will need a rental car, include the names and numbers of some agencies in their invitations. If they'll be relying on public transportation, send them a map of the subway or train system in your city.

Another way to make your out-of-town guests feel welcome is to invite them to the rehearsal dinner and to any other wedding events that are going on while they're in town. Inviting them makes them feel like the trip was worth it and that you're *really* glad they could make it . . . and it certainly beats staring at the four walls of a hotel room, or sitting in your aunt's living room watching television while *she's* off whooping it up at the rehearsal dinner. The rehearsal dinner is actually the perfect time to touch base with out-of-town guests. You won't be as busy as you will be at the wedding—you'll have time to actually finish a conversation with your guests.

Where's Main Street?

Don't forget to enclose detailed maps to all the events for those unfamiliar with the area. You don't want guests to have traveled across the country for your wedding only to miss it because they got lost a few miles from the ceremony site. As a further precaution, consider putting a trustworthy friend or relative in charge of rounding up the out-of-town group and transporting them from place to place. This person would also be in charge of airport pickups and dropoffs.

If out-of-town guests must bring children with them who are not invited to the wedding, talk about finding a babysitter well in advance. Children can be invited to the rehearsal dinner even if they're not going to the ceremony.

Filling Their Time

If it's clear that your out-of-town guests are going to have some free time on their hands, try to come up with some suggestions to pass that time effortlessly. The last thing you want guests to remember about your wedding is how bored they were while sitting in their hotel room waiting for the reception to start.

Some suggestions might include the following:

- **Movie theaters.** Include a map and a phone number.
- **Restaurants/clubs.** In the event that your reception is wrapping up early and guests will be looking for additional entertainment, give them some suitable options.
- **Parks.** Having an autumn wedding? Perhaps your guests would enjoy a drive (or a walk) through the state park to see the foliage.
- **Regional events.** Is something special happening in your neck of the woods on your wedding weekend? An outdoor concert, craft show, county fair?

Feel free to include as much information for your guests as you can find. The more they have to choose from, the more likely they are to remember their trip to your wedding as an adventure. Ⓔ

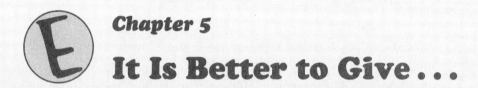

Chapter 5

It Is Better to Give...

Need them or not, you will get gifts when you get married. Maybe you have absolutely nothing to stock your kitchen with, or maybe you have everything. Whatever the case, you'll probably want to register for some things, and you'll be buried in a landslide of gifts in the end. Even though you'll be writing thank-you notes until your hand cramps, the best way to show your appreciation is by having a long, happy marriage.

The Gift Registry

Though some of your closest friends and family members have probably already decided on the perfect gift for you, there are most likely others—those outside your immediate circle of friends and relations—who would appreciate a few hints. That's where the gift registry comes in.

Gift registry is a free service provided by many department, jewelry, gift, and specialty stores. You and your groom register for a list of gifts you would like to receive. When friends and family go into these stores, pulling up your registry is as easy as finding the touch-screen computer that houses the information. Many registries are also available online, as part of a store's Web site. As each item is bought, it is removed from the list, helping to prevent duplication.

Which Stores?

You and your fiancé should put some careful thought into which store or stores you will register with. Make sure each store has a variety of quality items in the colors and styles you want. You might consider registering with a specialty shop, but remember that the point of the registry is to make gift-buying as convenient for your guests as possible.

To prevent receiving gifts intended for a bride with your same surname, make sure the store uses your groom's name and/or your wedding date as an additional point of reference when your friends and family log on to the store computer or the Web site to purchase their gifts for you.

Even though *you* don't mind making the long haul to your favorite little store downtown, some of your guests might. What's more, smaller stores, though they may offer a bridal registry, may not be set up to offer the convenience of purchasing gifts online. While you may choose to register for a few household goodies in a small boutique, you may want to reserve the lion's share of your registry for a store that is easily accessible to the majority of your guests.

It's best to register with at least one high-quality department store that is sure to have almost everything you need. Your registry will be sent to their branches in other cities and states and will also appear on their Web site—all key advantages, especially for out-of-town guests.

Before registering with a store, ask about the policy on returns and exchanges—you don't want to be stuck with duplicate or damaged gifts. Make sure the store will take responsibility if you receive gifts intended for another couple, and vice versa. Even brides with names much more exotic than Smith or Jones can still share their names with someone else out there. If they've both got bridal registries at the same store, there can be a mixup.

You'll Take One of Everything!

Take your time and browse through the store. Items you are likely to want to register for include a formal dinnerware (china) pattern, a silverware pattern, glasses, pots and pans, linens, small appliances, and various household items (measuring cups, candlesticks, and so on). Many brides know exactly what they're looking for before they step foot in the store, while others don't have the foggiest notion.

Fortunately for the brides in the latter category, most stores have preprinted registry sheets. These not only alert you to what you should be looking for, they'll practically walk you through the process of the entire registration process.

FACT

A carefully assembled gift registry can help put you on the road to a beautiful, functional, and well-stocked home. It will also help ensure that you don't get Art Deco when you wanted Victorian; and that you won't be sitting in front of a pile that contains five juicers, three blenders, and twelve can openers.

When you decide on the styles, patterns, and colors you want, simply add that item to the list, or check the box next to the item and fill in the brand name and quantity. And even though you may feel awkward about it, don't be afraid to ask for a few "big ticket" items like a television or

DVD player. You may be helping out friends or family looking to chip in for just such a gift.

Tableware

Though you and your fiancé may have found it perfectly acceptable up to this point to eat off paper plates, this can't last forever. When your parents come for dinner (and they will), they're going to want to see that you can put a table together. The best way to do that? Pick your tableware carefully. Tableware includes china, everyday dishes, flatware, and glassware, so you have a lot to mull over.

China

Dinnerware usually refers to fine china, although couples also usually request a set of "everyday" dishes. Obviously, the china is more expensive, and you may prefer to include only the china on your registry and pick up the everyday dishes yourselves. Only *you* know what your priorities are. Theoretically, you can register for as many goodies as you want; *realistically*, you're going to receive the most practical items (such as dishes) first, and the less practical items (like the entire home-facial kit you're just dying to have) only if every other item on the registry has been purchased already (or if you have an aunt who refuses to buy practical gifts). So if you have your heart set on both sets of dishes, check 'em off on your registry, but realize that you will only be receiving a certain number of gifts, and that set of everyday dishes will be yours in lieu of something else you might want even *more*.

There are two types of fine china: porcelain and bone. Porcelain is made from refined clay and minerals that make it nonporous, which means it cannot be stained by food. The main ingredient in bone china is bone ash. This china has an almost translucent glow. If you hold it up to light, you can see through it.

Hollowware refers to serving bowls and dishes, such as soup tureens, vegetable dishes, salt and pepper shakers, creamers, sugar bowls, and so on. The choices of style and composition are very broad here. Sterling silver, pewter, glass, wood, silverplate—the list goes on and on. Obviously, you'll be looking for what best complements the tableware scheme that you choose.

Plain Plates

"Everydayware" may seem self-explanatory, but there are actually several kinds to choose from, so your choice might be more complicated than you thought.

First, there's *stoneware*. Like porcelain, stoneware is made from clay, but the clay is grainier and rougher, making it very durable. There's *earthenware*. Earthenware is also made from clay, but it is less durable than stoneware, and it may be stained by food.

Then there's *oven-to-tableware*. From the name, you already know you can cook with it. Oven-to-tableware contains a little porcelain and a mixture of other clays. It is usually guaranteed to be safe and untarnished by the oven for a certain number of years.

The highest-quality *plastic* dinnerware is known as melamine, which is very durable and stain resistant. Not many couples use plastic these days, but you might consider it as a spare set for picnics, vacations, and camping trips.

QUESTION?

How many place settings should we register for?
That depends—on you. If you love to entertain, you'll need a good number of formal place settings (ten or twelve). If you entertain rarely, however, you may want eight settings for special occasions.

Silverware/Flatware

What most of us know as silverware is referred to as flatware in the stores and by those in traditional circles. As you would expect, flatware is just about anything that you eat with, short of chopsticks: forks, spoons, knives, and even serving utensils. Since you won't want to place your best china next to stainless steel utensils with plastic handles, you should put some thought into high-quality flatware.

The best flatware you can buy is made of sterling silver. Some families treat their sterling silver as an heirloom and pass it down through the generations. These days, many couples are bypassing the highest-quality silver and opting for something that is both elegant and less expensive.

There is no denying the elegance and style of sterling silver—but don't hide it away in a cupboard and use it only on special occasions. Regular use of your silver will help to bring out a special glow (called a patina) in the silver that is caused by small scratches. Since you can use it every day, and it tends, with good care, to get better with use and age, you may consider forgetting the middle-of-the-road stuff and going with sterling silver as your standard flatware.

Glassware

Glassware is anything you drink out of or pour a drink from: beer glasses, wine glasses, cocktail glasses, champagne glasses, pilsner glasses, brandy snifters, water goblets, wine decanters, you name it. Your glassware can be as elegant as crystal, right down to everyday juice glasses. The main divisions for glassware are based on how it's made and decorated.

Glassware can be hand-blown or machine-made. Pieces of hand-blown glass are so fine and delicate that they are considered works of art. If you and your fiancé live life like it's a roller derby, you might want to take a pass on the artwork and go for something a little sturdier.

Full-lead crystal is the highest quality glassware you can buy. (The glass must meet standards for its lead content.) Although you might wonder how lead could make such a difference (after all, they used to make pencils out of it!), it does provide an amazing sparkle—and also makes the crystal softer, which aids in the creation of delicate designs.

Other terms you might see in the glassware section of the department store include the following:

- **Pressed glass.** Molds are used to create raised patterns on the glass.
- **Etched glass.** Designs here are made using wax and acid.
- **Cut glass.** Decorated by hand using a stone wheel, or a machine that performs the same function.
- **Lime glass.** Made from combinations of lime and soda. This is the inexpensive, "everyday" glassware.

If you want a really different look, consider colored glass, milk glass (opaque), or cased glass, which looks two-toned.

Linens

Linens are another common registry item. Linens are not restricted to the kitchen. Yes, you should consider napkins (not the kind you use once and throw away), tablecloths, and place mats—but don't forget towels, face cloths, sheets, and pillow cases.

Most stores recommend that you register for three sets of bedroom linens. And you'll need six to eight bath towels for *each* bathroom.

Cookware

There's a wide range of pots and pans available. If you're a gourmet cook, you probably have preferences already. However, if you're waiting for marriage before you dive into regular stints in the kitchen, or if your groom is the one who does the cooking, you may not know the first thing about what you want—or need—in your cookware. Since you may be using these staples of your kitchen a lot, and since you'll probably have them for years and years, choosing the right items for your registry is crucial.

Most high-quality cookware comes in several different forms, depending upon what an item is made of. Before you sign up for anything, find out about the different options: Which one is most durable? Most likely not to fade or scratch? Best at conducting heat?

The Standards

Aluminum is the most popular variety on the market. It spreads heat quickly and evenly, and is the lightest cookware you'll find. (It's pretty easy to clean, too!)

Porcelain enamel conducts and spreads heat the way metal does, but it also has a surface that's extremely easy to clean. Porcelain enamel won't stain or scratch, and you certainly won't find little shavings from the pan's bottom in your food.

Stainless steel, alas, is not a very good conductor of heat. It is durable, though, and it will not dent, scratch, stain, corrode, or tarnish. Sometimes stainless steel can be combined with copper or aluminum, which takes care of the heat-conducting problem.

Remember to ask if the cookware comes with a nonstick surface and any sort of guarantee. You don't want to find that the nonstick surface on your incredibly expensive cookware *comes off* when you wash it.

Glass

Glass and pyroceramic cookware has an all-in-one quality that is ideal for someone with a hectic schedule (or a disdain for washing a lot of dishes). You can use it to prepare a meal in advance, freeze it for a later date, cook it in the oven, and serve from it on the table. It's also nonstick and easy to clean. Its downfall is that it won't behave the same way as metal if you drop it on the floor.

Copper

People have been cooking with copper longer than with any other metal. It is the best conductor of heat you can find, and it helps to keep food warm if it has to sit around a while. Copper is not for those who don't like expending a little elbow grease, as it has to be polished periodically to maintain its shine.

Make sure any copper cookware you buy is bonded with stainless steel, silver, or another surface, as it is dangerous for food to come in direct contact with copper. Mashed russet potatoes would turn into rusted russet potatoes in a straight copper pan, because copper will stain food.

Microwave

Microwaveable cookware has a name that speaks for itself. Since many men and women have grown up only using the microwave for cooking purposes (and since meals are often prepared and eaten on the run these days), you'll want to make sure that you have a few good pieces that will survive—and fit—in your microwave. Most pyroceramic cookware does double duty in the oven *and* the microwave.

FACT

Before you list cookware on your registry, get recommendations from friends, family, or even from Web sites. For instance, *www.epinions.com* offers opinions from consumers on just about everything you can imagine. You should lean toward following the recommendations of people with the same cooking habits as yours.

Gifts at the Reception

Gifts can get lost or damaged at the reception. Tell everyone who might be asked to pass the word that you'd prefer things be sent directly to your home. Any gifts that are brought to the reception are often placed on a gift table. Make sure that the table (or area) you're designating for gifts is out of the way (and away from the door) and won't be bumped into by out-of-control line dancers later in the evening.

Wait until you get home before opening anything. The chances of losing or breaking something at the reception are much greater if the gifts are opened. Ask that someone be in charge of watching the gifts—especially the gifts contained in envelopes (read, "Money") and making sure they find their way home. It's unfortunate but true—unattended gifts sometimes walk away.

Returning/Exchanging Gifts

What if someone sends you a lava lamp—with a matching fringe lamp-shade? Your first instinct, assuming your decorating instincts are in a completely different vein, might be to immediately throw it out, burn it, or exchange it for something else. But it's not as simple as that. The people who bought you that gift did so with the best of intentions, spending a good deal of their time, energy, and money on you. Imagine how hurt they'd be if they visited your house a week after the wedding, expecting the lamp to hold a place of honor, only to find that you'd exchanged it for some napkin rings.

The best thing you can do to avoid this awkward situation is to wait until about a month after the wedding to exchange any unwanted or duplicate gifts. Some brides display all of the gifts they've received somewhere in their home in the days before the wedding; anyone who visits you at that time is likely to look for their gift and even ask your opinion of it.

After the wedding, when everything is put away in its proper place, guests are less likely to make an issue out of their gifts (you hope!). This is also a good policy regarding gifts you receive at the reception. If your aunt, however, gives you a painting on black velvet, you may want to consider keeping it around so that she can see it when she comes to visit you.

ALERT!

If you do return an unwanted gift, don't let the giver know about it. Send a prompt thank-you note expressing your gratitude—and make it sound as sincere as you possibly can.

If you receive a damaged gift, try to track down the retailer who sold the item. If this item didn't come from your registry, you may need to let the gift giver know that the gift was delivered in a less-than-perfect condition. You may be directed to the store where the purchase was made, or the giver may offer to exchange the gift for you. She may still have the receipt, and in any event, she's in a much better position than you are to deal with the store in question. She's the customer, she's the one who spent her money there, and she's the one who is going to get the concessions she's looking for from the store manager.

You, on the other hand, are just a gal coming in off the street, claiming to have received a gift from this store that someone else claims to have purchased there. You have no idea when the gift was bought or how much it cost at the time. You want to experience a run-around first-hand? This is the way to do it.

If you're forced to make a blind exchange, be as firm as you can with the store's employees, but remember you're likely to only get so far with them. They have no idea who you are, after all, and smaller stores often won't make returns or exchanges if you don't have a receipt.

Thank-You Notes

As soon as you receive a gift, you should send out a thank-you note. As hard as it will be given the many notes you'll be writing, try to be warm and personal. Always mention the gift, and, if possible, how you and your fiancé will be using it. This small touch will prevent people from feeling that you just sent them a form letter (which, by the way, is completely unacceptable, no matter how busy you are).

When sending notes for gifts you receive before the wedding, sign your *maiden name.*

Samplings

Some examples of thank-you notes include these:

Dear Ann and Billy,

Thank you so much for the beautiful painting. We plan to hang it over the living-room fireplace for everyone to see. The colors really brighten up the room.

Fondly,
Ann

Dear Aunt Mary:

Thank you for the lovely wine glasses; they really round out our bar set. Jim and I are looking forward to your next visit, when you can have a drink with us.

Warmest regards,
Ann

Each letter makes mention of the gift in question and how it's being used. Notice the sincerity of each note, too. Ann might hate that painting over the fireplace—but you'd never know it.

The gifts may start arriving as soon as you announce your engagement and may continue in a steady stream until the wedding—and even after you're Mr. and Mrs. The gift organizer in the back of this book helps you to keep a record of what you receive, from whom, and when. Organizing things this way will be a great help when you sit down to write those thank-you notes.

Love It . . . Who Sent It?

Occasionally a gift without a card—or *any* clue as to the identity of the giver—will arrive in the hands of a bride. If this happens to you, you're not off the hook as far as writing a thank-you note goes. Put your keen detective skills to work. The sender assumes there is an identifying card with the gift (this isn't a little game someone's playing with you, and it's not from a secret admirer), and he or she is waiting anxiously to hear from you.

If the gift arrived in the mail, check for the return address. No luck? Check to see whether the gift was purchased from the store where you are registered. If it is, there may be a record of who bought it.

If the gift was brought to the reception, your job will be a little harder. Go through your guest list, and try to figure out which people hadn't yet sent a gift by that point. With any luck, there will be only a handful of people who went to the reception who hadn't sent their gift ahead of time. Perhaps you can narrow it down from there. Or perhaps the gift itself will be a clue about its sender. If your great-aunt has always sent demitasse spoons as wedding gifts, and you got a set with no name, you've probably found your culprit.

Proceed with your well-written thank-you notes.

If you hear (from your mother, most likely) that your Aunt Louise hasn't received a thank-you note and you have absolutely no idea what she's given you, it's better to fudge a little on the thank-you note than not to send one at all. ("Thanks so much for the gift. We really love it.")

When You'd Prefer Cash

Perhaps you and your fiancé would prefer gifts of cash to put toward buying a house, a car, or another big-ticket item. If this is the case, *do not* express this wish on your invitations. Ask someone responsible and tactful, such as your parents, to spread the word around. This approach keeps things low-key and helps to let people know what the money will be used for, so they don't think their generosity will be keeping you supplied with cigarettes and beer.

Honeymoon registries have become more popular lately. Your travel agent can help you and your groom set up an account for the honeymoon of your dreams. In many cases, contributing to these honeymoon funds is as easy as logging on to the travel agency's Web site.

If you do find that you are receiving vast amounts of money and you want to be absolutely sure that the money finds its way to its intended purpose (that down payment on a house, or on a car, for example), set yourself up a separate wedding fund. It will be much easier to keep track of the money (and where it's going) if it's separate from your other accounts.

> *Dear Ed,*
>
> *Thank you so much for your generous gift. Mark and I have narrowed it down to two houses and are having a hard time deciding between the two. When we do, we hope you'll be one of the first dinner guests.*
>
> *Cordially,*
> *Ann*

Writing a note for a cash gift is a little different than writing a note about a lamp. Observe the note to the left.

Still polite, but there's no specific mention of the money. Vague? Yes. Acceptable? You bet. The amount of a cash gift should not be mentioned in a thank-you note. Ⓔ

Chapter 6

Showers and Other Shindigs

One great perk of following the traditional road to your wedding day is that you'll suddenly find yourself in the middle of a gift-giving storm. Although you won't be hosting a party for yourself, whoever hosts your shower (or engagement party, for that matter) will probably be looking for your opinion on any number of issues—the guest list, the menu, games. Consider yourself a pinch hitter for your own pre-wedding parties; you're on deck!

It's Raining Presents!

Do you *need* presents from your friends and family to get married? Of course not—but shower gifts *do* go a long way toward helping you and your fiancé set up your household and your future life together. If the two of you have been living on your own (or together) for any amount of time, you may be thinking, "We have everything we need." But what about the things you *want*? And what about the things you don't need every day but do need for special occasions, like dinner parties? This is the time to stock your home.

Who's Hosting?

In the past, etiquette dictated that a bridal shower could only be hosted by your friends, not by family. Today, as with almost all things wedding, this has changed. Family, friends, coworkers, or anyone else who is so inclined can throw a shower for you. The most common hosts are your bridal party, in combination with your mother and other close family members—but who's to say which other generous (and ambitious) people might have a party up their sleeve(s)?

Typically a shower is held either at a small function hall or in someone's home, depending on the size of the guest list. The guests are usually women, but your fiancé can come along for the ride if he wants. He probably won't be nearly as excited as you are about the pots and pans and measuring spoons and place mats—but you never know.

If someone offers to throw a shower for you, don't look a gift horse in the mouth. You should only decline in the most bizarre circumstances (say, if your former boyfriend's new girlfriend wants to throw a party for you, and up to this point, you and she have only hurled accusations at one another).

When?

Time was, the specifics of the shower—time, date, location, and so on—were kept secret from the bride until the last possible moment. These days, however, it's common—and in many cases, necessary—for the bride to take an active part in planning the festivities.

Showers are usually held two to three months before the wedding date. If you absolutely cannot corral your most important guests within the confines of this time frame, shoot for a slightly earlier date (say, three and a half months prior to the ceremony)—or one that's a *little* closer to the wedding (but no more than a month before the big day). You're looking for a date within wedding range. A date that's too close, however, might set you up for feeling stressed over last-minute wedding details while trying to squeeze your shower in somewhere.

The Invites

Making up a guest list? Check with your host(s) first and touch base on the budget. If the plan is for your shower to be a small, informal affair to be held in someone's tiny apartment, your list will obviously be much different than if your hosts are renting out a huge banquet hall. And in either event, who should be invited, and who should be left off the list?

The Cardinal Rule

Any guest who is invited to the shower is automatically invited to the wedding. Period. You can't get around this one, and if you try to, you'll look like a greedy and insensitive Bridezilla. And even if you know *you're* sticking to this rule, it's in your best interest to make sure your *hosts* aren't inviting women who aren't on your wedding guest list.

All of this comes back to you. You can try to shift the blame onto the person who sent the errant invitation(s), but as the bride, you're the ultimate authority figure in this matter and the one who will be held responsible. If someone slips through the cracks, you'll be forced to add another place setting at your reception—which isn't the worst thing in the world. It's when you have to add twenty extra place settings that things start getting hairy.

Shower Size

Often, different groups will host separate showers for the bride-to-be. Perhaps your college friends will throw you a small shower; your coworkers will host another party; and the groom's family will have a third soiree for you. Is it all right for you to revel in such generosity? Of course it is.

Informal showers are generally a breeze to plan. Your host may want to send invitations (any showery-type invites from a stationery store will suffice), but it's perfectly acceptable for the hosts to make phone calls if your guest list is small enough.

No matter how small the shower, the guests should be treated to a nice little party. They will be fed, watered, and entertained. You might cringe at the idea of shower games, and if you're inviting a small group of women who feel the same way, you can encourage your hosts to do away with the games and the door prizes altogether. Just be aware that if your guest list includes ladies from an older generation, those games and prizes are part and parcel of a wedding shower, as far as they're concerned. Sitting around and drinking wine with you and your friends isn't going to fit their definition or expectations of what a bridal shower is all about.

FACT

If your hosts are aware of the other showers you'll be treated to, they may want to gear their own parties in specific directions. For example, your college friends may want to host a lingerie shower. Your coworkers may want to throw a pantry-stocking party, and your in-laws may want to have a domestic/housewares party.

The bride with a large family and many close friends often finds herself in the midst of a huge shower. Some brides feel overwhelmed by the attention and the sheer volume of gifts generated by a party of this magnitude. Here are a few tips for navigating the large shower:

- **Keep cool.** Even if you're completely overwhelmed, every guest wants to see you looking happy.
- **Mingle.** All of these women have come to celebrate your impending marriage, and they brought you gifts. Say hello to every single one of them.

- **Feed yourself.** You're going to have a long afternoon. If you know that you become easily irritated when you feel crowded or hungry, don't turn a potentially bad situation into a disaster.
- **Fudge it.** Every gift deserves a sincere (or at least sincere *sounding*) "ooh" and/or "ahh," even if you find you're losing steam when you're only halfway through the pile.

Some brides are on edge during pre-wedding parties. Unfortunately, these are the same brides who earn the labels "difficult," "bratty," and "spoiled rotten." Don't act as though someone forced you to come to this shower and collect all the goodies.

The In-Law Shower

How can you possibly attend a shower where you don't know anyone and act as though it's perfectly natural to be opening expensive gifts given to you by complete strangers?

If your future in-laws host a shower for you, you may be meeting many of your husband's relations for the first time—and you may feel incredibly awkward about accepting gifts from them. Don't. For starters, no one is forcing these women to come to your shower. For another thing, it's a sure bet that your mother-in-law has gone to bridal showers hosted by these ladies (and given for brides your mother-in-law didn't know yet) and that they're returning the favor.

The best thing you can do when you're surrounded by strangers at your own bridal shower is to smile and say thank you, and make as much polite conversation as you can. You'll leave those ladies saying, "Wow! We could use more of *her* type in this family!"

Food and Drinks

No matter the time of day or the number of guests, food and drink are required elements of the bridal shower. The shower menu can be as simple or as complicated as the hosts want it to be. If your shower is scheduled for noon, for instance, your guests will be expecting lunch.

If, on the other hand, the party starts at three in the afternoon, lighter fare is more appropriate than a large meal.

Good Morning!

A brunch shower is a lovely affair, and the menu couldn't be easier to plan. Whether your hosts are planning an at-home shower or a party in a banquet hall, there are quite a few safe bets that every guest will enjoy:

- **Breads**—bagels, croissants, rolls
- **Pastries**—muffins, Danish, doughnuts, coffee cake
- **Meats**—ham, sausage, bacon
- **Beverages**—coffee, tea, juices, mimosas
- **Other breakfast staples**—eggs, omelets, Belgian waffles, pancakes, fresh fruit

Here's a word to the wise: Don't try to substitute bowls of cereal for a classy brunch here. Your guests will suddenly remember that they left something at home and will leave to retrieve it. They won't be back.

Lunch Time

If your shower is a sit-down lunch in a banquet hall, your hosts will choose a meal from the menu that the caterer offers. If they're hosting the shower at home, it may be easier to put out a spread and let the guests feed themselves.

Suggestions for feeding the afternoon crowd include platters of cold cuts, rolls, various salads (tuna, chicken, pasta, potato, seafood, garden), condiments, and a variety of beverages (soda, punch, wine).

The In-Between Hours

Your shower isn't at lunchtime, and it's not at dinnertime, so no one will need to eat, right? Wrong. It's a party, and you just can't have a party without food—unless you don't mind a bunch of hungry and annoyed women on your hands. Fortunately for your hosts, hors d'oeuvres are popular with party-goers and relatively easy to prepare—or to find in any grocery store.

Consider feeding the masses chicken fingers or wings, stuffed mushrooms, crab cakes, crudités with dip, calzones, shrimp, or pizza cut into bite-size pieces. Pick up a menu from any take-out restaurant, and chances are you'll find a list of possibilities. Easy eats.

You're Not Finished!

You've fed them, but what's a meal (or a snack, for that matter) without dessert? Unless the guests will be having a sit-down meal, with a dessert served afterward, the sweets table should offer a wide variety of choices, which can be so-beautiful-you-hate-to-eat-them works of art or your basic cookies. Cakes, bar cookies, brownies, and fruits dipped in chocolate are easy desserts to prepare, and they're crowd pleasers, too.

FACT

Another featured dessert can be a shower cake. Your hosts can order a shower cake from a bakery, but they can also bake one themselves. It can be simple or elaborate, depending upon how ambitious and creative the hosts are feeling. The cake can be shaped like a heart, a basket, a gift-wrapped package, an umbrella, or anything else that seems appropriate.

Keeping Track

During the gift-opening part of the shower, put someone you trust (an organized bridesmaid, your mother, a friend—but not your six-year-old niece) in charge of recording each gift and who gave it. Choose someone who can keep things organized even if things get hectic, so that when you sit down to write your thank-you notes, you won't come off sounding like a confused bride. (You don't want to thank your Aunt Marion for the gift that Aunt Mary gave you, and vice versa.)

Make sure the person charged with keeping track of who gave you which gift understands the importance of the task. You *don't* want to see this person chit-chatting on her cell phone or hitting the buffet while you're working your way through the stack of presents.

There is a gift recorder included in the back of this book. You can copy it or make your own. All you need is a sizable pad of paper divided into two columns: Gift and Giver.

Let the Games Begin!

Everyone has a definite opinion on shower games: You either love 'em or you hate 'em. Unfortunately, your personal feelings and the opinions of your guests may be different, so in the interest of keeping everyone amused, showers often include games.

Think of this as a way to liven things up a bit for your guests. Alas, even the most engaging party games can encounter some initial resistance from a party pooper or two. If you offer prizes for the winners of these games, though, even the biggest wet blankets may be encouraged to play.

A word to the wise: Keep it clean, especially if you're in mixed company. It's one thing to play rowdy games when you're sitting around with your girlfriends—it's quite another to include Grandma and Great-Aunt Ruth. You'll send them packing, and they won't look back—ever.

Guess the Goodies

Fill a large decorative jar with white or colored candied almonds. Ask the guests to guess how many almonds are in the jar. They can take as long as they want to hazard a guess; at the end of the shower, they hand in their answers on a slip of paper. The person who comes closest to the number without going over wins the jar and the almonds. (You can substitute chocolate kisses, M&M's, jelly beans, or anything else you can think of.)

Make sure that whoever filled the jar knows how many what-have-yous are inside and has written the number down somewhere for safekeeping and for the ultimate last word on who has won. Otherwise, this contest could start to resemble the 2000 presidential election, with countless recounts and various contestants claiming victory.

Famous Couple Trivia

Try developing some trivia questions with a love theme for your shower. Chances are, your guests will do better answering these questions than inquiries about the first space launch, which always seem to be the stumpers in the board-version trivia games (unless, of course, your girlfriends happen to be rocket scientists—in which case, they may actually prefer some more challenging mathematic trivia questions, like figuring out how many different boyfriends a certain starlet has had).

Sample questions include these:

- Who was Tom Cruise's first wife? (Mimi Rogers)
- Who did Prince Rainier marry? (Grace Kelly)
- Who dies first in *Romeo and Juliet*? (Romeo)

Make up your own questions—it's a fun game and most of the guests will have an equal chance of winning, if you include questions about couples from every generation represented at your shower. Set a time limit for answers, and give a prize to the winner. The person with the most correct answers wins.

Pin It on the Groom

This certainly sounds like it has some potential, doesn't it? If your live groom is not willing to volunteer his services (which is very likely), draw the silhouette of a man on a large piece of paper. Attach a photo of the groom's face to the top. Blindfold the guests, spin them, and have them try to pin a flower on his lapel, or a bow tie on his neck.

Prizes

Prizes are the bribe you'll need to get some of your guests to play these games. For others, game-playing is nothing less than an expectation. But what kind of prizes? New cars? Small appliances? An all-expense-paid tropical vacation for two? Perhaps. (But most likely not.)

Winners of shower games expect something useful, but not something that's incredibly cheap. When your hosts (or you) are out looking for prizes, think middle-of-the-road. You don't want anything too expensive, but nothing should look like it came from the dollar store, either. Some suggestions include shopping list pads, recipe cards, note cards or stationery, coffee/tea mugs, candy, bubble bath/bath oils, decorative magnets, coasters, or houseplants.

To guard against the possibility of a riot, prepared hosts will have more than one prize on hand for each game, just in case there's a tie. If there are no ties, or if your hosts are particularly generous, or in the event that the "No Games" opinion wins out, your host can give away extras as door prizes. When the ladies enter, hand them a number (or a ticket—you can buy rolls of them at your huge warehouse/grocery/household goods store). If the tables have place cards, you can write small numbers in the corner of each guest's card. One of the hosts chooses a number, and whoever has the number chooses a prize.

The prizes should be wrapped, if possible (you can't very well wrap a plant, after all) to ensure maximum suspense for the guests ("Ooh, I wonder what she'll get!") and the prize winner as she makes her blind choice ("This one looks like it might be a magnet, but I *really* want some note cards").

More Parties (!)

The bridal shower is just one of several festive occasions that may occur over the course of your engagement. This means, of course, that you should be prepared to party heartily during your engagement—and be prepared for all of it to come to a screeching halt after the wedding. (So enjoy being the center of these good times while they last.)

The Engagement Par-tay

Although it is customary for the family of the bride to host some sort of an engagement party, it's perfectly acceptable for the family of the groom (or anyone else) to host such an affair—or do without one altogether if you prefer. Most engagement parties nowadays are very informal, with invites made via phone or a handwritten note. The party is usually held either at the host's home or in a restaurant. Guests do not typically bring gifts to an engagement party.

The first toast at an engagement party is made by the father of the bride to the couple. This might be followed by a toast from the groom, who will tell everyone how happy and lucky he is to have snagged you. Anyone else wishing to offer a toast may then do so.

The Bachelor Party

You've heard all about (and have probably dreaded) this. In the past, this party was held the night before the wedding, but too many hung-over grooms and weaving green ushers have led more and more rational adults to the conclusion that the bachelor party is better suited to an earlier date. If you can convince your groom to sow his last wild oats at least two weeks prior to the wedding, everyone will feel better about the whole thing. A week before the big day is the closest he should try to squeeze it in.

Bachelorette Party

Now you're talkin'! These days, the bride-to-be is getting a chance to shake her groove thing too, and the activities are bound to be a little livelier than those shower games.

Bachelorettes have come a long way in the past decade or so, and most brides fully expect to paint the town red with their best gal pals. The same time frame applies as for the bachelor party. You don't want to try to juggle a hangover and your wedding day. Since many women seem to be more on the ball as far as party planning is concerned, your friends may spend months planning the perfect bachelorette for you, complete with male strippers, great food, awesome music, a limo . . . and whatever else they can cook up.

Three rules for you:

1. Enjoy yourself.
2. No bachelorette night tattoos.
3. Leave the stripper with his dignity.

Attendants' Party

An attendants' party gives you the chance to turn the tables—to honor the people who've been honoring (and assisting) *you*. Usually this party is scheduled to take place a week or two before the wedding, to give all the harried planners a chance to relax. And it gives you a chance to thank them for all that they have done for you during this busy time.

This may be the perfect time to give your attendants the gifts you've bought for them (though if you want to wait till the rehearsal dinner, that's fine, too). The guest list does not have to be limited to the attendants; family and close friends can also be included. To keep the atmosphere relaxed, consider having a barbecue, a park picnic, or a day at the beach (weather permitting, of course). You might also want to consider having a moratorium on wedding talk. Make it a day (or night) to concentrate on what's up with your attendants' lives—you may have been missing out on some good stuff while you've been caught up in your own wedding whirlwind.

Chapter 7

I Do, I Do: The Ceremony

The wedding ceremony. It's that little thing you have to get through before you can get to the reception. The ceremony is where you make the official commitment—you'll go in as an engaged couple and come out a married one. The ceremony sets the scene for the rest of the day, so you don't want to leave anything to chance. The wedding of your dreams is in the details, after all.

Going to the Chapel?

If you're having a religious ceremony, consult with your officiant about premarital requirements as early as you can. Religions differ in their rules and restrictions, as do different branches within the same religion. If you're involved in your church (and/or have been to many weddings in it), you probably have some idea of what lies ahead. However, if you don't attend services regularly, or you're planning on marrying in your fiancé's church, you might not have the faintest idea of what's allowed and what's not.

Your first meeting with the officiant should clear up most of the technical details and give you the opportunity to ask questions. After everything is settled, the way will be clear for you to personalize your ceremony with music, Scripture readings, special prayers, and even your own vows.

During the meeting with your officiant, be sure to get all the details concerning rules and restrictions, your church's stance on interfaith marriages, any required commitments to raise children in your religion, and so on. Don't be afraid to ask questions. You want to make sure you and your church are on the same wavelength on these important issues:

- What are the requirements (including any premarital counseling) for getting married in this church/synagogue?
- Is the date (and time) you're interested in available?
- Who will perform the ceremony? (You may be close to a particular officiant, only to find that he or she is not available at the time you want.)
- Are visiting clergy allowed to take part in the ceremony? If so, who will be responsible for what?
- Are interfaith ceremonies permitted? What are the requirements or restrictions involved?
- Are there any restrictions on decorations? On music?
- Is another wedding scheduled for the same day as yours? Is there adequate time between the ceremonies so that your guests and the *other* guests aren't fighting for parking spots?
- Are there any restrictions on where the photographer and videographer can stand (or move) during the ceremony?

- Will you be allowed to hold the receiving line at the site—in the back of the church or synagogue, for instance, or in a courtyard?

You should also ask about the cost for the ceremony and for the use of church or synagogue personnel and facilities. This payment is typically referred to as a donation. It doesn't go to any single individual, but to the church or synagogue as a whole.

Religious Ceremonies

The specifics of religious ceremonies vary widely from religion to religion and denomination to denomination. Your officiant will be able to explain in more detail what's involved, but here's a quick rundown.

Roman Catholic Ceremony and Preparations

If you're getting married in the Roman Catholic Church, you probably already know that it has extensive premarital requirements. First, there's Pre-Cana, the premarital course that every engaged couple who is planning to marry in the church must complete. Basically, it consists of covering the big topics of marriage—sex, finances, children—in the context of Catholicism. This might take place at a Pre-Cana leader's home (with another engaged couple or two) over the course of several evenings, or it might take place in a much larger setting (a school cafeteria, for example), over the course of one long day. When you complete the course, you'll receive a certificate that says you're good to go—down the aisle, that is.

If you're a divorced Catholic and you're hoping to marry again in the church, you've got your work cut out for you. In order to be eligible for Catholic remarriage, you'll have to get an annulment, which is a long process (involving a church investigation and possible trial) proving that your first marriage wasn't valid in the eyes of the church for any one of a number of reasons.

Most annulments take at least eighteen months, and they aren't handed out like popsicles. If your first marriage was valid (as far as the church is concerned), then you're out of luck as far as getting remarried in the Catholic Church is concerned. And regardless of what you've been told, if you married (and later divorced) a non-Catholic, you're not granted an automatic annulment.

FACT

For more about the requirements surrounding annulments, talk to your priest—or do a Web search. There's plenty of information online that will give you a good idea as to what's involved with the process.

What about the ceremony itself? You'll be given the option to go through the entire mass, complete with the Liturgies of the Word and Eucharist, or you may choose to cut to the chase, which means your ceremony will consist of some readings and the vows.

The Protestant Ceremony and Preparations

The Protestant religion encompasses many different denominations, but the basic elements of the marriage ceremony are the same. Typically, you can expect things to happen in this order. A Prayer of Blessing is said; Scripture passages are read; there is a Giving in Marriage (affirmation by parents); vows and rings are exchanged; the celebration of the Lord's Supper takes place; the unity candle is lit; and the Benediction is given.

Protestant marriages, regardless of denomination, have far fewer requirements and restrictions than Catholic marriages. An informational meeting with the clergy is required, but premarital counseling is optional.

Jewish Ceremonies and Preparations

Judaism, too, has different "divisions" that adhere to different rules. However, in the Orthodox, Conservative, and Reform traditions, certain elements of the wedding ceremony are basically the same:

- The *kiddushin* (betrothal ceremony) is conducted under a *huppah*, an ornamented canopy (optional in the Reform ceremony).
- The Seven Blessings are recited. Relatives may be chosen to read some of them.

- The bride and groom drink blessed wine; the groom then smashes the glass (wrapped in a napkin) with his foot to symbolize the fragility of life.
- Following the ceremony, the bride and groom retreat to a private room for about fifteen minutes (*yihud*)—the perfect break in a hectic day.

Jewish marriages within the Orthodox and Conservative branches have a few stipulations that require rigid adherence. Weddings cannot take place on the Sabbath or any time that is considered holy. Both Orthodox and Conservative ceremonies are performed in Hebrew or Aramaic only, and neither branch will conduct interfaith ceremonies. Men must wear yarmulkes, and the bride wears her wedding ring on her right hand.

Eastern Orthodox Ceremonies

The Eastern Orthodox (including Greek and Russian Orthodox) wedding ceremony is very similar to the Roman Catholic one, but it features some additional rituals that have important symbolic value.

Many rituals in the Eastern Orthodox ceremony are performed three times—to represent the Holy Trinity. Wedding rings are blessed, then exchanged, three times. (Rings are worn on the right hand.) Crowns are placed on the couple's heads and switched back and forth three times. After the Gospel is read, the bride and groom each take three sips from a cup of wine. The congregation sings "God Grant Them Many Years," and the couple walks hand in hand around the ceremonial table three times.

If Yours Is an Interfaith Marriage . . .

The Catholic Church will sanction a marriage between a Catholic and a non-Catholic providing all of the Church's concerns are met. It is not necessary for, say, a Jewish person to convert to Catholicism in order to marry in a Catholic ceremony.

In marriages between a Protestant and a Catholic, officiants from both religions may take part in the ceremony if the couple wishes and if the church permits it. However, in a Jewish-Christian wedding, even the most liberal clergy rarely will perform a joint ceremony in the temple or church. These ceremonies usually take place at the actual reception site.

Let's Be Civil!

Some couples faced with the tension and potential family problems of an interfaith ceremony choose a civil ceremony. Other couples choose to go this route because they aren't particularly religious people, because they're looking to avoid the expense of a traditional church wedding, or because they're short on time. Civil ceremonies are usually quite a bit easier to pull together than a ceremony in a church.

FACT

The officiant in a civil ceremony is a judge or other civic official legally qualified to perform a marriage. Where will you find him or her? Call City Hall or your county clerk's office for information. They should be able to point you in the right direction.

Contrary to the stereotype (a barren scene in a judge's chambers that takes all of twenty seconds), a civil ceremony does not necessarily mean being boring, quick, or small. You can have a civil ceremony with all the trimmings of a traditional wedding. After all, your civic official isn't tied to a chair in City Hall. Get him or her out of the office—and into a hotel ballroom or a country club or on a yacht or anywhere else you feel like having your wedding.

Civil ceremonies not held at City Hall or the courthouse are usually held at the reception site, which tends to make things more convenient for all involved. It doesn't make much sense to rent a country club for the ceremony, then move everyone to a hotel ballroom for the reception. (See the section on receptions for more location ideas.)

Military Style

If either you or your fiancé is in the military, you may want to consider having a military wedding. These are very formal affairs. They can look quite impressive, what with all of those uniformed guests and wedding party members. This type of wedding features what is perhaps the most visually stunning conclusion of them all: the newly married couple walking arm in arm from the altar beneath an archway of crossed swords!

Spit-Shine That Sword!

A groom serving in the armed forces must wear his dress uniform in the ceremony. As part of his outfit he may wear a sword or saber, but never a boutonniere. If the groom does sport something with a long, sharp blade, the bride stands on his right, presumably to avoid getting blood on that nice white dress. If he doesn't wear a sword, she stands on his left.

A military bride has the choice of wearing her dress uniform or a traditional wedding gown. Other military personnel in the wedding party, male or female, usually wear military garb.

Sit Here, Sir!

As if the seating plan for a regular reception isn't stressful enough, the seating at a military wedding has to account for high-ranking officers and special officials. These people must be seated in places of honor. The remainder of the military guests should be seated by rank. And if you thought you'd seen enough of swords at the ceremony, you're not through yet. Tradition dictates that the bride and groom cut the first piece of their wedding cake with a sword.

With the exception of the attire, some matters of protocol, and the occasional use of weaponry, a military wedding can be as close to a traditional wedding as you wish.

Making the Ceremony Personal

You've been to too many weddings that looked like carbon copies of each other. You desperately want to avoid falling into this trap—but *how*? Get creative. Use your imagination. Do some brainstorming with your fiancé or your friends. If you're attending some weddings in the near future, observe everything carefully. You don't have to copy another bride's ideas, but you can easily take the *meat* of something and add your own spices.

Scripture

Scripture readings at your wedding will, of course, be religious, but you don't have to recycle the same ones you've heard at a dozen other weddings. If you're getting married in a church, your officiant will provide you with a list of recommended readings, most of which focus on some aspect of togetherness and marriage. You can choose from the list the passages that speak to you the strongest.

However, if you have a personal favorite passage that isn't included in the list of wedding readings, ask your officiant if it would be possible to include it in the ceremony. It may even be possible that he or she can build the sermon around your favorite Biblical passage, as long as it incorporates an appropriate message for the occasion.

The Music

Music can add a new dimension to your ceremony, enhancing both its spirit and its meaning. You will have a broad range of choices here as well. Most officiants request that the songs you select be religious, but generally that doesn't mean you're restricted to music you only hear in a church. If you can find commercially released songs that meet the criteria, there should be no problem in their making it onto this "play list."

If you have a friend or relative with a good singing voice or talent for playing an instrument, perhaps he or she can be persuaded to sing or play a special song. It would be best if he or she has experience performing in front of an audience; you don't want to have to give the soloist a pep talk just before the ceremony.

The Rest

How else can you personalize your ceremony? Some couples like to acknowledge their debt to their parents by offering special readings or prayers that focus on family themes. Or, as you walk up the aisle, you could give a single flower from your bouquet to your mother and your groom's mother. Consider including a wine ceremony or a ceremony for the lighting of the unity candle. You might also take your vows by candlelight, and have the church bells ring as you are declared husband and wife.

ALERT!

Be sure to consult with your officiant *first* about the possibilities that are open to you—once you know what's acceptable and what's not, it's up to *you* to be creative!

Writing Your Vows

You may want to formalize your commitment with something unique—something specific to your relationship or situation. If you want to write your own vows, check with your minister first to make sure that personalized vows are permitted during the ceremony. If, on the other hand, you're thinking, "*I'm* not writing any vows!" give it another thought. You get to stand at the altar once with your fiancé, and what better way to pledge your love than to do it in your own words? Get a pad of paper and a pencil with a big eraser, and let yourself go with the flow.

Start at the Very Beginning . . .

Where to start? Think about your relationship and the things that have the most meaning for each of you. For example:

- How do you, as a couple, define the following terms: love, trust, marriage, family, commitment, togetherness?
- How did the two of you first meet? What was the first thing you noticed about your partner?
- What was the single most important event in your relationship? (Or, what was the event that you feel says the most about your development as a couple?)
- Is there a song, poem, or book that is meaningful in your relationship?
- If you share common religious beliefs, is there a particular passage of Scripture that you as a couple find especially meaningful?
- Do you and your partner have a common vision of what your life as older people will be like? Will it include children and grandchildren? Take this opportunity to put into words the vision you and your partner share of what it will be like to grow old together.

Think of these ideas as seeds. It's up to you to make them grow into something more. If you're particularly creative and/or expressive, the possibilities are endless.

Having trouble getting started? Here are some sample wedding vows.

Religious Intro

Groom: *From the beginning of creation God made them male and female.*

Bride: *This is why a man must leave father and mother . . .*

Groom: *. . . and the two become one body. They are no longer two, therefore, but one body.*

Bride: *So then, what God has united . . .*

Groom: *. . . man must not divide.*

Bride: *John, today, in the gathering of this honored company, we unite in God's love. I pledge myself to you as your wife, and will be faithful to you for all of our days.*

Groom: *Kathy, today, in the gathering of this honored company, we unite in God's love. I pledge myself to you as your husband, and will be faithful to you for all of our days.*

Nontraditional Vows

(Both bride and groom recite the same vow.) *I come here today, (name), to join my life to yours before this company. In their presence I pledge to be true to you, to respect you, and to grow with you through the years. Time may pass, fortune may smile, trials may come; no matter what we may encounter together, I vow here that this love will be my only love. I will make my home in your heart from this day forward.*

Love Letters

Maybe this material isn't enough to get across the full meaning of what you want to say, or maybe you simply can't find the right words. Is it time to panic? Nope. Chances are someone else has said it already. William Shakespeare, Elizabeth Barrett Browning, John Lennon—you may just need to find the perfect quote, poem, or song lyric to complete the mood.

Fortunately, there are many books of quotes compiled specifically for this occasion in circulation—look online or at your local library. Once you find a book of suitable verses, look in its index under "love," "marriage," "wedding," "husband," "wife," and other key words—these will direct you to appropriate passages.

FACT

Remember, the right way to compose your own wedding vow is *your* way. The examples you have just seen are offered as general guidelines only. Let your imagination be your guide to developing vows that are meaningful to both you and your partner.

The Second Time Around

Although certain celebrities may be experts at the remarriage game, there are some things you may have questions about if you're heading into your second (or third, or fourth) marriage. There are a few rules of protocol to follow, but nothing you can't handle.

Clean Slate

If this is not the first marriage for either you or your fiancé, the main thing to avoid is the appearance of duplicating (or competing with) your previous wedding. You certainly don't want your fiancé to think you're trying to live in the past by recreating your first wedding. You want to start fresh.

If there was something you did at your first wedding that was particularly meaningful to you—if you wrote your own vows, for example, or if you carried roses because you and your mother grew them together in her garden—it's all right to include them in the second wedding. (*New* vows will be written with your future husband in mind, of course, and the roses are a lovely personal touch.)

Things you should avoid recycling include music, readings, the dress (or any part of the bridal ensemble), the rings, and the reception site. Do things as differently as you can without crossing into foreign, *this-is-not-the-wedding-I-want* territory. Your groom should be a great help to you in this regard.

Shh! Keep It Quiet!

Many people believe that if they had a large wedding the first time around, they must keep things very quiet and subdued for a subsequent wedding. That's not the case, particularly if either member of the marrying couple has never been married before.

In the past, second weddings were hush-hush, but these days they can include the same grandeur as a first wedding. The bride may still have a big wedding party and a big wedding dress; her father might walk her down the aisle, and there might be a slew of limos waiting for you and your attendants after the ceremony. You might also want to have the big reception with all the trimmings.

On the other hand, if you want to have a smaller second wedding, that's perfectly acceptable and not the sort of thing that will raise any eyebrows. It's up to you and your groom to decide what's appropriate for the two of you.

Gifts or No Gifts?

Another point of concern for some couples is the issue of shower and wedding gifts. They feel that if family and friends have already given gifts, it's not fair to ask them to do so again.

The answer to this dilemma is completely up to you and your fiancé. If the two of you are older and established in your lives, you might want to include a "no gifts, please" clause on your invitations (see Chapter 11 for details). But if this is a first marriage for one of you, or if the two of you really would appreciate some help in starting your new life together, it's perfectly acceptable to have a shower and for guests to bring gifts to the wedding. (Of course, guests are never obligated to bring a gift—even to a first wedding—but many may want to anyway.)

As far as the ceremony itself goes, you should consult with your officiant about any restrictions or requirements surrounding the marriage of a divorced person. Once you've handled those issues, the ceremony can pretty much proceed as if it were a first marriage.

If you're a real stickler for etiquette, you can consult any number of books dedicated solely to the issue of remarriage. But these days, it really doesn't need to be that complicated. You and your fiancé should handle a remarriage in a way that makes *both* of you feel comfortable. If that means finding a middle ground somewhere between the big wedding he wants and the tiny wedding you want, then you'll have to play the game of compromise very carefully.

Double Your Pleasure

Your sister, friend, or relative wants to share your wedding day. You, of course, tell her to get lost and pick another day. (There are only 364 others to choose from, after all!) Then you cool off and realize that maybe it's not such a crazy idea after all. And it sure would be *different*, wouldn't it?

Be Selective

Maybe you'd be glad to share this day with someone who's special to you. (And if it's your sister, your parents will certainly appreciate having to pay for only one wedding instead of two.) Whoever the other bride happens to be, the two of you will be forced to share memories of your joint wedding day for the rest of your lives—so make sure she's someone who's going to be in your life for a long time, not someone you'll regret sharing this incredibly special day with.

Obviously, no one can predict what will happen in the years to come. But some situations are easily dispensed with. If you have a friend (or a cousin, or even a sister, for that matter) who annoys you, and she's suggesting that the two of you share a wedding day, say no. Otherwise, you'll regret it in the long run. All the things that get under your skin *now* will be magnified a thousand times over as you plan this wedding with her. By the time you both walk down the aisle, the whole thing will have turned into a headache the intensity of which you could never have fathomed.

And as you can imagine, two full wedding parties take up a lot of room, so find a place that can accommodate everyone. Aside from the fact that everything is done twice, the double wedding can be just like any other wedding. As far as bridal showers and other pre-wedding events go, it's up to you and the others involved to decide whether or not to do things jointly. It's certainly easier on everyone else if the two of you have a joint shower, but if either of you feels the need to retain a sense of individuality, you might tactfully suggest doing some things separately.

Punk-Rock Polka Wedding?

There are some benefits to a double wedding—most of them financial. You send out one invitation for both couples, buy one set of flowers, have one DJ or band.

It would be best for everyone's eyes and ears if the level of style and formality between the two wedding parties were the same. Long, flowing purple dresses in one party and orange polka-dotted miniskirts in another will cause raised eyebrows—and potential eyestrain for anyone daring enough to look directly into the glare of this gathering. Similarly, it's doubtful that your DJ will appreciate alternating the latest tunes for one couple with classical recordings for the other.

Me First!

The main piece of protocol to be aware of in a double wedding is that the older of the two brides proceeds down the aisle first with her wedding party, and then proceeds to do other key things first—like saying her vows. And exiting the church first. And throwing her bouquet before the younger bride tosses hers.

If you happen to be planning a wedding with your younger sister, be aware that as far as she's concerned, this whole setup might get old real fast. You might want to let her have the privilege of taking the lead on some things—or *you* might end up being the first bride (in your family, anyway) to be trapped in the bride's room all night. (Hmm . . . Who wedged that chair under the doorknob?)

Now that you've got your ceremony planned, it's time to think about what you'll be wearing! Ⓔ

North Thurston High School
Learning Resource Center

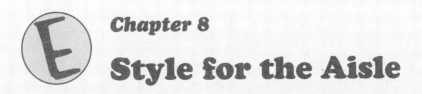

Chapter 8

Style for the Aisle

You're on a new reality show, *Wedding Style Scare Factor*. You have to describe your wedding in detail, and if you can do it correctly, you'll win a billion dollars. Easy money, you're thinking . . . but what kind of wedding *are* you planning? Formal, informal, white tie, black tie, no tie? Time's running out! All right. Relax. There aren't any plans to air this exciting new show (or *are* there?), but you will need to know what kind of wedding you're planning before you can dress your attendants—and yourself.

Man, Oh Man!

Wedding attire is subject to the degree of formality, the season, and the time of day of the wedding. As long as a groom knows the basics of the wedding details (how formal, which season, the hour), just about any formalwear shop can point him and his attendants in the right direction, while simultaneously steering him away from huge fashion errors. (Breathe your sigh of relief now.)

Though every tuxedo carries an air of formality, some are actually dressier than others. You wouldn't want your groom to arrive at your wedding completely overdressed (wearing a top hat at your beach wedding, for example), or way underdressed (wearing tuxedo *shorts* in the cathedral).

Another point to consider is this. If you're having a very informal wedding (on the beach or in a park, for instance), your groom may not need a tuxedo at all. Weddings are basically categorized by their pageantry (things like the setting, your dress, the formality or informality of the reception site), and each style carries its own rules about appropriate apparel.

- **Informal or semiformal wedding (daytime):** Dark formal suit (in summer, select a lighter shade), white dress shirt, dress shoes, and dark socks.
- **Semiformal wedding (evening):** Formal suit or dinner jacket with matching trousers (preferably black), white shirt, cummerbund or vest, black bow tie, studs, and cuff links.
- **Formal wedding (daytime):** Cutaway or stroller jacket in gray or black, white high-collared (wing-collared) shirt, waistcoat (usually gray), striped trousers, striped tie or ascot, studs, and cuff links.
- **Formal wedding (evening):** Black dinner jacket and trousers, white tuxedo shirt, waistcoat, black four-in-hand tie, cummerbund or vest, and cuff links.
- **Very formal wedding (daytime):** Cutaway coat (black or gray), wing-collared shirt, vest, gray striped trousers, ascot, gloves, and cuff links.

- **Very formal wedding (evening):** Black tailcoat, white pique shirt, white waistcoat, white bow tie, black trousers, patent leather shoes, studs, and cuff links.

Point this section out to your groom, and make note of the fact that there isn't any type of wedding (with the possible exception of a Vegas elopement) that advocates making bad fashion choices. Even though the tux will go back to the shop, you're going to be looking at pictures of it forever.

Your Wedding Groan, uh, Gown

You thought finding a bathing suit was tough? Just imagine the pressure you'll put on yourself (and on every bridal salon employee within a fifty-mile radius) to find the perfect gown for the most important day of your life to date. Before you leap into this challenging task, do a little homework. Know what you're willing to pay. Know the general style you're looking for, and know that not every dress shop is looking out for your best interests.

Style Guidelines

Brides, too, are supposed to follow the informal/formal and time-of-day guidelines based on the type of wedding they're planning. However, you should know that many brides are choosing the gowns that they want with blatant disregard for these guidelines (good for them).

ALERT!

You should try to avoid any serious fashion errors. In general, evening weddings are dressier (backless and/or sleeveless dresses would be fine for this type of event). Morning weddings are downright chaste (most of your upper body should be covered), and the longest trains and veils are reserved for the most elegant and formal affairs.

When buying a gown, your major considerations will be these:

- **Fabric.** While many fabrics do double duty as warm- and cold-weather coverings these days, you should save heavy fabrics—like velvet—for winter weddings, and choose from very light ones—like chiffon—for spring and summer.
- **Sleeves.** Can you wear a sleeveless gown in the coldest months? Yes. Just bring along some kind of formal wrap in case you find yourself chilled. Likewise, if you want to wear long sleeves in July, make it happen.
- **Length.** If you're having an informal ceremony, a lacy suit is fine. If you're having an ultraformal wedding, choose a floor-length dress with a very long train. For a semiformal wedding, either a tea-length or floor-length gown is a good choice.
- **Train.** There are many options for trains, which are a separate issue unto themselves and are discussed in the next section.

If your shape will be changing in a certain way between now and the wedding day, don't worry. There's no shortage of styles for the pregnant bride to choose from. Obviously, the style you choose will depend upon how far into the pregnancy you are and how far along you expect to be at the time of the wedding. Brides in their first trimester have a much broader range of choices than those in their second or third.

Train!

When talking trains, there are two things you'll want to keep in mind: length and style. The three most common lengths are sweep, chapel, and cathedral. The sweep train just touches (or *sweeps*—get it?) the floor. The chapel train trails three to four feet behind the gown. If you want the type of train that finishes entering the room five minutes after you arrive, the cathedral (or monarch) train is for you. It ranges from six to eight feet in length. And if you're looking for something *really* dramatic, take a look at a royal cathedral train, which will extend ten (or more) feet behind you. A Watteau train is a beautiful alternative to the more familiar styles—this one falls from the shoulder blades to the hem of the gown. You can also find shorter trains that fall to your fingertips.

If you don't remember ever having seen a bride tripping over her train during a dance with her groom, it's because most trains are bustled (if not detached) after the ceremony to give the bride the freedom to do the Funky Chicken.

The Dress Hunt

You've been looking through bridal magazines, passing the time, waiting for the engagement ring. Now you've got the green light to go out and find the dress. Should you trust yourself to make a dress? Is shopping in a random bridal shop a good idea? The truth is, there are hazards to both situations. But if you're aware of the risks, you're in a good position to head them off.

Starting from Scratch

Handy with a needle and thread? Got enough time (and self-confidence) to whip up a wedding gown? Making your own dress can save loads of money—a homemade dress can cost from a quarter to half the price of a store-bought one—and allow you to create the exact dress you want.

Even if you're not up to a do-it-yourself gown, maybe you (or a relative or friend) know of a seamstress whom you trust to make your gown for you. Of course, you'll be paying for labor as well as the fabric, but it's still likely to be less expensive than a store gown, and you'll have the "luxury" of complete design control. (In other words, you'll have no one else to blame if you don't like the style of your dress.)

Dresses made by hand can take even longer to make than manu-factured gowns (from six months to a year), so be sure you give yourself (or your seamstress) plenty of time to work—and make sure you're dealing with someone who will finish the job. If your seamstress flakes out just weeks before the wedding and decides she just can't go on with her work (and you discover how much she *hasn't* done), you're going to be in a tight spot as far as finding another dress goes. And if you're the one wielding the needle and thread, be honest with yourself. Are you capable of this? Do you have the time? Can someone else pick up the slack if find you're *not* capable and/or *don't* have the time?

Bridal Salons

If you're like most brides, you'll be hitting the bridal salons in your area to find your dream gown. Most salons require an appointment, which you can usually get with only a day or two's notice. Making appointments is worth the trouble, as they ensure that the staff will give you the proper attention. Don't be surprised if you feel like Cinderella being fitted for the magic slipper. The salon employees are hoping lavish treatment from them will turn into lavish amounts of money from you. Be careful. Smiles, compliments, and free coffee and tea (and, in some cases, champagne!) do not necessarily translate into quality dresses or reputable business practices. Read on . . .

Bridal Salon Bewares

Even if you have an unlimited amount of money to spend on a gown, you want to be sure you're shopping in a reputable store, one that won't leave you standing at the altar in your slip come your wedding day. (Eek!) Unfortunately, some bridal shops out there will try to get as much money out of you as they possibly can. In exchange, you'll find that they provide little or no quality. Be informed about some of the more common schemes (and don't assume that those smiles are genuine).

The majority of salons require a deposit equal to half the price of the dress. Rather than order the dress from the manufacturer right away, they'll hold your deposit and use the money for other things (like earning interest in the company checking account). They end up ordering your gown at the last possible minute, which means it may not be ready in time for the wedding.

In Chapter 3 we discussed the alteration scam as it pertains to bridesmaid's dresses. It's worth investigating in the context of your wedding gown. A shop may *grossly* overestimate the size a woman takes in order to charge a hefty fee for alterations.

Employees of dress shops make a valid point on this issue by reminding customers that most women are different sizes on top and on the bottom. This is true—and if you're a size ten on the top and a size twelve on the bottom, you may well have to order a size fourteen, because the dress runs small and it has to fit the largest part of your body. *This* isn't cause for alarm. A recommendation that you order a size twenty *is*.

Word of mouth is always your first line of defense. If someone whose opinion you've always respected tells you that she had a major problem with a shop, *listen* to her—even if the store has a dress you love. She's giving you the benefit of her firsthand experience.

Get every aspect of your gown's purchase down in writing, including the delivery date. Find out the store's policy regarding late or damaged gowns. Find out exactly when the shop plans to order your dress. Ask for written verification of the order, and call periodically to check on progress.

If (God forbid) something should go seriously wrong, don't be afraid to take legal action—or to at least threaten it. You may be surprised at the action you'll see once the word "lawyer" enters the conversation.

Let the Fun Begin!

Now that you're armed with the facts, you're ready to shop. Get going as early as you possibly can. Wedding gowns can take six months or longer to arrive after the order is placed, so start making your way through the racks of satin, silk, taffeta, chiffon, brocade, shantung, and organza (it's like a carnival of fabric!) as soon as that ring hits your finger.

Leave yourself time for alterations and unforeseen glitches. No book can tell you what style and fabric are best for you. Instead, those are strictly judgment calls for you (and your mother, of course) to make. When you find the right dress, you'll *know*.

You'll want to take along one person (your mother or a close friend, for instance) to consult with on matters of style and appearance. It's also this person's job to baby you when you get frustrated because you don't like any of the dresses you've tried on. It's not wise to take more than one or two people, however. The situation can be stressful enough even without adding in the opinions of five other people.

QUESTION?

Should I bring a camera with me to the bridal salons?
Taking a camera along when you try on gowns seems like a good idea. You could take pictures of yourself in your favorite gowns and look at them at your leisure. Unfortunately, it's a prohibited practice in many stores. Bridal shops are brutally competitive with one another. They don't want you to have a picture that you could take to another salon—or to a dressmaker.

Accessories

You've found the perfect dress. You're thinking, "I'm done, I'm done! Hooray!" Hold it right there, sister. You're not done. (Silly girl—you thought this would be as easy as finding a *dress*?) You need a veil and headpiece, and all the little things to complete your ensemble. Summon up your strength. You're heading back into the trenches.

Although salons offer slips, nylons, bras, and shoes, the items they sell are often overpriced. You're better off buying them elsewhere. The key is starting early enough so that you can find what you need without being pressured for time.

Where's Your Head?

Your headpiece and veil should complement the style of your dress. Don't pick something so ridiculously elaborate that it overpowers you and your dress. You want all eyes focused on you—the complete package—not a little body and tiny head under a massive headpiece.

Today's wedding veils owe a lot to the invention of one of the world's most popular modern conveniences: Velcro. Thanks to Velcro, veils can now be removed from the headpiece after the ceremony, which frees the bride from worrying about ripping her veil during close encounters with family and friends. It may not sound classy, but talk to a bride who has had her head almost snapped off because a hand or ring got caught in her veil, and you'll gain a new appreciation for the concept.

FACT

Although a headpiece takes only eight to ten weeks to arrive after you order it, try to give yourself more time than that. Having the headpiece well in advance gives you a chance to go through one or two trial runs with your hairdresser.

Your Handbag

You won't be carrying a handbag during the ceremony, but you will need a bag to carry your personal things—lipstick, mirror, comb, tissues for your tears of joy. The purse should also complement your ensemble, so leave your navy-blue work handbag at home. Think little, white, lacy, beaded, or bowed. (Some dressmakers will make drawstring bridal bags from fabric that matches or complements your dress.)

Savvy brides who don't want to be bothered with a purse can request an extra alteration to their wedding dresses: deep pockets. For about the same price as an ornate bridal purse, you could have your lipstick *really* handy for the entire evening.

Your Tootsies and Gams

Your footwear should be silk or satin, and the same color as your dress (all whites are *not* the same). Choose a pair you can dance and stand in comfortably—remember, you'll be on your feet for hours!—and break them in by wearing them around the house before the wedding. One way to save a bundle on bridal shoes, if you're crafty, is to purchase a pair of plain, inexpensive shoes and decorate them yourself with lace, beads, or whatever suits you and your dress.

When it comes to hose, avoid opaque white stockings! Instead, go for the sheerest champagne, nude, or pale blush color you can find (depending on your dress color, sheer white or ivory are fine, too). Sheer stockings are classier looking and are flattering to legs, whereas opaque stockings can make perfectly fine gams look like tree stumps. Have an extra pair handy on the big day in case of disasters just before the ceremony.

Intimates

You'll want to purchase undergarments that work specifically with your gown. These may include a strapless or pushup bra, a corset, special tummy reducing underwear, and a slip.

If your gown requires a petticoat, don't try to get away without wearing one for the sake of saving yourself a few bucks. The gown is designed to fall a certain way (that is, over a petticoat). If you go without the proper undergarments, you will have wasted the money you spent on the dress, because it just won't look right.

Bridal Bargains

So you're a real bargain shopper, are you? Hope you have some mettle—looking for bargain bridal dresses is hard work (especially as this practice grows in popularity). For every bride who finds the dress of her dreams at a fraction of the price she would have paid in a bridal shop, there are ten others who have nothing but frustration to show for their bargain hunting.

ALERT!

If you're determined to find something cheap, start looking as early as you can and remember—if it's cheap but it's not the least bit flattering (and you'll *know* whether it is or not), leave it for someone else.

Used/Consignment Gowns

One way to get an inexpensive gown (provided you don't care if you're not the first and only person to wear it) is to pop into a consignment shop. There are even some shops that are dedicated solely to wedding apparel. A previously worn wedding gown can be yours for a fraction of the cost of a new dress, and you can take it home with you the same day.

Of course, finding a quality wedding gown on consignment may require some tenacity, as well as a little detective work, since they don't come down the pike every day. If you're serious about finding a gently used dress, check the classified section of the local newspaper. One bride's broken engagement could be your coup.

The downside to purchasing a previously worn gown is that it will probably need some alterations. Bridal salons may not work on gowns that are not bought at their store, so you'll have to search for a reliable seamstress to do the alterations for you. Be forewarned: Talented seamstresses who can tackle your alterations and have them completed in time for the ceremony are few and far between. And unfortunately, the expense of these alterations *may* nullify the money you saved buying the used gown, depending on how much (or how little) you saved in the first place.

Outlet/Warehouse Sales

Maybe you've seen television news coverage of a local warehouse's one-day wedding gown sale. Brides-to-be line up as early as six o'clock in the morning to get first crack at wedding gowns, many boasting top designer names, marked down to as little as $100 each. When the doors open at nine, it's as if a dam has burst. Women grab as many dresses as they can handle, regardless of size, to increase the odds of finding something they like. No one bothers much with dressing rooms; they try the dresses on right next to the rack. If a woman doesn't like a gown, you can bet there's someone standing next to her ready to grab it.

The obvious advantage of these sales is financial. You can get a new gown for the price of a previously worn one, but you still have to hustle to find a seamstress to do the alterations, and she won't come cheap. And it goes without saying that you won't get the pampering of a bridal salon. Why, you'll be lucky to get space at the mirror!

Shopping this way for a wedding gown is not for everybody. However, if you can endure the madhouse atmosphere, the competition, and the possibility that you might come away empty-handed, getting up extra (*extra*) early to get your spot in line might work out swell for you.

FACT

If you have a good eye for fashion, an inexpensive alternative to a formal bridal gown is to find a suitable bridesmaid's dress. You may have to dress it up a bit with some lace, buttons, and so on. For a less formal occasion, this can be a thrifty and inventive way to go.

Wedding-Day Beauty Tips

The dress is perfect, the shoes are divine, your pantyhose are the perfect complement to your legs . . . hey, wait a minute . . . What happened to your hair? And why is your face all blotchy? Have you been doing some last-minute beauty rituals—things you've never tried before? Word of warning: Don't! While you want to look your best, you also want to look like you. This is not the day to try to jump-start that new beehive hairdo trend you've been reading about. Stick to what's been working for you all along. If you must try something new, give it a trial run (or two or three) before the big day.

Pre-Wedding Hair Prep

You know that there's a time lapse between the *cut* and the *look*. For many women, it's a week or two from the time their hairdresser's scissors crop their locks until they feel truly comfortable working with and styling their hair. If you've made any drastic changes to your hairstyle, it could take even longer for it to feel like *your* hairdo.

If heeding that warning is prudent in everyday life, the advice quadruples in value when talking about your wedding. Never, *ever* get a haircut or change your hairstyle right before your wedding. Not only do you run the risk of looking and feeling self-conscious in the new 'do, but you could absolutely hate the new style, upsetting you to the point that you can't truly enjoy the big day. (There's a reason that the phrase "bad hair day" carries with it the unspoken message of "Leave me alone!") Do you really want these emotions captured on film?

ALERT!

The same rule of thumb applies to highlighting, coloring, perming, or straightening your hair. If you want to have an updated look for your wedding day, try it out well in advance— and have it professionally done. No one but Mother Nature can grow back the hair you burn off your head with an at-home perm.

Change is a wonderful thing, of course, and it's understandable that you want to look a little different on your wedding day. Just make sure to allow enough time before the wedding to get acquainted with your new hair (or to learn to live with any disasters). Start experimenting with your hairdresser six months prior to the wedding. And don't forget that you'll need to bring your headpiece to the beauty shop for at least one trial run before the big day.

Wedding-Day Hair

If you're like many brides, you'll want to reach for the security of the stylist on your wedding day, either because you feel no one can make you look better or because your hands are too busy shaking to wield a brush.

Brides walking out of a salon, wearing an up-do, a veil, a *button-up* shirt (because you can't pull a T-shirt over your perfectly groomed hair, after all), and jeans are a fairly common sight, especially during the busy wedding months. However, if you don't want to be seen in public this way, ask whether your hairdresser would be willing to make the trip to your home (or wherever you'll be preparing for the ceremony). This might also save you the trouble of exposing your perfect hairdo to any nasty weather—a virtual guarantee of a bad hair day.

Put Your Face On

If you've always wanted to sit down at one of those department-store cosmetic counters and say, "I challenge you to make me *more* beautiful!" now's the time. Like your hairdresser, a cosmetologist can help you feel more confident in your appearance—or give you a completely new look. Even if you're completely happy with your daily makeup selection and application skills, you may want to try something special for your wedding day.

A department store cosmetologist will gladly give you a consultation and a makeover, especially if it impels you to buy some of her products. If you're impressed by her abilities and her advice, buy whatever items you want or need and go home and practice.

The alternative to a department store cosmetologist is a professional cosmetologist. She'll cost more, of course, but she won't be worried about selling you a specific line of cosmetics. She'll use whatever looks best on you (and she'll try to sell you that).

This is the woman you can hire to come to your home before the wedding—if she does a great job, book her. She'll be worth every penny.

"You're Soaking in It"

Does your concept of a manicure include Madge dipping your hand in Palmolive? Having someone file your nails and attend to your cuticles may seem frivolous, but consider this. After admiring your dress, your hair, and your new husband, friends and family are going to want to see your ring finger. Your photographer might also suggest a "ring shot," in which you and your groom clasp left hands over your bouquet. If your fingernails are misshapen, bitten, or just plain unattractive, consider salvaging them for this one day. (E)

Chapter 9

The Ins and Outs of Receptions

If weddings simply involved standing before a religious or civic official and saying, "I do," there would be precious little to have a nervous breakdown over. Brides wouldn't pull their hair out over every detail, and parents wouldn't start putting aside money to pay for their daughter's wedding on the day she was born. A typical reception has finery, etiquette, cakes, and dances—and this is only a partial list. This chapter takes you on a ride through planning the big party.

Start Looking *Now*

The first thing you have to do is find a place to have your reception. Religious officiants will tell you to set the ceremony date first and then find a reception site. Many couples, however, try to do just the opposite. Of course, this is like the chicken-and-the-egg question. What it really comes down to is whether you are more particular about the site of the wedding ceremony or of the reception. If you just have to be married in the church where you were baptized and confirmed, and *its* available dates don't coincide with the dates available at the reception site you're considering, then you'll just have to find another banquet hall.

On the other hand, if you want your reception in a certain location, but the location of the actual ceremony doesn't really matter to you (you'll even consider a civil ceremony on the premises), your choice is obvious.

During the peak wedding months of April through October, competition for wedding sites can be fierce. If you're marrying in this time frame, plan on looking for your ceremony and/or reception sites at least a year in advance.

Off the Beaten Path

While function halls, country clubs, and hotel ballrooms are still the most popular sites for receptions, these days there's no limit (except your imagination—and your tolerance for the unusual) to where you can hold your reception. As long as people can gather there to eat, drink, and be merry, it will do.

Get Creative

Looking for someplace really different for your wedding reception? What kind of unusual, original settings can you choose from? Consider the following:

- Castles, estates, or historic mansions
- Observatories
- Museums/art galleries
- Scenic mountain resorts
- Historic battleships, boats, or yachts
- Gardens, greenhouses, or public parks
- Country inns
- Concert halls or theaters

There are also baseball parks, football fields, marinas, and other spots connected to hobbies or anything of common interest. Your creativity is your best source. Follow up your instincts with some phone calls to the appropriate people—the manager of the historic movie theater, for example—to find out what's available in your area.

Odds are you'll pay a bit more to secure one of these nontraditional sites than you would for a standard venue. But be sure to weigh the cost against all that you'll get for your money. In settings like these, your surroundings won't be part of an insignificant background. They'll say something unique about you and your new husband.

FACT

The availability of some of these more unusual options will depend on the season and the weather. But if Mother Nature cooperates, sites like these can make for a beautiful and memorable wedding day. (For outdoor sites you will, alas, need to establish a backup site elsewhere—or incorporate a large tent into your plans—as a precaution against inclement weather.)

Theme On!

A theme wedding is another step away from the traditional that will make your wedding something special. Depending on the theme you choose, you can live out your fantasies of living in another time or another place. (Just make sure to give your guests a heads-up so that they aren't shocked to see your groom in tights at your Renaissance-themed wedding.)

Some ideas include the following:

- **A period wedding.** Emphasize the traditions, costumes, music, and customs of an earlier period.
- **An ethnic wedding.** Perhaps you and your fiancé would like to highlight the culture and costumes of your ethnic backgrounds.
- **A holiday wedding.** A wedding during a holiday season can take advantage of the decorations and spirit of that time. (Valentine's Day and Christmas are popular choices.)
- **The all-night wedding.** This is a wedding celebration that's planned to last through the entire night. The wedding usually comes to a close with breakfast the next morning.
- **A weekend wedding.** You've heard of an all-nighter? Well, this is an all-weekender. Usually, a weekend wedding is set up like a mini-vacation for you and your guests, taking place at a resort or hotel.
- **A surprise wedding.** The wedding is a surprise not to you, but to your guests. Invite people to a standard-issue party—your guests will be completely surprised when they arrive at a wedding.

What about a wedding with a sports theme? A beach party wedding? How about a hoe-down weddin' theme? Pick something and go all the way with it.

Traditional Style

All right, so you don't have to dress up like cowpokes just to have a memorable wedding. In fact, wherever you decide to receive your guests as husband and wife will seem like the perfect spot to you on your wedding day.

Home-Sweet-Home Reception

For many couples, the perfect solution to a reception dilemma is having a party at someone's home. If you're lucky, you, your parents, or someone you know will have a house and yard big enough to accommodate your reception. What better way to celebrate the most important day in your life than in the house where you grew up or the backyard where you used to play? Placed in a unique context, and surrounded by family and friends, you'll have an incredible reception experience.

ALERT!

Don't assume that having a home reception means your parents have to sweat in the kitchen all day preparing and serving food. If you're expecting more than fifty guests, it's best to bring in a professional caterer for the job.

Because a home or backyard reception is so informal, you won't be tied down to traditional entertainment (play some CDs instead of hiring a band), menu items, or even a dress code. If the festivities are in the backyard, have a barbecue or a clambake and tell the guests to wear shorts.

Stay Right Where You Are!

Some receptions are held on the same grounds as the ceremony— the ultimate in convenience for you and your guests. Many churches and synagogues have a function room on the premises that you can rent without much fuss, at a cost that's much less than a commercial site. The reception is typically small and informal, and the menu is usually quite scaled back (maybe as light as cookies and punch, or a small buffet).

Bear in mind that a site with a religious affiliation may not allow alcohol and may also restrict the kinds of music you can play at the reception.

While You Wait

You've found the perfect place for your ceremony and the perfect place for your reception. The only problem is that the reception site is booked until two hours after your ceremony ends.

Relax. There's no law that says receptions have to immediately follow the ceremony. However, if a delay is inevitable, make sure that your guests, especially those from out of town, are entertained between the ceremony and the reception. Set up a hospitality suite at a nearby hotel, or ask a close friend to have cocktails or hors d'oeuvres at his or her house.

Your Reception Investigation

Now that you're aware of all of the reception options open to you, it's time to consider some sites and put them through the wringer. This is the part of your wedding you will likely spend the most money on. Take the proper steps from the very start to make sure you get every penny's worth.

A Few Inquiries

Because this is a business transaction (not the most romantic way to think of your wedding day, but perhaps the most practical), you should treat your interview with the banquet manager as such. Here are some questions to ask of him or her:

- How many people can the facility comfortably seat? How big is the dance floor?
- Is an in-house catering service offered? Can you bring in your own caterer? (See Chapter 10 for more catering details.)
- How many hours is the site available for? Is there a time minimum you must meet? Are there charges if the reception runs overtime?
- Is there free parking? If there is valet parking, what are the rates and gratuities?
- Will there be coatroom and restroom attendants? A bartender? A doorman? What are the charges?
- If you've arranged for an open bar, do you have to bring the alcohol, or does the site provide it? If you've arranged for a cash bar, what will the prices be?

- Does the facility have more than one reception site on the premises? Is yours the only reception happening that day, or is there one before or after (or at the same time in the next room)?
- Will your deposit be returned in the event of a cancellation?

There are other issues to address as well, such as where your musicians will set up, how and where your decorations will be displayed, and how many guests will be seated at each table.

FACT

A good banquet manager will walk you through the entire reception from start to finish. A not-so-good one will simply ask if you have any questions. Don't be shy—lay them on him or her. It's in your best interest to ask as many questions as you can come up with to make sure you're spending your money in the right place.

Comparison Shopping

You can start your search for the ideal reception site by asking friends for their suggestions and comments. Visit the places you're considering, go through all the questions listed above in your preliminary conferences, and write down the answers for easy comparison later on. Note carefully whether the people you will be dealing with are courteous and responsive to your wishes.

If you like a hall and the prices quoted, go back to see a wedding or a formal dinner in progress, especially if you have never been to a function there. If you are considering a restaurant or a country club, it is a good idea to have dinner there on a Saturday or Sunday, when presumably the kitchen and staff are putting forth their best efforts at their busiest time. Take note of the activity. Will your party have adequate privacy if the rest of the place is full? What kind of ambiance is projected by the clientele the place draws, the physical setting, and the quality of service? Carefully check the maintenance of (and the lines forming inside) the restrooms on a busy evening.

If a place seems like a good possibility, have the site manager give you a preliminary estimate in writing, spelling out the details of menu, service, and everything else you've discussed. Then compare your various estimates and impressions before you commit yourself.

That Costs *How* Much?

Make sure you're aware of all reception-related charges up front. A deposit (usually a great big one) will reserve the site you want. Many sites won't refund this deposit if you decide you don't want them anymore. Before you sign on the dotted line, review the agreement carefully, and get references from people who have used the facility for a wedding reception. As always, make sure every part of your agreement, including date, time, services, and policies, is in writing.

Sales tax, an item sometimes overlooked, adds a hefty amount to the already large reception cost. Cancellations, changes, and last-minute additions may also cost additional money. You don't want to come home sunburned and exhausted from your honeymoon only to discover that your wedding money will go toward paying off the hidden fees associated with the reception.

Receiving Your Guests

On to the actual reception. You'll be faced with the issue of whether you should have a receiving line. This tradition receives a fair amount of bad press these days, and it's usually the first to get the ax. But consider this. A receiving line doesn't have to take up an agonizing chunk of time, and many of your guests may be expecting you to have one. It enables you, your groom, and key members of the wedding party to meet and greet your guests—which is *very* important, since you won't have time to socialize at length with everyone at the reception.

Imagine your Aunt Gert's disappointment in this scenario. She has chosen *the* perfect wedding gift for you, traveled across the country to watch you walk down the aisle. And yet, since there isn't a receiving line, and since you're so busy having your picture taken and being whisked off every which way during the reception, she never has the opportunity to wish you and your groom well.

ALERT!

Disappointment will be the least of it, if you're lucky. Some guests (particularly older ones) view the omission of the receiving line as a rude gesture, as if the bride and groom were saying, "Just eat your dinners and leave us a gift. We don't have time to say hello."

Receiving Line 101

The present-day etiquette on receiving lines is short and sweet. You should have one, but keep it simple. The order of the line is not even something that must be adhered to—as long as you include the essential players, you're in good standing.

The receiving line should form after the ceremony but before the reception. If you're worried about the line taking up too much time on your big day, or if you and your groom are not immediately proceeding to the reception (because you're taking photos, for example), try to have the receiving line at the church or synagogue.

If you elect that option, be sure to check with your officiant first. Some have restrictions concerning where the line may be formed. The most convenient spot is often near an exit or outside, where guests can move through easily on their way to the reception. If you choose to have the line at the reception site, have refreshments and entertainment available for guests while they're waiting.

Who Is Included?

Your attendants do *not* need to be included in your receiving line. This speeds things up and eliminates a whole lot of the very phony, "Oh, so nice to meet you!" comments from all parties involved. Though at one time only women were expected to stand in the receiving line, fathers are more than welcome—unless they're needed to greet guests at the reception site.

If you're including all of the parents, your line can form in this order: mother of the bride, father of the bride, bride, groom, mother of the groom, father of the groom. If there's been a divorce and lingering bad feelings between one set of parents, do a little shuffling.

If a guest is a complete stranger to you, introduce yourself. Be friendly but brief. A simple "Thank you so much for coming! It's so good to see you!" or, "I've heard so much about you," in the case of meeting new relations for the first time should suffice. If you have someone who's chewing your ear off, don't be afraid to point out the appetizers and the bar to them.

All in a Day's Reception

You're probably already familiar with the traditions of the first toast, the first dance, the cake cutting, and the garter and bouquet throwing. But just in case you're a little foggy on them (or up in the air over whether to include them in your reception), here's a refresher.

Toasts

After the guests have been seated for dinner, everyone is served a glass of champagne or another sparkling beverage for the toast. Toasts, of course, are an important part of the wedding reception—and, like every other wedding ritual, toasting has its etiquette.

Brides rarely give toasts at their own weddings, though they may if they're inclined to do so. Best men are the first in line to present a toast. However, they usually don't read up on wedding etiquette. You or your groom may need to give *your* best man a few pointers—such as less is *always* more, and a randy limerick has no place in a room full of elderly relatives.

You and your groom should know that the recipient of a toast does not drink at the end of the salute, but simply smiles at the person offering the kind words. All toasts except the best man's toast are optional. Once the toasting is over, the dinner is served, and your best man can stop his profuse perspiring. He's done.

FACT

If everyone is chomping at the bit, waiting to hail you and your groom, the order of toasters is as follows: best man, groom's dad, bride's dad, groom, bride, friends and relatives, maid or matron of honor, groom's mom; bride's mom . . . and then anyone else.

The Opening Dances

The bride and groom's first dance is often one of the most romantic parts of your reception. You and your new husband will dance to a song the two of you have carefully chosen for its message of undying love while your guests look on and smile.

After the first dance, the bride dances with her father, and then the groom dances with his mother. Afterwards, the bride and groom's parents dance, the bride dances with her father-in-law, the groom dances with his mother-in-law, and the bridesmaids and ushers dance with each other.

That's a whole lot of dancing, you say? Yes, it is—and it can be incredibly time consuming, especially when you see your guests itching to hit the dance floor. Feel free to eliminate or combine some or all of these dances, and when you're ready to mambo with the masses, have the bandleader or master of ceremonies announce when *everyone* is welcome on the dance floor.

The Cake-Cutting Ceremony

Aside from being a tasty little treat, the wedding cake performs a very important function as the centerpiece of the cake-cutting ceremony, when the bride and groom cut the first piece of cake together and feed each other a bite as the crowd watches to see if either of you has the guts to smash the other one's face with it. At a sit-down reception, the cake is usually cut right before the dessert, if any, is served. However, if you have a photographer who is trying to move things along, don't be surprised if he or she wants to move the cake-cutting up a bit. The caterer or baker will cut the rest of the cake and distribute it to the guests.

The Bouquet and Garter Toss

Once widely accepted traditions, these reception elements have gradually lost favor in some sectors. If you've never been a witness to this merry little convention, it starts with the bride tossing her bouquet (usually a throw-away bouquet provided by the florist for this occasion) to a group of single women. The groom then removes a garter from the bride's leg and tosses it into a crowd of single men. The two "winners" come together in the middle of the dance floor, where the woman is seated, and the man with the garter slides it up, up, up her leg. The men cheer, and the other women are grateful that they didn't catch the bouquet.

Today, many brides find the tradition degrading, especially to the women involved. As a result, many brides decide to eliminate it, in whole—or just in *part*. There's no such thing as a reception ordinance requiring your female guest to allow a strange man to push a garter way up her thigh. If you want to toss your bouquet, go for it—and leave it at that.

Turning the Tables

Unless you're planning a cocktail reception with hors d'oeuvres or an informal buffet, you're going to need a seating chart. Guests (especially those who don't know many people) often feel uncomfortable without assigned seating.

It's best to realize early on that no matter how hard you try, someone—your mother, your fiancé's mother, your cousin Marta—is bound to be unhappy with some aspect of the seating plan. The easiest way to approach this project is to get input from your mother and future mother-in-law; if possible, the three of you should sit down and come up with the plan together. Both moms will know those relatives who want to sit together and who should be seated at opposite ends of the room—which will make *your* life infinitely easier.

Placing People

If you're planning a very formal wedding, place cards are necessary for all guests. At less formal receptions, place cards are used only at the head table. The easiest way to alert guests to their table assignments is to place table cards on a table near the reception room entrance. Table cards simply list the name of the guest and their table assignment. Another option is to set up an enlarged seating diagram at the reception entrance.

One idea for creative seating assignments is to decorate the tables with centerpieces and other goodies that go along with different themes, and name the tables accordingly. If you put a different type of floral arrangement at each table, for example, you can tell your guests that they'll be sitting at the Daisy table or the Rose table.

Save Me a Seat!

The head table is wherever the bride and groom sit, and is, understandably, the focus of the reception. It usually faces the other tables. The table is sometimes elevated, and decorations or flowers are usually low enough to allow guests a perfect view of you and your groom kissing and gazing into each other's eyes, even as the two of you scarf down your filet mignon.

Traditionally, the bride and groom, honor attendants, and bridesmaids and ushers sit at the head table. The bride and groom sit in the middle, with the best man next to the bride and the maid of honor next to the groom. (The seating of the attendants should follow male-female-male-female around the table from there.)

You may also choose to have a table for two—just you and your groom. Or you could sit with your honor attendants at the head table and seat the rest of your attendants together at a smaller table.

Child attendants should sit at a regular table with their parents. Spouses of attendants don't sit at the head table with their husbands or wives. If they won't know anyone else at the wedding, try to seat them with someone they might have something in common with.

The Parents

Parents of the bride and groom sit at separate tables with their own families. There's no single correct seating arrangement for the parents' tables. The bride and groom's parents can sit together with the officiant and his or her spouse at the parents' table, or each set of parents can host their own table with family and friends.

The officiant is seated in a place of honor at the reception. Make sure that one of the parents' tables includes the officiant and his or her spouse. Seating the person who pronounced you husband and wife near the kitchen is a no-no.

Not-So-Musical Chairs

Where do you seat your divorced, actively warring parents? As far away from each other as possible without offending either of them. The trick here is to place each of them at separate tables that are in the vicinity of the head table, but not so close to each *other* that they'll have to hear their ex-spouse's voice.

Here's an example. If your groom's parents are not divorced, you could reserve three tables in front of the head table for seating the parents—one for your mom and her family, one for your groom's parents, and one for your dad and his family. Your in-laws' table would be smack dab in the middle in this scenario—neutral territory.

Party All Night?

After the guests have been whooping it up at your reception all day (or all night, as the case may be), it can be tough for them to stop having fun and go home. Sometimes the parents of the bride or groom will host a small after-party for very close family and friends. This way people get to wind down—or continue on with the fun they were having. The after-party is usually at the parents' home, but these days it is also common for the family to rent another reception site, or to extend the time at the original one. The danger of the latter situation, of course, is that the parents may end up hosting many more guests than they had intended. (E)

Chapter 10

Food, Glorious (Catered) Food

Although you and your groom will probably be too excited to eat much on your wedding day, it would be wrong to assume the same about your guests. The two of you will be dining on love, excitement, and romance. Your guests, on the other hand, will probably be looking forward to beef, chicken, a sandwich—*anything*, in short, to stave off starvation. Enter the caterer. His or her mission is a simple one: Prevent the guests from gnawing each other's arms off.

What Do You Need?

Catering can be basic or complex. It might involve two people in a kitchen making sandwiches and hors d'oeuvres for an at-home reception; a traveling company complete with cooks and a waitstaff who will serve you at your rented reception site; or a full-service caterer supplying tables, chairs, linens, dinnerware, and a full bar, and coordinating your whole reception for you, from flowers to photos. Your head may begin to spin as you consider the options, but if you don't want your *guests*' heads spinning from hunger, settle down and take stock of the situation. Along with your budget, the type and location of your reception will help you determine the kind of caterer you need. After that, all that's left is to find out who can do it best at a price you can afford.

A caterer might be friendly, inexpensive, and cooperative, even downright artistic. But if his food doesn't *taste* good, he might as well be serving your guests oil on canvas . . . on a plate. Don't subject your guests to bad food for the sake of a great deal. You don't have to serve an extravagant dinner featuring prime rib or filet mignon, but you do want food that's worth the money you'll pay for it. Don't hire anyone without tasting the food first. If no samples are available for you in the initial consultation, ask to visit an actual catered event. You'll get to sample the cooking and see the whole troop in action.

In-House Caterers

If you're lucky, the reception site will have an in-house caterer who fits your budget, serves great food, and knows how to work with you. Hotels offer these services, as do most country clubs. There are several advantages to using an in-house caterer, the biggest being that you don't have to go through the trouble of finding one yourself. (Hooray!) The in-house caterer is already familiar with the particulars of the room, which itself is a perk with many advantages. For instance, linens and dinnerware that complement the overall atmosphere are already in rotation, and the wait staff has already carefully choreographed their serving routine.

But the in-house picture isn't *all* roses. In-house catering is usually more expensive than independent catering, often charging you for lots of little extras (read: things you may not want or need) as part of one all-inclusive package. So to find the best value, you just shop around and bring in your own people, right?

Unfortunately, it's not always that simple. Some reception places with on-site caterers may allow you the option of bringing in another catering service, but with most others, it's their way or the highway. If the food is good and the price is reasonable, you might find this arrangement completely acceptable. However, if during your taste test you find yourself gagging on something that *might* be chicken (but might *not* be, considering that gray coloring), you won't want to leave your wedding meal—and the gastrointestinal fate of your guests—up to these particular people.

ALERT!

If your reception site offers in-house catering *only,* and the food is not up to your standards, you'll have to make a very difficult choice. Serve your guests rubber chicken in the setting of your dreams, or find another caterer—and another site—for your reception.

Independent Caterers

Before you go searching for an independent caterer, find out what your reception site provides and what it doesn't. Some sites offer linens, glass and dinnerware, tables, chairs—everything but the food. Others provide nothing but the space you'll be standing in. Know what you need before you go looking for an independent caterer. As you read through this chapter, you'll find that there are a variety of services available to the needy bride, as long as she's first able to identify her needs.

Bare-Bones Caterers

Some caterers specialize in keeping it simple. They provide food, period. Everything else—beverages, linens, dinnerware, glasses, even waiters and waitresses—is left up to you. Sometimes this can work out to your advantage. Caterers like these may offer great food at a low price, and you may be able to find a good deal on anything else that you'll need.

You can save quite a bit of money this way. If you purchase alcohol in quantity, for instance, you'll avoid the outrageous markups that usually accompany liquor provided by caterers.

The disadvantage, of course, is that this could be very inconvenient for you. What you could be getting in one fell swoop from a complete catering service, you're going to have to go out and do yourself. If you're a savvy businesswoman who doesn't mind making lots of calls, this will be a project for you. If you absolutely abhor this type of thing, it could be a logistical mess.

There are businesses that specialize in renting party goods and equipment. If your reception site doesn't provide tables and chairs, for example, you'll have to do some research to find out what you'll need and to determine a fair price for the cost of these rentals. Then you'll have to orchestrate getting it all to the site on the day of your wedding and getting it back afterwards. This is not impossible, but the job may require more work than is apparent at first glance.

Meat-on-Their-Bones Caterers

This type of caterer, which most people associate with a wedding reception, provides food, beverages, a waitstaff, and bartenders. Most also offer linens and dinnerware. If you need tables and chairs, these caterers will usually do all the legwork for you and simply add that to the cost of your total bill. If you're lucky, they'll charge you exactly what the rental agency charged them, but it's not uncommon for them to add a fee for their trouble, so get a written estimate before you authorize anything. Some of these caterers will let you supply the alcohol, but others prefer not to worry about the potential liability (or their loss of liquor revenue).

Fat Cat(erer)s

As you would expect, this type of caterer offers just about every item and service you could imagine, and a few you probably couldn't. Many of these caterers have branched out into the reception coordinating business. Basically, if you choose to pay them for it, they'll take on the entire responsibility of planning your reception, including music, flowers, photographer—the whole nine yards. This may sound like a dream come true, but unless you're careful, it has the potential to become quite a nightmare.

ALERT!

If you're searching for a caterer for a wedding at home, make sure the catering service checks out the kitchen, the appliances, and the storage and electrical capabilities to ensure that everything is adequate in size and power. Your mother's tiny kitchen may be fine for the family, but how will it handle ten people trying to prepare and serve massive quantities of food?

First, there is the cost. This kind of service doesn't come cheap. Second, you're flying blind. How are you to know whether you'll get a high-quality photographer or a close (amateur) friend of the chef who happens to have a nice camera? Third and most important is the question of quality. With so many irons in so many fires, even seasoned veterans can make horrendous mistakes. If you find a "fat" catering service that really appeals to you, consider contracting them for the traditional catering services—but keep a tight rein on everything else.

Finding the Right One

No matter what type of caterer you decide on, you'll need to ask questions to make sure that they can provide the services you want. Don't play the part of the shy bride—your wedding (and your hard-earned money) lies in the balance. You don't want to kick yourself later for not asking a relatively obvious question when you had the chance.

The Cost

You'll want to know about the price of the food. Caterers can give you an estimate based on current food prices. Closer to the wedding, they should be able to give you the final price, reflecting the prices at that time. Ask about how much of a difference you should expect. For instance, you don't want to end up paying $50 for a meal if the estimate you're given initially is $25. You should also ask about price guarantees.

You'll want to know if your overall estimate includes meals for your disc jockey (or an entire band), your photographer, your videographer, and anyone else you'll have on the clock that evening. Also ask whether the cost covers gratuities for the staff and the cost of the bartender, coatroom attendant, and anyone else who will be working at your reception.

If you're looking for a caterer who can serve up killer hors d'oeuvres in plentiful amounts, get a price list. You'll also want to know the price difference between setting the appetizers out on a table (for the guests to help themselves) and having the wait staff pass them around on trays.

Don't forget to ask about the refund policy. It's not a pleasant topic to broach, but what if, for example, a hurricane blew into town on the same weekend as your wedding? Or what if you and your fiancé decide next week that you're going to elope? What will happen to your down payment? Will you be held responsible for any additional payments?

The Food

Does the caterer offer a sit-down meal? A buffet? Stations? No matter how simple or fancy the service, you want to know whether this caterer can meet your needs. Ask if there are different options. Can your guests choose between fish (a popular choice among health-conscious folks) or red meat (popular among the more daring)? If you have vegetarian or kosher guests attending the reception, can special meals be prepared for them? What about the wedding cake? Can this caterer provide one, or will you need a baker on the side?

What about the leftover food? Time was, folks frowned upon their hosts taking that food home. Now it's more commonplace to see a caterer wrap up any extra meals—and considering what you're likely to pay for those meals, you shouldn't feel funny about asking about this option. Another idea is to have those meals donated to a local soup kitchen.

The Contract

When you decide on a caterer who meets your budget needs and who has answered these questions to your satisfaction, *get every part of your agreement in writing.* Don't leave any stone unturned—you might get tripped up later. If you're not familiar with a caterer's work, or if he or she is new in the business, ask for references—the names of those who have used the facilities recently. This is most important when you're planning almost a year ahead. You'll be asked to give a sizable deposit, and you want to make sure the caterer will still be in business when the date arrives!

FACT

You'll want to know what the ratio of staff to guests will be and what the staff will be wearing. You'll also want to ask about the linens, dinnerware, and related items. If you're planning a pink wedding, you don't want brown tablecloths.

Feeding the Masses

"Chicken or beef?" "Sit-down or buffet?" These are the two most common dilemmas in planning your reception menu. You'll hear opinions from everyone on these issues, and every opinion will be different. Even those who agree with each other will do so from entirely different angles. Your mom will prefer a buffet meal because it's less expensive, but your friend might tell you that buffet foods taste like warmed-up leftovers (which she should know . . . given that's her favorite meal). How's a bride to choose?

Choosing the Menu

Chicken is less expensive than beef. What's more, in this time of diet and health awareness, chicken (as long as it's not fried or wrapped up in bacon) is the healthier option. Many people simply don't eat red meat anymore.

On the other hand, some hosts (your parents, for example) may feel they're being cheap if they don't serve beef, although it's doubtful that choice will make or break your wedding. If you're really concerned, offer your guests a choice of several meals. On their response card, give them the option of checking off poultry or beef (or fish, or vegetarian—whatever you have worked out with your caterer).

Sit Down? Line Up?

There's a bit more to consider in the sit-down versus buffet debate. A sit-down meal is generally considered more formal than a buffet. In addition, many people feel they're treating their guests better by not making them stand in line for their food. Buffet service, if you're leaning that way, does have its advantages, though. Because it eliminates the need for waiters and waitresses, it's usually less expensive to serve than a sit-down meal. A buffet can add a relaxed touch to a morning or afternoon wedding.

If you do decide to go with a buffet, consider having two lines instead of one. Your guests will get to the food twice as fast, an especially nice touch if you're planning a rather large wedding. Though buffet service saves you the cost of a waitstaff, it does require more food than a sit-down meal, since portions are not controlled. You will want to have plenty of food visible so that no one will feel shy about taking enough to eat. The caterer should assign a few staff members to watch the table and replace any food that starts to run low.

Semi-buffet service is another option. With this service, the tables are already set with plates, flatware, and glasses. The waitstaff clear the tables and serve drinks; the only thing the guests pick up at the buffet table is the food.

Stations

This option is gaining popularity with the buffet crowd. Rather than presenting your guests with warming trays of food that could start to look unappetizing once the bulk of the line has attacked, this option calls for several manned food stations to be set up around the reception hall. Some common types of stations include these:

- **Pasta station:** Tortellini or fettuccine are good pasta choices, with marinara, pesto, and alfredo sauces covering most appetites. A stack of small plates or shallow bowls sits on the table. Waitstaff ask guests their choices, then scoop a small amount of the pasta into a saucepan, add the sauce, and toss it all together. The guests get just the kind of pasta they want, and they know it's hot and fresh.

- **Carving station:** Pasta alone will not suffice at a wedding reception. The carving station offers a selection of meats carved right from the bone. Large roasts of turkey, beef, or ham are good choices. Guests are given a slice of their choosing, and again, because it's carved right in front of them, they know it hasn't been sitting under a warming lamp for an hour.

- **Skewer station:** The best combination of vegetables and meats or seafood. Guests watch as their skewer of chicken, beef, or scallops, onion, pepper, mushroom, and zucchini is flame-broiled to perfection, then laid on a bed of rice. This can be a little more time-consuming than the pasta or carving stations. The alternative is to have the skewers flamed ahead of time, then presented buffet style.

The beauty of the stations buffet arrangement is that guests get the hot, fresh food they want prepared by a professional. Make certain to arrange a serving time frame with your caterer and agree that when that time is up, the food stations will be cleared.

Salads, fresh fruit, steamed vegetables, breads and rolls, and other side dishes can be laid out on a separate table and self-served with plates provided. Tables are set with silverware and linens so guests have to carry only their plate of food. Condiments that complement the pasta, meats, or skewers, such as grated cheese, cranberry sauce, and au jus, should be placed near the foods they accompany, but far enough away so that the line moves steadily along.

Liquor's Quicker, But It Ain't Cheap

One of the hottest topics surrounding any wedding is whether to host a cash bar or an open bar.

At the open bar, guests drink for free, courtesy of you or whoever is footing the bill. At a cash bar, they have to pony up for their own drinks. Some people will suggest to you that it's rude to expect your guests to pay for their own drinks. After all, you wouldn't normally host a party and expect your guests to pay for what you serve them.

On the other side of the debate is the sobering (as it were) fact that open bars can end up being extremely expensive. People are often wasteful with liquor that they haven't bought. Someone might order a drink, take a sip, and go off to the powder room. The drink is forgotten, or the guest assumes it's gotten warm and orders a fresh one. And why shouldn't this guest take full advantage of your generosity?

Another thing to consider with an open bar is that you're more likely to have drunken guests wandering about the room. People who would never pay eight bucks for a glass of wine in a bar suddenly find that vino tastes much better when it's on the house.

Other Options

If you really don't want to make your guests buy drinks, there are a few options that might work for you:

- Have an open bar for the first hour of the reception only. This will ease your guilt, help your guests pass the time pleasantly while you're off taking pictures, and minimize any problems with guests.
- Serve free champagne punch. This punch is fairly light, in terms of alcohol content, and people aren't likely to pound down glass after glass.
- Place bottles of wine on the tables. A typical bottle of wine holds four to five glasses. At a table seated for eight, a bottle of red and a bottle of white ensures that everyone gets a glass or two with their meal. You control the expense and consumption by purchasing a set number of bottles of the wines of your choice, and your guests get a free glass of wine to raise in your honor.

If your reception site allows it, you may be able to save some money by purchasing a few kegs or several cases of high-quality beer plus some cases of good wine. Offer other alcohol or cocktails for cash for those who prefer something harder.

Tray Cool

You didn't see anything you liked in the previous section? How about offering tray service? Your guests don't have to pay for their drinks, and you don't incur the massive expense of an open bar. You choose a few drinks that you feel will be popular with the majority of your guests (include beer and wine as sure bets). The waitstaff will pass these selections around on a tray and offer them to your guests. The servers do not float around with drinks all night, but serve them on a schedule to keep costs (and overconsumption) to a minimum. You might send the servers around before dinner, when dinner is being served, and at other times during the course of the reception.

QUESTION?

What does it cost to have drinks passed by waiters?
Tray service will obviously cost you more than a cash bar will, but it will also cost you much less than an open bar. Think of it as a happy medium. As a bonus, you can regulate how much liquor your rowdy guests consume.

Make Your Own Bar

If you're having a home or backyard reception, and instead of leaving it to the caterer you have chosen to provide alcohol yourself, you'll need to know what you need and how much of it to have on hand. For the setup, there are stores that will rent you a bar for the day. If you don't want to spend the money, ask around to find if anyone you know has a table that would suffice. Make sure that any table you use is sturdy and steady. Draping the table with a nice white tablecloth that extends all the way to the ground not only dresses things up, but also hides excess bottles and trash stored underneath. Now, what will you need . . . ?

The Soft Stuff

Always include nonalcoholic options on hand for guests who prefer to steer clear of the hard stuff. Every bar should stock soft drinks, but you might also add a nonalcoholic punch. (Punches look very inviting when served in an elegant bowl or fountain.) Don't think you're restricted to that bright red stuff you drank as a kid. There are plenty of nonalcoholic options, including sparkling grape or apple juice.

Champagne or *Non*?

Though we commonly refer to any sparkling white wine as champagne, only the wine made in the Champagne region of France carries this title. As you might expect, you'll pay more for good champagne, but you can pick up a decent sparkling wine for around $10 a bottle. Unless you have a champagne connoisseur on your guest list, nobody will know the difference, and you'll be saving yourself a bundle by buying the other stuff. If you're like most people, you'll only want enough champagne to fill everyone's glass once for the opening toast.

FACT

If your caterer is responsible for procuring the champagne and other liquor, all you have to worry about is the bill. If you have to buy it yourself, assume that each bottle of champagne will yield seven glasses.

Set 'Em Up

If you're setting up your own bar, you'll need more than liquor. You'll need garnishes, like maraschino cherries, lemons, limes, celery, and olives. You'll need mixers, like soft drinks, soda water, tonic water, and milk. You'll need ice, swizzle sticks, and cocktail napkins.

Now for the hard stuff. You'll need beer, wine, vodka, gin, rum, tequila, vermouth, and blended whiskey. This should be enough to please everybody, but if you know that you're inviting a crowd that enjoys schnapps or brandy, adjust your shopping list accordingly.

For anyone concerned about guests having a little too much to drink, here's a tip. Don't serve salty foods. They only make people thirstier. Do serve meat, fish, cheese, and other high-protein foods. They restore blood sugar, which is depleted when someone drinks alcohol, and they help sober up guests who have had too much. Coffee will only wire a drunk—it won't sober him or her. You'll be left with someone who is still very drunk, probably a little edgy, and much too eager to dance. If you're trying to sober up some guests, have them drink water to flush out their systems.

ALERT!

If you're serving alcohol at an at-home reception, it has to be an open bar. It's against the law to sell liquor without a liquor license. (And you don't want the fuzz breaking up your reception, do you?)

Doing the Numbers

You may not care if you have a lot of liquor left over at the end of the reception. Somehow, some way, you'll probably find something interesting to do with it, no matter how hard it may be. (Actually, liquor stores usually buy back unopened bottles of alcohol, but not loose cans or bottles of beer.) But how do you know how much to buy in the first place? There are some standard guidelines of consumption.

On average, each guest will have four to five drinks in an evening. You'll get twenty-five drinks from a fifth of liquor, providing you're using a one-ounce pony to make them with one ounce of alcohol each. Using one and a half ounces of alcohol (that is, a one-and-a-half-ounce jigger), you'll get eighteen drinks per fifth. A single case of liquor contains twelve bottles. Assuming that you're using one ounce of alcohol to make every drink, then one case will yield 300 drinks.

For the beer drinkers in a crowd, half a keg will give you 260 eight-ounce glasses of beer. If you're serving beer in bottles and cans instead of on tap, seven cases is the equivalent of half a keg. (Note: For those swing-from-the-chandelier wine drinkers, figure that each one will drink the equivalent of one full-sized bottle.)

Have you ever been to a wedding where the bride or groom was incoherent because he or she had had too much to drink? Not only is this embarrassing for guests to witness, but nine times out of ten the drunken newlywed regrets the experience mightily. If you do drink, be sure to eat something and to drink nonalcoholic beverages, too. It's up to you to know when you're about to cross the line from happy newlywed to obnoxious drunk bride—and to stop yourself in time.

Your Liability as a Host

Rejoicing with the bride and groom does not have to mean drunken reveling. But it does sometimes happen that a few guests go beyond the limits of common sense and wind up incredibly trashed. In recent court decisions, this has become a serious problem for both hosts and caterers. Be aware of your responsibilities.

Liquor may not be served to anyone under the legal drinking age, even at a home party. Courts have ruled that hosts are financially liable when teenagers who are served liquor at parties in private homes become involved in auto accidents or criminal matters. Caterers and restaurants have been held to the same standard.

If any of your adult guests are too drunk to drive but do so anyway, and then have an accident after being served drinks at your party, the damage they cause is your responsibility and liability. As a good friend, you should call a taxi or find someone else to drive the car in these cases. Caterers and bartenders as well are liable in this situation.

To avoid these situations, discuss with your caterer ways to limit alcohol consumption at your reception. Reliable caterers are happy to cooperate and to suggest options, especially since they are even more accountable than you are should there be an unfortunate accident, be it a bad fall or an auto crash.

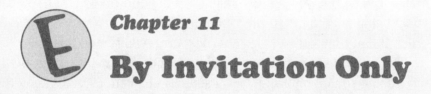

Chapter 11

By Invitation Only

Although nine out of ten people you'll invite to your wedding will probably already know the date, the time, and the place, you still have to send out invitations. Some people *need* something to stick on the refrigerator as a reminder of the upcoming event. Sending out invitations is also a good way to keep track of who's coming and who's not, provided people pay attention to your request (nay, *demand*) to RSVP.

Where Do You Get 'Em?

It used to be that any bride who was sending invitations was forced to haul herself down to a stationery shop (or a craft shop or department store that also sells stationery) in order to make the necessary arrangements. Nowadays, of course, there are many other options available. The one you choose might just depend on whether you care about being able to physically touch the invitation before you place an order. If that's important to you, don't worry—you're not alone.

The look of your invitation gives people their first hint as to the type of wedding you'll be having. If you send out invitations with a colorful bunch of balloons on the front that proclaim "We're Having a Party!" it's doubtful that your guests will expect a formal affair with top hats and tails. And conversely, an elegantly engraved invitation is bound to give people the message not to show up in jeans. Make sure you choose invitations that are appropriate to the occasion you're planning.

The Old-Fashioned Method

Most brides still find their invitations by going to a stationery store and browsing through the catalogs. These catalogs contain samples of predesigned invitations—the paper color, paper stock, borders, and ornamentation have already been set. You pick out the color of the paper and ink, the style of the script, and the words you want to use. Many invitations come complete with phrasing. All you do is supply the information for your wedding, and the manufacturer does the rest.

FACT

If you normally have a hard time choosing between many options, take someone along for the ride who can help you narrow down the choices. Though the store employees will be of great assistance, your mom (or your maid of honor) will be the voice of reason if you find yourself overwhelmed by all the options. ("Why are you ordering red lettering? Your wedding colors are fuchsia and gold!")

These sample catalogs are created by a handful of large printers that dominate the invitation market. By printing several lines of mass-produced invitations, these companies are able to offer a greater variety and a cheaper price than a private printer. Because these companies are the main source of wedding invitations, you'll probably see the same sample catalogs in the majority of places you look.

The Internet

Of course, if it exists, you can probably find it online. There are countless Web sites that sell traditional and unique invitations, and if you're looking for a real deal, you'll find it here. The downside, of course, is that you're taking a chance. Many brides like to see and feel their prospective invitations. (Is the paper heavy enough? Is the lettering raised enough? Are the die cuts crisp enough?) If you receive a box of 200 invitations that turn out to be very flimsy, you'll instantly regret this choice. One way to prevent an error like this is to educate yourself in matters like paper stock, acid-free paper, and various printing methods.

The upside is that Internet orders can be processed within a week in many cases, so if you're short on time, this may be your best option.

ALERT!

If you know you don't have the time (or the interest) for a crash course on the finer points of paper and ink, you're better off ordering from a store, where you can ask questions and actually see what you're ordering.

That Printer Guy

You may have heard about personal stationers or printers—the people who will design a unique invitation for you and then print it. Because of the ease and popularity of the catalog and Internet methods, creating invitations this way is becoming a thing of the past. Private stationers and printers simply can't afford the overhead costs that come with the broad selection that large manufacturers offer.

If you can't find an invitation you like online or in a stationery store, or if you want something very specific, there are private printers out there who can do the job for you. These printers may be a bit harder to find and more expensive than the big guys, but if you want your invitations to feature lions on roller skates instead of the traditional doves and bells (hey, they're *your* invitations), they might be your best bet. Check the business section of your phone directory under "Printers."

Printing Methods

You may not know the first thing about printing methods, and what's more, you don't *want* to know. But when it comes to ordering your wedding invitations, the type of print you choose is a big factor in how much or how little you end up spending here.

Engraving is the most elegant form of putting ink on paper. The paper is "stamped" from the back by metal plates the printer creates, which raises the letters up off of the paper as they're printed. Unfortunately, you'll pay extra for all that elegance, so unless you have a humongous invitation budget, engraving may be off limits.

If you're inviting fifty people or fewer, the etiquette gurus will allow you to write your invitations out by hand. That may not be good news for your hand, which will probably start cramping after invitation number ten, but it's very good news for your pocketbook.

A great way to get the look of engraving without the cost is through a process called thermography. Most mass-produced invitations these days are done using this method. By using a special press that heats the ink, the printer creates a raised-letter effect that is almost indistinguishable from engraving. What is distinguishable, however, is the price. It's about half the cost of engraving. Offset printing, also called lithography, produces flat images and is the starting point for thermography.

Calligraphy, that fancy formal script, is an up-and-coming approach in the world of invitations. If you've always loved the look of calligraphy but didn't think you could afford to have a calligrapher letter your invitations by hand, recent developments might cause you to reconsider. Printers are now able to reproduce calligraphy using software—a method considerably faster and cheaper than the human hand. Any sadness you may feel about the computerization of yet another art form (tsk, tsk) is likely to be tempered by your sudden ability to afford it (hooray!). If you're interested in hiring a *human* calligrapher, ask your local stationery store for referrals or check the Yellow Pages.

What Are You Saying?

Having trouble figuring out how to word your invitations? You're not alone. With all the mixed families in the world today, many brides find themselves wondering how to print invitations without offending anyone. But you can relax—there are as many options for styles of wording as there are invitation styles.

Formal/Traditional

Mr. and Mrs. Roger Parker
request the honor of your presence
at the marriage of their daughter
Elizabeth Elaine
to
Mr. Justin Clark
on Saturday, the fifth of August
Two thousand and five
at two o'clock in the afternoon
Fairview Baptist Church
Fairview, Pennsylvania

Bride's parents hosting the wedding

Mr. and Mrs. Robert Clark
request the honor of your presence
at the marriage of
Miss Elizabeth Elaine Parker
to their son
Mr. Justin James Clark
on Saturday, the fifth of August
Two thousand and five
at two o'clock in the afternoon
Fairview Baptist Church
Fairview, Pennsylvania

When the groom's parents host the wedding

Mr. and Mrs. Roger Parker
and
Mr. and Mrs. Robert Clark
request the honor of your presence
at the marriage of their children
Elizabeth Elaine
and
Justin James
on Saturday, the fifth of August
Two thousand and five
at two o'clock in the afternoon
Fairview Baptist Church
Fairview, Pennsylvania

Mr. and Mrs. Roger Parker
request the honor of your presence
at the marriage of their daughter
Elizabeth Elaine Parker
to
Justin James Clark
son of Mr. and Mrs. Robert Clark
Saturday, the fifth of August
Two thousand and five
at two o'clock in the afternoon
Fairview Baptist Church
Fairview, Pennsylvania

When both the bride's and groom's parents host the wedding

The honor of your presence is requested
at the marriage of
Miss Elizabeth Elaine Parker
and
Mr. Justin Clark

Miss Elizabeth Elaine Parker
and
Mr. Justin James Clark
request the honor of your presence
at their marriage

When the bride and groom host their own wedding

Note that in all cases you should spell everything out—names, the year, the time, and so on. It's all right to abbreviate common titles (such as Mr. and Mrs., for example), and it's also fine to use the numerical representations for the address of the church or synagogue, but only if you must. Generally, the address (including the street name) of the church can be omitted altogether, unless doing so will cause extreme amounts of anxiety for your guests (if, for example, you're getting married in New York City and no one would know *which* St. Andrew's you've chosen for your wedding site). If your entire guest list knows your smallish hometown area well, you can simply opt for the name of the church (for example, St. Paul's Roman Catholic Church), followed by the town on the next line (Bedford, Illinois). Zip codes are never included.

QUESTION?

If you are including the actual address of the church on the invitation for practical reasons, should you spell the street number out?
You'll see invitations done both ways. If you're shooting for a more formal look, a good rule of thumb to follow is the one writers use: Spell out numbers under 100. And remember, don't use abbreviations. Words like "Street" and "Road" are never abbreviated.

Divorced Hosts

Circumstances will probably vary when divorced parents host a wedding. Use these examples as general guidelines.

When the mother of the bride is hosting and is not remarried

Mrs. James Parker
requests the honor of your presence
at the marriage of her daughter
Elizabeth Elaine

> *Mrs. David C. Hayes*
> *requests the honor of your presence*
> *at the marriage of her daughter*
> *Elizabeth Elaine Parker*

> *Mr. and Mrs. David C. Hayes*
> *request the honor of your presence*
> *at the marriage of Mrs. Hayes' daughter*
> *Elizabeth Elaine Parker*

When the mother of the bride is hosting and has remarried

> *Mr. Roger Parker*
> *requests the honor of your presence*
> *at the marriage of his daughter*
> *Elizabeth Elaine*

> *Mr. and Mrs. Roger Parker*
> *request the honor of your presence*
> *at the marriage of Mr. Parker's daughter*
> *Elizabeth Elaine*

When the father of the bride is hosting and is not remarried

When the father of the bride is hosting and has remarried

Deceased Parents

Deceased parents are usually not mentioned on wedding invitations because only the hosts of the event are listed. However, if you want to mention your late mother or father, no one is going to fault you for it.

When one parent is deceased and the host has not remarried

> *Mrs. Ann Parker*
> *requests the honor of your presence*
> *at the marriage of*
> *Elizabeth Elaine,*
> *daughter of Mrs. Parker and the late*
> *Roger Parker*

> *Mr. and Mrs. David Spencer*
> *request the honor of your presence*
> *at the marriage of Mrs. Spencer's daughter*
> *Elizabeth Elaine*

When one parent is deceased
and the host has remarried

> *Mr. and Mrs. Frederick Parker*
> *request the honor of your presence*
> *at the marriage of their granddaughter*
> *Elizabeth Elaine Parker*

When both parents are deceased,
a close friend or relative may host

Religious Ceremonies

The following are general guidelines for those who wish to emphasize the religious aspect of marriage. If you have any questions, consult your officiant prior to having the invitations printed.

> *Mr. and Mrs. Parker*
> *are pleased to invite you*
> *to join in a Christian celebration*
> *of the marriage of their daughter*
> *Elizabeth Elaine Parker*
> *to*
> *Justin James Clark*
> *on Saturday, the fifth of August*
> *Two thousand and five*
> *at ten o'clock in the morning*
> *St. Phillip's Methodist Church*
> *Fairview, Pennsylvania*

For Protestant ceremonies

> *Mr. and Mrs. Roger Parker*
> *request the honor of your presence*
> *at the Nuptial Mass*
> *at which their daughter*
> *Elizabeth Elaine*
> *and*
> *Justin James Clark*
> *will be united in the*
> *Sacrament of Holy Matrimony*
> *on Saturday, the fifth of August*
> *Two thousand and five*
> *at six o'clock in the evening*
> *St. Joseph's Catholic Church*
> *Fairview, Pennsylvania*

For Catholic ceremonies

Mr. and Mrs. Samuel Sherman
and
Mr. and Mrs. Jonas Goldsmith
request the honor of your presence
at the marriage of their children
Abigail
and
Daniel
on Sunday, the eleventh of June
Two thousand and five
at four o'clock in the afternoon
Congregation Shearith Israel
Two West Seventieth Street
New York

Mr. and Mrs. Samuel Sherman
request the honor of your presence
at the marriage of their daughter
Abigail
to
Mr. Daniel Goldsmith
son of Mr. and Mrs. Jonas Goldsmith

For Jewish ceremonies (Approaches will differ by ceremony, and by Orthodox, Conservative, or Reform affiliation)

Military Ceremonies

In military weddings, rank determines the placement of names. If the person's rank is lower than sergeant, omit the rank, but list their branch of service. Junior officer's titles are placed below their names, followed by their branch of service. Titles are placed before names if the rank is higher than lieutenant, followed by their branch of service on the next line.

Mr. and Mrs. Roger Parker
request the honor of your presence
at the marriage of their daughter
Beth Elaine
United States Army
to
Justin James Clark

Mr. and Mrs. Roger Parker
request the honor of your presence
at the marriage of their daughter
Beth Elaine
to
Justin James Clark
First Lieutenant, United States Navy

When the person's rank is lower than sergeant

When the person has a junior officer's title

When the person's rank is higher than lieutenant

> *Mr. and Mrs. Roger Parker*
> *request the honor of your presence*
> *at the marriage of their daughter*
> *Beth Elaine*
> *to*
> *Captain Justin James Clark*
> *United States Navy*

Invitation Extras

As though choosing the invitations and carefully wording them isn't enough! You'll have choices to make about the envelopes, and you'll also need to alert your guests to the particulars of the reception.

Envelopes

Like the invitations themselves, the envelopes you choose can range from simple, with plain, high-quality paper, to fancy, with foil-laminated inner flaps or flaps with a colorful design. Beautifully packaged invitations are a nice touch, but as you might expect, the more you add to the envelope, the greater the cost.

ALERT!

Before you break the budget, keep in mind that the envelope is a throwaway item. Ask yourself if it really makes sense to spend extra on something most people rip to shreds and then toss in the garbage can.

Preprinted Return Address

Plan to have the return address preprinted on the outer envelope and on the response cards. Whose address should it be? Traditionally, whoever is listed as the host for the wedding receives the RSVPs—but if *you're* the one communicating with the reception site coordinator or caterer (even though your parents are the actual hosts) you might prefer to have the responses sent directly to you. That way, you don't have to bother your parents every week (or every day as the big event draws near) to see who has accepted and who hasn't. Before you make a decision to put yours as the return address, make sure you tell whoever is hosting the wedding, just so you don't step on any toes.

Reception and Response Cards

If the reception is at a different location than the ceremony, you will need to include these cards in your invitations. Remember to include the full address of the reception site for out-of-town guests. If dinner will be served, make it clear, or some guests may brown-bag it. You'll also need to include response cards. These are the cards that the guests send back to you so that you can add them to your final list or scratch them from it.

Mr. and Mrs. Roger Parker
request the pleasure of your company
Saturday, the fifth of August
at three o'clock in the afternoon
Fairview Country Club
1638 Eastview Lane
Brookdale, Illinois

Sample formal reception card

Reception
immediately following the ceremony
Fairview Country Club
1638 Eastview Lane
Brookdale, Illinois

Less formal reception card

M_____
_____accepts
_____regrets
Saturday, the fifth of August
Fairview Country Club

The favor of your reply is requested
by the twenty-second of July
M_____
_____will attend.

Sample response cards

The response cards also need an envelope with a first-class postage stamp (provided by you). One way to save some money here is to order response postcards—they obviously won't need envelopes, and the cost of stamps for postcards is quite a bit less than first-class stamps.

As for those oblivious souls who neglect to return your card . . . try not to be too hard on them. Make a simple phone call, one that tactfully passes over their failure to RSVP, and ask whether they will be attending or not.

Addressing the Envelopes

This is a project of massive undertaking. Give yourself plenty of time, and be realistic. Don't think you're going to write out several hundred envelopes in one sitting. Remember that this is supposed to be fun and exciting—you're sending out your wedding invitations, for crying out loud!

Be Prepared

To address your invitations, you will need all of the following:

- Several pens (use black ink only)
- Several friends and/or family members with good penmanship
- Stamps
- Invitations, inserts, and envelopes
- Plenty of food, drink, money, and whatever else it will take to bribe friends and/or family members into helping you

It's a good idea to ask a few people to help you address your invitations, but don't ask so many that things become chaotic. Make sure the same person who writes the information on the inside of an invitation also addresses its outer envelope. This makes the invitation package look uniform and convey that it was put together with care.

Know how to address people of various professions. On the outside envelope, a judge is addressed as "The Honorable George Smith." A member of the clergy is "The Reverend George Smith." A lawyer is addressed as "George Smith, Esq." Medical doctors are addressed as "Dr."

(but Ph.D.s do not require any title). Everyone else is "Mr.," "Mrs.," or "Ms." These are the only abbreviations (aside from "Jr.") that are acceptable. Everything else (with the exception of street numbers) is written out.

ALERT!

Never use a typewriter or printed label to address an invitation envelope—it looks as if you were too busy to take the time to personally invite your guests. You may *feel* this busy, but don't let your guests know it.

Formal or Informal?

When addressing the outer envelope, include the full name of the person or persons you are inviting. On the inner envelope, you can be more casual. If you're addressing the outer envelope to Mr. and Mrs. Stephen McGill feel free to write "Steve and Linda" on the inner envelope, but only if they happen to be your close friends. Otherwise, drop the first name and simply address the inner envelope to Mr. and Mrs. McGill.

If you are inviting the whole family, the approach is pretty much the same. (Children's names should come after their parents'.)

Mr. and Mrs. Stephen Michael
McGill and Family
(**or** ... The Smith-McGill Family)
16 Maple Drive
Chestnut Hill, Massachusetts 02555

Outer envelope

Mr. and Mrs. McGill
Andrea, Paul, and Meg

On the inner envelope

Children who are over eighteen and are invited to the wedding should receive their own invitations, whether they're living at home or on their own.

One more note on those inner envelopes: Remember how careful you had to be when addressing members of various professions on the outer envelope? You're not off the hook yet. While you addressed the judge's outer envelope, "The Honorable George Smith," on the inner envelope, he is simply "Judge Smith." The Reverend George Smith is transformed into, simply, "Reverend Smith."

And Guest

When you invite a single person with a guest, you're faced with two schools of etiquette: old school, and actual world. Old school etiquette soundly denounces the use of the phrase "and Guest" on the outer envelope of an invitation *or* on the inner one. In the actual world, however, invitations are addressed this way all the time—and everyone understands it.

Bottom line: If you want to toe the etiquette line, you'll address separate invitations—one to the guest you're inviting, and one to his or her guest. This will require a considerable amount of effort, in that you'll have to track down your guest's *guest's* address at a time when you're incredibly busy—which is why most brides shun this practice. If you just want to make things easier on yourself (because, after all, isn't it nice of you to allow your friend to invite a guest in the first place?!), go ahead and address the outer envelope with the name of your friend or relative. Then add the phrase "and Guest" on the inner envelope following his or her name.

Packaging the Invites

Now that you've got everything addressed and ready to go, what's the best way to fit it all into the envelope? Packing up the invitation and its extras can be as confusing and time-consuming as everything else you've done for your wedding. What goes where, and why? Here's a method that should make things easier for you:

1. Place the response card face-up under the flap of the response card envelope.
2. Place a small piece of tissue paper over the lettering on the invitation.
3. Put any extra enclosures (reception cards, maps, directions, and so on) inside the invitation. Put the response card and envelope inside the invitation as well. The lettering should be facing upward.

4. Place the invitation inside the inner envelope with the lettering facing the back flap. Don't seal this envelope. (The inner envelope is not typically gummed anyway.)
5. Put the inner envelope inside the outer envelope. Again, the writing on the inner envelope should face the flap of the outer envelope.
6. Seal the outer envelope. Make sure the envelope is properly addressed and contains your return address. Stamp and mail.

Instead of wearing out your tongue and the tongues of your friends, purchase a water applicator wand from an office-supply store. These wands are filled with water and stopped with a small sponge that, when pressed to the back of an envelope or stamp, releases a small amount of water. Or place a damp sponge in a bowl and dab stamps on its surface to moisten. (This method is not recommended for envelopes since the whole flap might get wet.)

Include directions and maps to the ceremony and reception sites in the invitations you send to out-of-town guests. Print out maps from your computer, and make sure they're large enough to be read without a magnifying glass.

Before you stamp all those invitations, find out how much postage you will need to mail your invitations. Sometimes, due to heavy paper and lots of inserts, the whole package requires more than a standard first-class stamp. To be on the safe side, take an invitation—one that's completely packaged up and ready to go—to the post office and have it weighed. An invitation that's an odd shape (square instead of rectangle, for instance) might also require extra postage and a little extra time.

Additional Stationery

Your business with printers and stationery suppliers may not end when you order your invitations (oh, they're going to *love* you). Depending on the type of wedding you're having, and where, you may need various cards for entrance to the ceremony, special seating, or weather-related contingencies. You'll need some thank-you notes with both your and your new husband's names on them, and you just might want to print some formal announcements.

Ceremony Cards

Ceremony cards guaranteeing entrance into the proceedings are not necessary for a traditional wedding site. However, if your wedding is being held at a public place, such as a museum or a historic mansion, you may need some way to distinguish your guests from the tourists (aside from the fact that they will be better dressed than the people hanging out in the snack bar—you hope).

Pew Cards

You will need pew cards (also called "Within the Ribbon" cards) if you wish to reserve seats at the ceremony for any special family and friends. Have them sit as close as possible to where the action is. Your special guests can pass the pew cards to the usher at the ceremony, who then knows to seat the special guests in the sections marked as "Reserved."

FACT

Worried about your outdoor wedding? If you're having your ceremony and/or reception outdoors, rain cards notify people of an alternate location in the event of rain.

Thank Yous, Thank Yous

You can order thank-you notes that match your invitations, or you can choose something completely different. The note cards can be as formal or informal as you like. If you already have personal stationery, you might consider using that for your thank-you notes instead of ordering something new. It's perfectly proper as far as the rules of etiquette are concerned, and you might save some money.

Announcements

If you and your fiancé are like most couples, you were not able to invite everyone on your original guest list. Business associates, friends and family living far away, and others may have been squeezed off the list due to budget or space constraints. Wedding announcements are a convenient way to let people know of your recent nuptials. They are not sent to anyone who received an invitation. (Note that people receiving announcements are under no obligation to buy you a gift.)

Announcements should be mailed immediately after your wedding. You and your fiancé should have them ready before you leave for your honeymoon, and your maid of honor or best man can mail them while you are gone.

The traditional wording of announcements	*Mr. and Mrs. Joseph Moran* *proudly announce* *the marriage of their daughter* *Margaret Ann* *and* *Mr. Justin James McCann* *on Saturday, the third of July* *Two thousand and four* *Holy Trinity Lutheran Church* *Chicago, Illinois*

Whoever is named on the invitation as the wedding's host should also be the person or persons announcing the marriage.

When to Order

Order your invitations three to four months before the wedding, and always order more than you need. Don't fool yourself into believing you won't make mistakes while you're addressing all of those envelopes. The last thing you need is a fistfight with your maid of honor because she messed up the last one.

Ordering at least twenty extra invitations will lessen the tensions among those writing them out and will save you the cost of having to place a second order. (The majority of charges for your invitation are for the initial start-up of the press and such; adding a few more to your initial order is much cheaper than ordering again.) Even if you don't make any mistakes, you'll probably want to have a few invitations as keepsakes.

When tallying up the number of invitations to order, don't forget to include all of the people who will be at the rehearsal. This includes attendants, siblings, parents, and the officiant, along with their respective significant others. Although a reply is not expected or required, these people may like to have the invitation as a memento.

Plan to mail out invitations about six weeks before the wedding, with an RSVP date of two weeks before the wedding. This will allow you time to give the caterer a final headcount.

Be sure to leave yourself plenty of time to address and stamp all those envelopes. If you're planning a wedding near a holiday, mail out your invitations a few weeks earlier to give your guests some extra time to plan. If you plan on inviting more guests as regrets come in, send your invitations out at least eight weeks in advance, with a response date of at least three weeks before the wedding.

Pressed for time? Ask your printer to provide you with the envelopes in advance. That way, you can write them out while the invitations are being printed.

Do-It-Yourself Projects

Now for some good news. You can print the little "extras" yourself. These are the things you probably don't want to drop a huge amount of cash on but that are nice for your guests to have. If you're talented and have some time to spare, you can even make your own invitations.

Ceremony Programs

Ceremony programs are to your wedding what a playbill is to a concert or play. The program lays out the order of the ceremony, the participants, the music, and the readings. You can add all the personal touches you want. Perhaps you have a favorite poem, quote, or song that can't be included in the ceremony itself, or maybe there's a special memory you'd like to share, such as how you and your groom met. Why not print it on the back of the program to give your family and friends something meaningful to read while they wait for the ceremony to begin?

Programs are easy to print on your own computer, and that makes them relatively inexpensive, too. Stationery stores have program covers and papers to choose from. The rest is up to you.

Making Your Own Invites

If you're artistic, or if you're having a less-than-incredibly-formal wedding, you might be thinking about gathering some supplies together and making your own invitations. If you're up to the challenge and you have the time, there's no reason you can't. Nothing is more interesting than receiving a wedding invitation from a bride or groom who made it lovingly with his or her own hands. A handmade invitation is personalized, obviously—you are, after all, choosing everything that goes on it.

Make sure you have the time to do this before you buy all of the supplies. If you haven't started this project at least six weeks before the wedding, you're either going to freak out from the stress of it all, or you'll end up ordering rush-job invitations. Either way, you won't be happy.

Before you decide to do this, recognize your limitations. If you are not artistic in the least (or you have no patience for crafty projects), *don't* try to make your own wedding invitations. Though handmade invitations, as a rule, look as though they were handmade, they shouldn't look like a four-year-old designed and glued them together. ("Is this *crayon*?" your horrified guests will wonder if they receive a less-than-ideally-crafted invite.) The money you save on a printer will never restore your good name when people realize that *you* are responsible for those unfortunate mailings. Ⓔ

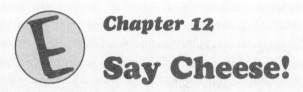

Chapter 12

Say Cheese!

A picture paints a thousand words. At no time in your life will this statement seem truer or more appropriate than on your wedding day. You'll be feeling things you can't even recognize, never mind describe—and thanks to the art of photography, you won't have to. A good set of wedding prints will preserve all the emotions, excitement, and memories (of the insane hat Aunt Betty wore to the ceremony, for example) for you and your family. Make sure those pictures turn out to be keepers.

Don't Skimp on the Pics

Good photography is not about simply clicking on the autofocus and shooting away with the family camera. It's an *art*—it requires skill and planning. Needless to say, you don't want to put this huge responsibility in the hands of just anyone, so be very careful about whom you choose as your wedding photographer.

Beware of "professional" photographers who really aren't—or at least aren't *yet*. Imagine how you'd feel after finding out the entire ceremony was photographed with the lens cap on. There are countless stories of couples that have received less-than-quality work for their money, like photos that were blurry or ill-composed; pictures with colors that never appeared in nature (and definitely weren't included in the wedding); shots of family and friends with a demonic red glow in their eyes.

ALERT!

Don't take a risk on an unproven entity. Take the time to find a photographer who will do justice to you and your wedding. There is no substitute for the education and experience of a professional.

Until you sit down with the photographer to map out a battle plan for the wedding, you will probably be dealing with price ranges rather than concrete amounts. The final price will depend on the approach to the wedding you develop with the photographer. Go ahead and look for the best value, but remember: You will do yourself a big favor by opting to pay a little more for a quality job.

Any Photographers out There?

Finding the right professional may not be a walk in the park. It's quite common for the best photographers to be booked a year or more in advance, so start your search early. Begin with the word-of-mouth approach. Ask your friends, family, coworkers, or anyone else you know who's been married or who has coordinated a wedding recently. Their opinions and their wedding albums will go a long way toward helping you find some options.

Personality Test

If you're going on word-of-mouth advice, make sure to ask your friend about her overall experience with the photographer or studio in question. The pictures may have turned out like a dream, but the person behind the lens could have been a nightmare—rude, pushy, sloppy. If that's the case, keep looking. Your aim is to hire someone who takes great photographs and does so in a way that makes everyone feel at ease. If you've ever been to a wedding where the photographer has fallen drunk into the punchbowl or made a pass at the maid of honor, you already know that you don't want this happening to you (never mind what your maid of honor wants).

If you can't find a good photographer by using the word-of-mouth approach, go to some bridal fairs and/or photography shows. Both are likely to yield plenty of good candidates in a variety of styles and price ranges.

You're looking for someone who makes you feel comfortable, someone who is willing to work with you every step of the way—and on *your* terms. A good photographer is able to relate to you, your groom, and your families, and will bring out the best in everyone and preserve it forever on film.

The Ex(perience) Factor

It also goes without saying that you're looking for someone who knows what he or she is doing. How can you grade the photographer's abilities if you don't know how to work the flash on your own camera? For starters, look for crispness and composition. Did the photographer make good use of lighting? Were a variety of backgrounds and settings used, or is everyone shown standing in front of the cake? Is there a good balance of formal and candid shots? This should give you an idea of what to look for, but if you have a friend or family member who knows photography, try bribing them into going along with you.

When interviewing a photographer who hasn't been recommended to you (in other words, if you're checking out a guy you found in the Yellow Pages), ask for references. The photos in the portfolio he's showing you might be incredible, but it's always possible that the person you're talking to bought them from someone else. This philosophy is called "wedding season cynicism," and it may save you a lot of headaches down the road. Ask for the names of former clients whom you can contact to get another customer's point of view.

The Digital Revolution

You may be a gadget-crazed girl, or you may be marrying a gadget-crazed guy, in which case your thoughts on photography may leap immediately to the digital revolution. The newest way is always the best way, you say.

Digital pictures do have their advantages. Generally speaking, digital wedding packages are often a little cheaper than those using the traditional film cameras. You'll likely have many more pictures to choose from in the end, and the pictures can easily be put onto a CD. This lets you easily e-mail them to friends and family. You can create your own wedding Web site, or you can have the images stored on DVD. With this last option, and some inexpensive software, you can create a moving photo album with soundtrack and everything so that you and the family can sit and watch the pictures parade past on your television. Having the pictures on a CD is also the equivalent of having the negatives. You can make all the copies you want.

The downside of most digital photos is that as you enlarge them, they lose their clarity, with enlarged photos often coming out blurry. If you can live with that possible consequence, digital may be something worth looking into.

The Interview

You'll need to ask a lot of questions to help you choose the best man, woman, or studio for the job. If there's anything about a potential candidate that makes you nervous, or if for any reason you don't trust this person to do the job correctly, move on. There are a lot of other photographers out there who are just waiting for your call.

The Right Questions

Don't be afraid to put your photographer through the wringer a bit. You're probably going to drop a big chunk of change into his or her pocket if you decide to hire him or her, so find out *before* you sign a contract what you're getting into.

FACT

Remember: A photographer's high price tag does not necessarily mean you'll be getting high quality. A low price tag, however, is a pretty reliable sign that you're likely to see low-quality results. This is one wedding expense that really is worth the money, time, and effort that it requires.

You probably won't be dragging your wedding dress out of storage very often, and you may not even remember what kind of flowers you carried, but you can bet that you and your loved ones will be going back to your wedding photographs time and time again.

Questions for your photographer include these:

- How long has he or she been in business? Does he or she specialize in weddings? Is he or she a full-time photographer?
- What kinds of packages does he or she offer? What's included in each package? What are the costs for additional photos?
- How many pictures does he or she typically take at a wedding of this size?
- Is there an hourly fee? Fee for travel?
- Will you be able to purchase additional pictures in the future?
- Can you see some of his or her recent work? Can you have the names of some former clients so that you can ask about their experience with this photographer?

The Answers You Want

There's more to this than asking the questions, of course, and since you may not have any experience in working with professional photographers, an explanation of these questions follows.

Steer clear of part-time photographers who only occasionally handle weddings. They're not likely to have the equipment and experience of an expert in the field, and their lack of commitment to this line of work will show in the final product. You want a full-time photographer, not someone who does this as a hobby, and not someone who's trying to line their pockets by doing this as a side job.

If you're planning on working with a studio, choose one that specializes in weddings. You may love the studio that did your high school graduation picture . . . but if portraits are all they do, they'll probably flunk out at your wedding. Only experienced wedding photographers know all the nuances of photographing a wedding, like how to avoid problems, when to fade into the background, and the best way to compose a great shot when working with a crowd.

Avoid very large studios that appear to use the assembly-line approach. Often they employ as many as 100 photographers and won't guarantee which one will show up on your wedding day, or how qualified he or she is to do the job.

If you find a studio you'd like to work with, always ask to see sample wedding photos that were taken by the same photographer who will be working your wedding. If this studio can't or won't supply them, find another one to work with.

A high-quality studio or photographer will take three times as many photos as you signed on for, to give you the best and broadest selection. If you ask for the thirty-six-photo album, you certainly don't want the photographer taking *only* thirty-six pictures.

Some studios will charge you a basic hourly rate. Others charge a flat fee based on the photographer's time and a certain number of photographs, such as seven hours of work and a thirty-six-picture album. Studios may also charge for the photographer's travel time, or for overtime if the job runs longer than expected.

Ask for prices up front. Complete fees for photographers range from several hundred to several thousand dollars, depending upon the quality, type, and number of photographs. Be sure to find out what the prices are for additional photos you may want to order beyond the original package. The studio may give you a very reasonable price for your package, but may also charge $100 for every extra photo. Some studios include albums, frames, and special parents' books as part of the deal.

Some other areas you may want to address, assuming you know the first thing about photography or can fake it really well, include these. Does the photographer use a variety of lighting techniques and backgrounds? Will he or she mix formal and candid shots? Will he or she be open to your ideas?

Being in Pictures

After you've chosen the photographer, sit down with him or her and discuss your wants, needs, and expectations. It's important to establish a good relationship well before the wedding so that everyone feels comfortable when the big (and usually nerve-wracking) day comes around.

There are, of course, the traditional wedding poses and shots, which will almost surely be included in your wedding album. If you have anything *else* in mind, let your photographer know—ASAP! Give him a list of all the special people you want included in the pictures, especially anyone who isn't in the wedding party. Your photographer may be exceptional, but he's not a mind-reader. If your eighty-year-old aunt is famous (or infamous) for her particular rendition of the Twist at family functions, make sure to tell your photographer that you want that moment captured on film.

Formal Photos Before the Wedding

Although it's considered bad luck for the groom to see the bride before the ceremony, many couples feel comfortable doing away with this superstition and taking the formal shots before the wedding. This makes life easier for a lot of people. The photographer doesn't have to rush to get all the shots on your list before hungry guests start a riot; the guests don't suffer from starvation or boredom while they wait for you to pose . . . pose . . . and pose again; and you get to enjoy more of the reception.

If seeing the groom before the ceremony is absolutely out of the question for you, try to take as many of the formal pictures as you can without him—you alone, you and your parents, you and your attendants, and so on. At the reception, speed things up by making sure everyone who's going to be in a picture knows where he or she is supposed to be.

ALERT!

If you don't want your photographer to bother with some of the standard poses (the groom with his ushers, the groom with bridal attendants), speak up. Why waste time and film on pictures you don't want?

Shooting on Location

Some couples opt to take their formal wedding photos at a location other than the reception site. Sometimes the spot they select is of great sentimental value; sometimes it's chosen just because the scenery is gorgeous. Some popular on-location photo shoot possibilities include a beach, lake, or garden (in the spring and summer), near foliage (in the fall), and in a snow-covered wood (in the winter).

If you do plan to take your photo shoot on the road, remember that your guests will have to wait even longer than usual to see you (and their dinner) at the reception. As a way to ease their impatience (and their stomachs), make sure that the reception site will be offering bar service and hors d'oeuvres while they wait for you to arrive.

Black and White

Though you may associate black-and-white photos with your parents' and grandparents' weddings, they can add a special touch to yours. Color may be brilliant, but black and white is classic. It creates atmosphere and style. Black and white lends itself best to formal portraits; it gives them a timeless feel that's perfect for an occasion like this.

For a really distinctive look, the studio can add some hand-colored tinting to your black-and-white photos—the same process used for movie star stills in the 1940s. If you thought you felt special on your wedding day, imagine how you'll feel seeing you and your groom looking like two of the silver screen's greatest lovers!

Of course, while you're adding all this style and atmosphere, remember to add a little more money to your overall bill. As odd as it may seem, black-and-white photos (even the untinted variety) usually cost more than color prints. Be sure to ask. Some studios will include black-and-white wedding pictures at no extra cost.

FACT

Some of the best photos from your wedding may not even come from the photographer. Place a throwaway camera on each table and ask your guests to click away at the people and action around them during the reception. You'll end up with candids of people and events the photographer probably wouldn't dream of shooting—at a fraction of the cost.

Keeping Your Negatives

Ask whether the studio will hang on to your negatives, and if so, for how long. You may want or need a picture from the wedding years later, and you'll want to know how to get one made. Most studios will keep the negatives for only a few years. If having them forever is important to you, ask about buying them. Don't forget that if you're going the digital route, a CD containing your pictures is as good as having the negatives, as far as reprints are concerned.

Photographic Extras

Aside from working with you on the wedding day, you may want the photographer to take an engagement photo and/or a formal bridal portrait. If so, you'll want to iron out the details with the photographer in your initial meeting. Some brides have portraits taken as a gift to their parents. Photos can also be used as part of a wedding announcement in the newspaper. If you plan to send a copy along to the paper, be sure to order a 5" x 7" black-and-white shot from the photographer.

Bridal portraits are usually taken either at the photographer's studio or at the bridal salon on the day of your last fitting. Most photographers will meet you at the salon, but you should double-check to make sure.

If your photography budget is overflowing with extra funds, you might consider thank-you notes that feature a picture of you and your groom. You can get one standard photo that goes on every note, or, if you're really ambitious, personalize each one with a photo of you opening the person's gift.

For your bridal portrait, you'll need everything you plan to wear on your wedding day. This means your gown and veil (of course), stockings, shoes, jewelry, and gloves (if you're covering your arms). You'll also want to have your hair styled the same way that you plan on wearing it at your wedding.

Videography

Despite the clear and present danger of winding up on one of those embarrassing home-video shows, videotaping your wedding is pretty much a given these days. Many couples consider their wedding video more valuable than their wedding photographs. This may be because the bride and groom are, ironically, the two people who usually remember the least about their wedding. They're in a fog of emotion and excitement, in which hundreds of sensory impressions go by in a blur. Still photographs will show them a few staged poses, but videotape will show how things *were*.

Unlike a still camera, the video camera records not just images, but time—taking in all the sound and action of a scene. Rather than focusing in on a few key friends and family members, video captures everybody. You can have a record of the guests as they sing, dance, eat, kiss, cry, laugh. When a bride and groom finally sit down to watch their videotape, it will certainly bring back memories but it will also show them many things they hadn't seen before.

Don't leave the videotaping to a friend or relative unless you've seen a sample of his or her work and were impressed by it. Your groom's brother may have the best intentions and even own a good video camera, but odds are he won't have the necessary sound and editing equipment to make a tape for posterity. He may miss some key moments while he's schmoozing your maid of honor, too.

Your Videographer

When searching for a videographer, apply the same basic guidelines you would for a still photographer. The pictures may be moving this time, but the images should still be crisp and clear, and colors should be true-to-life. You want to be comfortable with your videographer, and confident he won't be ordering your guests in and out of shots because he fancies himself the next Big Man on the Hollywood Scene.

Confirm that your videographer has up-to-date, quality equipment, and not a forty-year-old eight-millimeter camera. Also ask about editing and dubbing capabilities, microphones (will you both be wearing one during the ceremony, for instance, or will only the groom be wired for sound?), and lights. Find out how many cameras he or she has, and how many people will be assisting on the job. Some video formats require the simultaneous use of two cameras; one person with one camera will bring you up short.

Ask to view sample tapes. You're looking for smooth editing, clear sound, and an overall professional look and feel to the tape. With all of the technology available today, you don't have to settle for anything short of broadcast quality production values.

Where should I start searching for a videographer?
If you're working with a studio for your wedding pictures, they may also offer videography services. If not, they might be able to recommend someone. And don't forget your most precious resource in these situations: word of mouth. Friends, relations, and coworkers should be able to help out with some referrals.

Once you've found someone and verified references, get a written contract stipulating costs, services, manpower commitments, the date, the time, and the place.

Interviewing Candidates

Again, you'll be putting on your bold bride cap and asking questions of a total stranger. Remember that it's in your best interest to ask as many questions as you feel are pertinent to the candidate at hand. The previous section covered information about the videographer's equipment. Here are some other things to ask him or her:

- How long has he or she been doing this professionally?
- Can you see some of his or her recent work? Is he or she working on a tape that you can see? (Again, this is the wedding cynicism philosophy—you want to make sure this person has actually done the work that you're looking at.)
- What kinds of packages does he or she offer? What are the rates? Are there any other fees, such as travel, hourly, and so on?
- What formats does he or she offer? Can you have a DVD instead of a tape (or vice versa)? What is the price difference?
- Does he or she use any special effects in the final product, such as titles, credits, music, and so on?
- Can you have several copies made?
- Ask for the names of former clients so that you can talk to them about their experience with this person.

When you're viewing samples of the videographer's work, consider whether the segments tell a story. In other words, does the tape make sense to you? Is everything in chronological order? Are the "big events," like the ceremony, the cake cutting, shown clearly? How's the sound? Is the editing smooth? Is the picture steady and focused?

There are some very elaborate video formats out there, some featuring special lenses and special effects. You can get an Oscar-caliber videotape, but it won't come cheap. Before you get carried away with the idea of seeing your name in lights, remember that little technicality called a budget. Like the photo package, the typical wedding video package costs anywhere from several hundred to several thousand dollars, depending on the quality of the equipment, the number of hours you've contracted the videographer for, the number of cameras, the amount of editing, and other factors. Remember to determine what's most important to you, figure out what you can afford, and go from there.

Formats

There are various format options for wedding videos. Your videographer may or may not offer you a choice, but asking for a certain style could open a door that otherwise would have remained closed to you.

A nostalgic format usually starts with a photo montage of you and your groom as children or young adults. From there, it might show the two of you sharing your lives together and then move right into your wedding. You will have to provide pictures from your youth and your groom's awkward teenage years, as well as your wedding invitation and program. The action will then follow the ceremony and reception. Because it takes a little more work to put together, this type of video can be more expensive than the others.

A straight shot format uses only one camera, thus making it the least expensive video option offered. No editing is required, but the videographer can still add small touches, such as names and dates, to help spice up the film.

A documentary format is the standard for wedding videos, and gives you a documentary-style account of your wedding day. It usually starts with you and your groom preparing for the ceremony, then proceeds to scenes of the wedding and the reception. Interviews with family and friends are sometimes added. Prices vary widely depending on the type of equipment used, the number of locations that the videographer has to schlep his or her equipment to, the number of hours you're contracting him or her for, and the amount of editing needed.

If your videographer will be using a format that requires editing, ask if you can have the unedited footage as well. You may not watch this tape as often, but you'll probably want access to the uncut version for those memorable moments that didn't make it onto the "official" tape.

Remember to take your videographer to your ceremony and reception sites ahead of time to check out the lighting, possible angles, and so on. You should also acquaint the videographer with the photographer, if they haven't crossed paths at a wedding before yours. This way each person can get an idea of how the other works and an understanding how to work together to get shots instead of stepping on each other's toes all evening.

Chapter 13
Right in Tune

Have you ever been to a wedding where the music was so bad you wished there hadn't been any? You certainly don't want anyone to remember your wedding this way, so you'll put some careful thought into this part of your big day. Remember that the right music adds emotion and drama to the moment; the wrong music kills anything you've got going. Take your time in choosing not only the perfect music, but also the perfect musicians.

Coming and Going

Carefully selected music can provide atmosphere and enhance the mood and meaning of your ceremony. You may already have an auditory fantasy of the music that will be playing as you walk down the aisle, as you take your vows, and as you leave the church.

This section offers suggestions for your church music—but remember that they are only suggestions. If, for example, you'd like a slow, somber (read: dramatic) piece to play while you walk down the aisle, instead of a chirpy little tune, go for it. It's your wedding day; choose the music that will make it feel special to *you*.

The Processional

The processional is the music that accompanies the wedding party in their jaunt down the aisle. A traditional march helps to set the pace for some nervous feet—but a lighter, airy piece might lift your heart as you take those first steps toward your soon-to-be-husband.

When it's time for you to make that l-o-o-ong trek down the aisle, you can walk to the same piece that you've chosen for the bridesmaids or to your own music. Sometimes the piece is the same but played at a different tempo, or with an audience-captivating pause before it begins.

Brides differ wildly in their preferences for their processional pieces. Here are some suggestions:

- Wagner's "Bridal Chorus"
- Mendelssohn's "Wedding March" (from *A Midsummer's Night Dream*)
- Bach's "Sheep May Safely Graze"
- Stanley's "Trumpet Voluntary"
- Pachelbel's *Canon*
- Handel's "Hornpipe" from *Water Music*
- Charpentier's "Processional"

Wagner's "Bridal Chorus" is the processional that many people think of when they picture a bride marching down the aisle; its bookend is

Mendelssohn's slightly more upbeat "Wedding March," which is often used as recessional music.

ALERT!

Getting married for the second time? Music for a second wedding ceremony is not an issue that breeds much controversy—unless you repeat everything you did at your first wedding. Unless you have a real connection to a song, choose *different* music for this ceremony.

The Recessional

The big exit! The song should be joyous and upbeat, reflecting your happiness at being joined for life to the man now accompanying you down the aisle and out of the church. An up-tempo song will also help move your guests along more quickly than a sedate piece, and if the reception is following the ceremony, they'll be happy for an excuse to bound (rather than stroll) out of the church.

Take another look at the titles listed in the section on the processional. Many of these pieces can be used at either the beginning or the end of the ceremony. Some other suggestions include:

- Widor's "Toccata"
- Purcell's "Trumpet Tune"
- Willan's "Finale Jubilante"
- Handel's "Sinfonia (Arrival of the Queen of Sheba)"
- Vierne's "Finale" from *Organ Symphony no. 1*
- Wesley's "Choral Song"

Ceremony Soundtrack

If additional musicians, singers, and songs are an option you'd like to consider, consult with the officiant in charge of your ceremony. Some religions place restrictions on secular selections during the ceremony, but others may be very open. Ask about this well in advance. You don't want the officiant running you out of the place when the soloist belts out her rather sassy rendition of "Love and Marriage" during the rehearsal.

Don't worry if you think you don't know enough about classical or "church" music. The musicians you eventually choose can offer suggestions based on guidelines you offer them, and some suggestions are offered in this chapter, as well.

The Prelude

The prelude lasts from the time the guests start arriving until all of them are seated and the mother of the bride is ready to make her entrance. The options for music here are very broad: upbeat, slow, or a mixture of both. The prelude establishes a mood as well as entertains the guests while they wait. The end of the prelude, right before the processional, is usually a good time for a soloist or choir to sing a song. During the final song of the prelude, the mother of the bride is seated.

Some good choices for the prelude include:

- Handel's *Water Music*
- Mozart's "Adagio" from *Ave Verum*
- Vivaldi's "Largo" from *Winter*
- Bach's *Brandenburg Concertos*
- Bach's "Jesu, Joy of Man's Desiring"
- Bach's preludes and fugues for the organ
- Mendelssohn's "Adagio" from *Organ Sonata no. 2, op. 65*
- Peeters's "Aria" from *Trumpet Sonata, op. 51*
- Massenet's "Meditation" from *Thaïs*

Ceremony Music

Music played during the actual wedding ceremony is called, oddly enough, ceremony music. The right music here can enhance the mood and emphasize the meaning of the service. Consider playing a short piece during the lighting of the unity candle, for example. If Communion is being incorporated as part of the ceremony, this is a good time for another vocal performance.

If you're getting married in a church, chances are your musical choices will be limited to religious songs. Paul Stookey's "The Wedding Song" is one former radio hit that will probably make the cut in your house of worship. Some other, non–Top-40 (at least not from the past hundred years) songs to consider:

- Schubert's "Ave Maria"
- Artman's "Wedding Prayer"
- Malotte's "The Lord's Prayer"
- Weatherill's "A Marriage Prayer"
- "The Irish Wedding Song" (traditional)
- Franck's "Panis Angelicus"
- Callahan's "Wherever You Go"
- Dvořák's "God Is My Shepherd"
- Peeters's "Wedding Song: Whither Thou Goest, There Will I Go Also"

Now, whether your church organist and/or soloist *knows* any of these songs is another matter altogether. He or she (or the musicians you've hired for the ceremony) will sit down and discuss your wedding music possibilities before the ceremony.

If any of these titles strikes your fancy, take some time and hunt them down in the music section at your public library before you meet with the musicians just so you can suggest some specific titles and names to them (*and* so you can be sure you want these songs included in your wedding).

Finding Your Church Musicians

Before you hire a full orchestra to accompany the church choir, though, remember that the cost of musicians and singers for the ceremony must fit into your overall music budget. In other words, you don't hire a $1,000 string quartet when you have only $1,200 allotted for ceremony *and* reception music. It may take some fancy footwork, but don't be intimidated. You can have wonderful music for both events with a little compromise and ingenuity.

If you regularly attend a church that employs a God-awful organist and/or singer, he or she is the last one you want commandeering the music for your ceremony. Most churches will allow you to bring in your own musicians, provided they meet the church's guidelines. In other words, unless you belong to a very progressive church, your favorite local hard-rock band probably won't be allowed to set up in the choir loft.

If your friends are no help, and your church doesn't have a wedding coordinator, you'll have to hit the wedding circuit in town. Sit through some weddings—if you hear a great soloist, grab him or her after the ceremony and make arrangements to meet and discuss your wedding. The great thing about attending other weddings is that you'll also hear *other* musicians (string quartets, trumpet players), and you'll get a million musical ideas for your own big day.

Still at a loss? Ask the music department at your local high school if there are any students who sing (or play the trumpet, piano, violin) at weddings. Seek out the director of the music program at a local college. Look in the classified section of your newspaper. The musicians are out there—you just have to hunt them down.

QUESTION?

Where can you find a good, reasonably priced soloist?
Word of mouth is, you'll remember, always your best bet. If your friends can't recommend anyone, your next best bet is to ask your church's wedding coordinator for guidance. He or she has seen the good, the bad, and the indescribable.

Who Will Rock Your Reception?

The size, formality, and budget of your wedding will help to determine the type of entertainment you have at the reception. At a formal affair, there may be a strolling violinist or a piano player who will provide background music as the meal is served. If you're having your reception in a private home or a backyard, you can use your own CDs and pipe them through a good stereo system. That will provide plenty of music to dance to.

Once you decide on the kind of music you want at your wedding, you need to find someone to provide it. You may already have someone in mind, like the DJ who played at your cousin's wedding or your favorite local band. If you don't have a clue, ask friends, relatives, and coworkers. Perhaps they've been to or hosted a wedding recently and can recommend—or steer you away from—a certain band or platter-spinner.

Many bands and DJs don't advertise, so word of mouth is probably the only way for you to hear about them. If you still come up empty, talk to your reception site coordinator. He or she has probably seen a lot of musical entertainment come and go and may be able to recommend someone who fits your needs.

These days, the big musical decision is whether to hire a band or a DJ. When it comes to price, the DJ is definitely the less expensive option, but there are other factors that may influence your choice. Whichever you select, you will want to finalize arrangements approximately six months in advance of your wedding date.

Live Bands

Assuming you can find a charismatic, golden-throated singer backed by talented, enthusiastic musicians, there is no substitute for a live band. If you're lucky enough to find live musicians who can work within your budget, snap them up quickly—before another bride hires *your* band for *her* wedding.

If you're not so lucky, plan to spread yourself pretty thin, making many treks to bars, lounges, and function halls—anyplace where you might find some decent live music. When you find a group who strikes your fancy, go back and listen to them again. Some bands will impress you the first time—but you have no idea whether they're having an especially good (and lucky) night or whether they always sound like they should be on the radio.

In addition to the band's sound, look for a variety of musical styles and tempos in their repertoire. Do they play seven slow songs, one fast number, then two more slow ones, or do they know how to vary the pace? Do they appear to be enjoying themselves, or do they look like they'd rather be somewhere else?

Nail 'Em Down

Once you find a band you like, make arrangements with the leader to sit down and talk about exactly what you want concerning your wedding. Have a list of songs ready that you have to hear at your reception. If they don't know the songs already, will they attempt to learn them in time? Ask about their sound system and equipment needs. If your reception site is too small, or doesn't have the proper electrical outlets and fuse power, it's better to know before you hire the band.

FACT

At most weddings, the bandleader doubles as the master of ceremonies. If you want your bandleader to perform this duty, find out whether he or she will be willing and if any extra cost is involved.

Make sure whoever will be acting as emcee has the poise and charisma to handle the responsibility. You don't want the microphone in the hands of someone who will insult your guests, make jokes as you cut the cake, or mumble your names unintelligibly as you enter the reception site for the first time as husband and wife!

Get It in Writing

Before you sign a contract with the band, make sure the following commitments are stipulated in writing:

- The band's attire. You don't want them showing up at a formal wedding in ripped jeans or gym shorts.
- The band's arrival time. Make sure the band is set up, with

instruments tuned, before the guests arrive. The band's sound check will probably not make for soothing dinner music.

- The exact cost of hiring the band . . . and everything included for that price. Some bands charge you if they have to add an extra piece of equipment; others charge a fee for playing requests.

This is also the time to make sure the band knows the exact location of the reception. There have actually been instances where the musical talent has shown up at the reception site with the right name, but in the wrong city.

Disc Jockeys

Disc jockeys are fast becoming the wedding music option of choice. DJs can provide more variety than a band. They give you the original version of a song, and they're less of a logistical headache. DJs are seen as slightly less formal than bands, but they're also considerably less expensive, which adds a great deal to their appeal.

It's just as important to see and hear a disc jockey in action as it is with a band. Look for the same things you would in a band: balance, variety, a good mix of fast and slow songs, a good personality, and first-rate equipment. Could this person perform the duties of master of ceremonies? Does he talk way too much or far too little?

Find out how big his or her music collection is, as your disc jockey should be able to accommodate the majority of your guests' requests. Provide a list of what you want played at the reception, and if you have some songs you absolutely, positively, upon penalty of death do *not* want played, give him or her a hit list of those, too! If some of the music you want isn't available, is the DJ willing to purchase it?

Some other questions to ask your DJ include the following:

- How many weddings has he or she provided music for? What size weddings does he or she typically work?
- Will he or she provide appropriate music for the cocktail hour?
- Does he or she provide a wireless microphone for any toasts or speeches?
- Is the gratuity included in the price?

The DJ's exact cost, including possible extras, the time of arrival and departure, the place, and his or her proper attire should all be spelled out in the contract that you sign.

The Songs

No matter what kind of musical talent you decide on in the end, you'll need to have an idea of the music you want played during the reception. If you're following tradition and including the first dance with your groom, and then a dance with your dad, and the groom's dance with his mother, you'll have to tell your bandleader or DJ which songs you want to hear at those moments.

Your choices for reception music are limited only by your imagination. The only guideline you should be aware of is that you want to entertain your guests—not drive them away. It's an added bonus if the music complements the theme and style of the day. In other words, for a very formal wedding, a swing group or jazz quartet might go over a bit better than an alternative-music-type band. Whatever type or types of music you do decide on, remember that this form of entertainment is like a little gift you're giving to your guests, to add to their enjoyment of your wedding. Your best bet is to go with an all-inclusive song list that covers a broad spectrum of musical tastes—some slow, some dance tunes, some rock, some soul.

Don't forget about *your* entertainment! Aside from pleasing the guests, you and your fiancé should make sure your own favorite music is played during the reception. Could you imagine celebrating your wedding without dancing with your new husband to "your song"?

The First Dance

You might already have a song that's special to the two of you that you'll want to use for your moments in the spotlight on the dance floor.

If you don't, though, or if you don't want to use it because you don't want anyone else *stealing* it from you, consider some of these songs:

"In My Life" (Beatles)
"I Swear" (All 4 One)
"From This Moment" (Shania Twain)
"I Do (Cherish You)" (98 Degrees)
"At Last" (Etta James)
"Grow Old Along with Me" (Mary Chapin Carpenter)
"Here and Now" (Luther Vandross)
"It's Your Love" (Tim McGraw and Faith Hill)
"Silly Love Songs" (Wings)
"It's Love" (Lena Horne)
"She" (Elvis Costello)
"Woman" (John Lennon)
"Just the Two of Us" (Grover Washington)
"My One and Only Love" (Louis Armstrong)
"Forever and for Always" (Shania Twain)
"A Moment Like This" (Kelly Clarkson)
"Annie's Song" (John Denver)
"I Could Write a Book" (Harry Connick, Jr.)
"Time in a Bottle" (Jim Croce)

Obviously, the possibilities are endless, not only because there are millions of songs to choose from (Old? New? Fast? Slow? Blues? Country? Any and all of these are fair game), but because your personalities *should* come into play in choosing the right one for you. If you're a silly, playful couple, you might want to choose something that's a little more lighthearted than you would if the two of you were very serious-minded people. The important thing is to choose a song that you both love. Don't worry about whether anyone else will feel it's an inappropriate or odd choice.

Dancin' with Dad

Here's where you might want to get a little more traditional—unless you and your father have a special song already, or your dad is a real ham who wants a goofy song instead of a nice one. "Daddy's Little Girl" is an old fave for this one, but other possibilities include these:

"Because You Loved Me" (Celine Dion)
"The Way You Look Tonight" (Frank Sinatra)
"Thank Heaven for Little Girls" (Maurice Chevalier)
"I Am Your Child" (Barry Manilow)
"You Are the Sunshine of My Life" (Stevie Wonder)
"Little Miss Magic" (Jimmy Buffett)
"Forever Young" (Rod Stewart)
"God Only Knows" (Beach Boys)
"Butterfly Kisses" (Raybon Brothers)
"A Song for My Daughter" (Ray Allaire)
"My Girl" (Temptations)
"Isn't She Lovely?" (Stevie Wonder)

Again, base this choice on your relationship with your dad, and not on what your mom (or anyone else, for that matter) would like to hear during this dance.

ALERT!

A word to the wise: If you can find out where the speakers are located in the reception room, try to seat your older guests away from them and away from the area where the musicians will be playing. Hopefully, this will prevent you from hearing any complaints from your elderly relatives concerning the volume of the music.

Other Dances

If your groom is going to dance with his mother, he should really choose the song himself. His mom might have a little song that she used to sing to him, or she might have a favorite song now that could be used. If all else fails, ask the band or DJ to play "Close to You" by the Carpenters. It's a safe bet and a tearjerker, all rolled into one neat little package.

If you're getting the whole wedding party out onto the dance floor, you might want to choose music that lets them cut loose a little and gets the party rolling. Consider these:

"It Had to Be You" (Harry Connick, Jr.)
"We Are Family" (Sister Sledge)
"Ain't No Mountain High Enough" (Marvin Gaye and Tammi Terrell)
"How Sweet It Is (To Be Loved By You)" (James Taylor)
"Everybody Have Fun Tonight" (Wang Chung)

Again, the choices are really endless. You don't have to pick a song about friendship—you can keep the music in the love vein. If you do choose to go with a peppy song here, make sure it's one that your wedding party can actually dance to (instead of trying unsuccessfully to catch a beat for several minutes).

A Little Ethnic Flair

To add some spice to the usual bag of "wedding" songs, consider featuring some music from your homeland (even if, technically, *this* is your homeland). If either you or your fiancé is Polish, for instance, play some polkas. If one of you is Italian, a couple of tarantellas are bound to light up the dance floor. If your guests have strong ethnic ties, they'll appreciate the nostalgia, and guests of a different culture will enjoy learning something new.

Chapter 14

Love in Bloom: The Flowers

To many people, flowers are the ultimate symbol of love. The beauty, the fragrance, the romance—everything about flowers, it seems, has captivated the imagination throughout history. Flowers are such an important part of the wedding décor that some might say they make or break the scene. The wrong flowers say, "Ho-hum," while the right ones shout, "I'm pretty!"

Flower Bud(get)

Before you get swept away by all the beauty and romance of flowers, calculate your flower budget. Flowers are one of those wedding expenses that can get out of hand quickly. The tab for this expense just tends to add up in a hurry, even when you're trying to keep things under control, but that doesn't mean that you have to lose your shirt on the flowers. If you're careful (and maybe a little crafty), you can bring your pretty posies in under budget—without sacrificing anything in the way of atmosphere.

Finding the Florist

An honest florist, when presented with a set-in-stone budget, will steer you in the most practical direction given the dollars you have to spend. Good florists know there's nothing to be gained by making you miserable by showing you things they know you can't afford. But if you don't have the slightest idea of your budget, then you can't really fault a florist for showing you his or her most expensive arrangements. Once the budget has been settled upon, you can concentrate on choosing the actual flowers.

Start searching for a florist at least three months before the wedding. Like everything else concerning the planning of your wedding, word of mouth is the best way to find someone reliable.

If you have trouble getting florist referrals from friends, consult the Yellow Pages, ask your reception site coordinator, or visit florists' booths at wedding exhibitions. Ask for photos of previous displays that the florist has done, and check references to make sure that there is a history of quality work for actual customers.

Once you decide on a florist, you'll need a written contract stipulating costs, times, dates, places, and services. Make sure the florist is scheduled to arrive before the photographer on your wedding day, so that you won't end up with a wedding album filled with you, your bridesmaids . . . and an eerie *lack* of nosegays.

When Your Florist Talks . . .

Before you meet with your florist, decide on the color scheme of your wedding. Bring color swatches (of bridesmaid's dresses and/or decorations) along to your meeting with him or her so the florist can recommend flowers that will either match or complement the overall scheme.

Your florist will also guide you to the flowers that most suit your style, taste, even your coloring. If you're very petite, for instance, the florist will probably advise that you not carry a huge, elaborate arrangement as it might overwhelm you. If you're particularly fair-skinned, you might be advised against an all-white bouquet, because the lack of color in your flowers will only emphasize the lack of color in your cheeks.

He or she will also tell you which flowers will look best in the ceremony and reception locations you've chosen. If you're getting married in a huge cathedral, for example, you'll need much more substantial pieces than if you're saying your vows in a teeny tiny chapel. If the florist has never done work at either site before, take a trip there together so you can both look around and discuss what will be needed—and where.

Delivery

Your fiancé is buttoning up the last button on his tux, and his ushers are joking with him that this is his last chance to make a getaway. Your makeup and hair would make a movie star jealous, your bridesmaids are admiring themselves in the mirror, and your flower girl hasn't stopped talking about the special basket she's going to carry down the aisle. And then it hits you: Where *is* that basket? And where are all of the *other* flowers?!

ALERT!

Any florist worth his or her salt will know (based on the time of your ceremony) when to have your flowers at your home, but it can't hurt to double-check. Make sure he or she knows when your photographer will be arriving at your home.

When hammering out the final details with your florist, make sure you're both clear on the delivery schedule. If you plan to take pictures two hours before the ceremony begins, chances are you want to be photographed holding your flowers, instead of standing there empty-handed. Communication is vital. Make sure your flowers are where you want them, when you want them.

What Do They Mean?

You might love a certain type of flower simply because it's beautiful, but do you have any idea what the meaning behind it is?

Flower	Meaning
Chrysanthemum (red)	Love
Daisy	Innocence
Forget-me-not	True love
Gardenia	Secret love
Iris	Affection
Ivy	Fidelity
Lily	Majesty
Lily-of-the-valley	Happiness
Rose (red)	Love
Rose (pink)	Perfect happiness; gratitude
Rose (yellow)	Friendship; joy
Rose (white)	Innocence; purity
Rose (peach)	Desire
Rosebuds	Beauty; youth
Violet	Modesty

You and your florist may be thinking of a certain type of flower because of its appearance. However, knowing its meaning might take a flower that you didn't previously love or admire and give it a new shine in your eyes.

Years ago, a bride might have been restricted from using certain flowers because they weren't in season at the time of her wedding. Today, most florists stock fresh flowers that have been imported from Europe, the Middle East, South America, and other foreign regions. How does all this importing affect you? It means that "in season" is no longer an issue and that all but a few of the most delicate flowers are available at any time of year. If you do decide to take a chance on one of the delicate flowers, have a second choice to fall back on.

FACT

Planning a Valentine's Day wedding? Those red roses might cost you a bit more than they would at another time of the year. Traditionally, orders that are set for delivery within the first two weeks of February are priced differently (read: higher) than they would be during the other fifty weeks of the year.

Do It Yourself

You just don't understand all of fuss surrounding a florist. You can arrange flowers as well as any professional, and you just hate to shell out all that extra money to have someone else complete the task. Oh, and you have lots of time on your hands.

Does this sound like you? If you're thinking of tackling your wedding flowers all by yourself, here are some things you should know.

Wholesalers

You'll need to find yourself a good wholesale dealer. What's your best resource? Word of mouth, of course. If you don't know anyone who's ever dealt with a wholesale florist, look in the phone book. Visit wedding fairs, and keep your eyes and ears open. Many wholesalers will even whip up your entire arrangements and deliver the flowers to your church; they just do it for a lower price than the fanciest flower shops.

I Want Cheap Flowers . . . dot-com

There are also plenty of Internet floral wholesalers that cater to thrifty, crafty brides. In addition to selling flowers at deep discounts, many of these Web sites also offer instructional videos on how to arrange, tape, and wire your flowers (some also offer e-mail support in case you have a little trouble with your arrangements).

The upside to this arrangement is that you stand to save yourself a lot of money. The downside? It's a little risky. The flowers are shipped overnight and are refrigerated so that they arrive fresh on your doorstep on the morning of your wedding, but *what if . . . ?* What if there's a storm, and the plane carrying your flowers is grounded? What if you get the wrong flowers? What if the flowers arrive dead? These are not easy fixes.

ALERT!

If you're going to order your wedding flowers on the Internet, and you honestly don't believe that any mishaps are likely to occur, make sure you have nerves of steel. It's one thing to be confident about it now. It's another to remain confident while you wait for your flowers.

If you think you might have been born under a bad sign (or that maybe you're on the wrong end of some kind of curse)—your new car is a lemon; every piece of clothing you buy goes on sale right after you lose the receipt for your price adjustment; you find yourself getting ripped off time and time again—buy your flowers from someone in town. It will make your life infinitely easier.

Ceremony Flowers

Flowers are an important part of the ceremony. They accent key points and create atmosphere. If you're getting married in a huge church, you'll need a few large, elaborate arrangements to compete with the surroundings; small displays would simply be swallowed up. Likewise, small accent displays would be a perfect complement to a quaint country church, where large arrangements would overpower the place.

How much of the ceremony site do you want to decorate with flowers? Some couples simply have one large or a few small arrangements placed around the altar. Some also place flowers on the pews, the windows or windowsills, on the doors, and on anything else that's standing still.

Try to pop in on a wedding in the same church (or hall) you'll be using; try to get a look at a wedding that your florist is doing, too. You'll get some ideas as to what looks good, what doesn't, and what you just have to have at your own wedding.

Christmas and Easter are good times to take note of church flowers. Take a look at how the altar arrangements are presented. Are the flowers on the floor or set up on small tables? Are those tables available to you? If not, can your florist provide something similar? If your church permits you to, take some pictures. This will give you a record of how the church *can* look dressed up in flowers.

Presentation

Have you ever received a box of beautiful roses and were afraid to take them out of the box? You knew that after you tried arranging them in a vase, they wouldn't be beautiful anymore. Most women can choose attractive flowers in colors that complement each other, but many of those same women couldn't *arrange* flowers in a visually appealing way to save their lives. That's why your florist is your pal. He or she can take weeds from your backyard and bunch them together so that they look like a million bucks.

Aside from having the talent to arrange flowers in pleasing combinations, florists also know how to *present* flowers. A good florist would not, for instance, put a beautiful bouquet to water in a soda can. (Even with nothing else to put those flowers in, he or she would figure out a way to make the can hold the bouquet as if it were a crystal vase.)

When presenting flowers at the ceremony, your florist may choose to use decorative baskets, glass bowls, or vases. Loose flowers can be tied into ribbon for decorating pews and chairs. Ivy can be wound around railings or placed with bows on candelabras. In season, potted flowers such as lilies, tulips, daffodils, hyacinths, and poinsettias can ornament windows or areas at the front of the church that need a little more flair.

Floral Road Trip!

Many couples use their ceremony flowers at the reception as well. By using the same flowers, you save yourself the expense of having to decorate both locations. You'll need to corral a responsible friend or relative to transport the flowers from the ceremony to the reception. While guests are milling around outside of the ceremony and traveling to the reception site, this trustworthy person will be unloading floral displays. By the time everyone arrives, everything will be all set for the photographer and the guests.

If you decide to go this route, make sure the reception site coordinator knows your plans. Your friend will have enough on his or her mind, loading and unloading expensive and possibly fragile arrangements into his or her car. He or she doesn't need the aggravation of arguing with the reception people about moving furniture, plates, and pianos to make room for the flowers. You'll also want to make sure that your friend knows where you want the arrangements placed. Having them dumped just inside the door probably isn't what you have in mind.

If your bridesmaids are willing to part with their bouquets, you could use their flowers to decorate the wedding cake table or the head table. Discuss this possibility with your florist, to get recommendations on types of bouquets that would work best for this dual purpose.

One caveat: Some churches require that any flowers that are used in a wedding ceremony must be "donated" to the church (so that the church doesn't have to shell out any bucks for flowers on that particular weekend). If that's the rule in your church, there's really nothing you can do about it. You don't really want to go *without* flowers, because the pictures of your ceremony will look barren without them. One thing you can do is to find out if there's another wedding in the church on the same day as yours and contact the other bride. If the two of you can agree on color and style, you might be able to share the same flowers.

Flowers at the Reception

The flowers at the reception are meant to highlight the overall design scheme. Place flowers atop the buffet or wedding cake tables; you'll give people something to look at while they think about food. (Flowers can also be used to decorate the cake itself. See Chapter 15 for ideas.)

Depending on the atmosphere of your reception site, hanging plants, small trees, or even topiaries can add splashes of interest to the surroundings. If your budget allows, consider small flower arrangements for the guest tables; they make wonderful centerpieces. Keep in mind that your guests should be able to see one another across the table, so avoid the tall crystal vase with the beautiful flourish of cut flowers and greenery. Keep the arrangements low, especially if your tables are round.

FACT

If you use a lot of floral arrangements at your wedding, put someone in charge of dispensing them after the reception. You may want to give the flowers to close friends or relatives, or perhaps to nursing homes or charitable organizations. You might also want to send thank-you flowers to mothers, friends, and relatives as a way of expressing your appreciation for their help.

For less formal weddings, small potted plants such as English ivy or philodendrons arranged in decorative baskets make attractive (and affordable!) table decorations. They have the added attraction of being something guests can take home with them and enjoy for years to come.

For a theme wedding (or just for fun), you could add a creative element to your table arrangements. If your theme is the beach, place a small arrangement in a wide dish of sand, shells, and colorful sea glass. Fall weddings could be dressed up with bright silk maple leaves, assorted nuts in the shell, Red Delicious apples, and tiny gourds. For a Christmas wedding, arrange flowers in wooden toy sleighs, include gilded or snow-covered pinecones, or perhaps place a small decorated wreath flat on the table with a candle in the middle.

Get Creative

Whether you decide to work with a florist or to do your wedding flowers yourself, you don't have to stick to the same old thing you've seen at every other wedding you've ever been to. But there's something to be said for following the old traditions, like those of carrying a bouquet or decorating the church altar with lots of arrangements. Assuming you're working with an adequate budget, there's nothing stopping you from taking your floral fantasies to the absolute limit. This section contains some ideas for getting imaginative with your wedding décor.

Centerpieces

Many brides choose *not* to include flowers in the centerpieces at the reception, which is one way to save yourself a lot of money. A crystal or glass bowl with floating candles is an illuminating option—and the light is doubled if you place the bowls on mirrors.

Instead of going with a traditional arrangement, one trend you'll see nowadays is placing flowers in several small silver vases and grouping them together as one centerpiece. You can invite your guests to take the vases home. You might also want to take small candies—conversation hearts or candied almonds, or even rose petals—and sprinkle them around the centerpieces.

Cover It!

If you're a bride who just can't have enough floral and greenery and tulle in your life, take a good look at your ceremony and reception site. Does either have any pillars? Banisters? Railings? Pews? If so, start swagging! You can add garlands, ivy, and/or tulle to any of these structures and really bring them to life. (You can find garlands of faux greenery in any craft shop, and tulle is relatively inexpensive). This is also a great idea if you're getting married outdoors in a pavilion or gazebo and need to dress it up a bit.

If your reception site is looking a little barren, think about placing some potted trees near the entrance. Or maybe you'd prefer a balloon arrangement. Keep wedding balloons as simple as possible. Consider using a combination of gold, clear, ivory, or white balloons as the main colors and then adding a few balloons that match your bridesmaids' dresses. You can also buy colored confetti to put inside the clear balloons.

How can I dress up plain-looking chairs?
Add some fabric overlays or ribbons to the backs. It's a fairly simple task, and your guests will feel as though they've been invited to the Wedding of the Year.

QUESTION?

Twinkle, Twinkle

So you've draped everything you could get your hands on in ivy, flowers, and tulle, and it still isn't enough. How about adding some little white lights to the mix? They're pretty, they're understated, and they give everyone the feeling that they're looking at a starry sky. If you're adding any potted trees to your reception site, these lights are a particularly easy way to dress them up a bit.

Flower the People

What about flowers for people? Along with that bouquet you will (or won't) be tossing, you'll have to choose arrangements for the wedding party, your mother, your groom's mother, and for any grandmothers.

The Maids

In most weddings, the bridesmaids carry their flowers rather than wear them. These arrangements can range from elaborate bouquets to simple groupings—or even single long-stemmed roses. (You may decide to add something special to the maid of honor's flowers as a way of making her stand out in the crowd.) Communication is key here. Provide your florist with either a swatch of fabric or an accurate color picture of the bridesmaids' dresses.

ALERT!

Without a visual reference, your idea of "mostly pink" could vary greatly from your florist's. He or she might picture a brilliant solid fuchsia dress—but in reality, the dresses are a floral pattern of barely pinks and whites. These very different dresses would require different flowers to complement their looks.

Floral hairpieces can be a lovely touch for your bridesmaids and also as part of your veil. Be sure to discuss hairstyles with your bridesmaids and your florist. It would be very frustrating to spend money for flowers that won't stay in your maid of honor's hair because she's decided to wear it loose, or because her hair is too short.

If you're having a flower girl, she'll need a basket of flowers or petals, or a small bouquet. Again, be sure the florist has a good idea of what the flower girl will be wearing so that she chooses appropriate flowers.

Who Else?

The mothers of the marrying couple usually receive special corsages just before the ceremony begins. You might also want to include flowers for anyone who's playing a special role in the ceremony, such as your readers, the guests who will bring the gifts to the altar, and so on. You won't forget wedding flowers for the mothers and grandmothers (you hope), and make sure you also remember to include any great-grandmothers and godmothers.

Flowers for the men are pretty simple. The ushers wear boutonnieres. Sometimes the boutonniere is dyed to match the bridesmaids' dresses. Sometimes it's white, and often it's a flower that complements the bridesmaids' dresses and/or bouquets. The groom wears a lapel spray to match the bride's bouquet or a traditional boutonniere. The fathers usually have boutonnieres similar to those worn by the ushers.

Smooth as Silk

Well, you thought you could meet your budget. But now you realize that you could really use more flowers in more places, and the issue of money is rearing its ugly head. If you want more than you think you can afford, consider silk. When done well, silk flower arrangements can be as beautiful as the real thing—and they even look real. Silk gives you a broader choice of colors (ah, the magic of dye), and while real flowers die quickly, leaving you to lament money spent on something that didn't last (the agony!), silk flowers can be kept as decorations or keepsakes long after the wedding.

If you can't bear the thought of not being able to smell the wedding flowers, but you dig the advantages of silk, compromise. Use live flowers where it's most important to you, and use silk where it won't disturb you. Some brides have two bouquets made—one real and one silk. They keep whichever they prefer and use the other one for the infamous bouquet toss.

Preserving the Bridal Bouquet

Many brides choose to preserve their bridal bouquet as a memento of the wedding. The odds are very strong indeed that your bouquet will, after a time, end up in storage (which often means "someplace where you seldom look at it"). Keep this in mind if you decide to take your bouquet to the florist for preservation. The process will probably cost you more than the bouquet itself. There are, however, cheaper and more practical ways for you to preserve your bouquet by yourself. If you decide to take advantage of them, you can spend the money on something else, like your honeymoon.

Pressing

Pressing is the most popular method of bouquet preservation. The first step is to take a picture of the bouquet—you'll need it to refer to later. Take the bouquet apart (that's right: *Take it apart*) and place the separate flowers in the pages of heavy books, between sheets of blank white paper. (If not cushioned by blank paper, ink from the book's pages will ruin the flowers.) The flowers should be kept in the books for two to six weeks, depending on the size of the blossom. The bigger the flower, the more time it needs. When the flowers look ready, glue them onto a mounting board in an arrangement that closely resembles the original bouquet—here's where that photo comes in handy. Place the board in a picture frame and hang it.

FACT

The process of pressing the wedding flowers works best if you start it fairly soon after your wedding, *before* your flowers have had time to lose their fresh appearance. Don't plan on putting the flowers in storage until you have the time to tackle this project. It's now or never.

Hanging/Drying

Again, snap a photo for reference and take the bouquet apart. To preserve shape and prevent drooping, hang the flowers upside down to dry. Some color may be lost in the drying process—the loss is less if the flowers are hung in a dark room. When the flowers are completely dry, spray them with shellac or silica gel for protection. Then reassemble them to match the photo. Like pressing, the earlier you start the process, the more successful it's likely to be.

Potpourri

For this method, you'll need to buy some netting or lacy fabric. Dry the flowers by hanging them, and gather the petals together. Place small piles of the petals into four-inch squares of the netting, then tie the squares into little pouches with ribbon. These little sachets can be placed anywhere, filling the air with a little reminder of your wedding day.

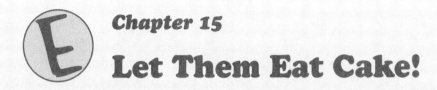

Chapter 15

Let Them Eat Cake!

The wedding cake—it's so pretty, you hate to cut into it and eat it. But alas, your guests will be clamoring for their slices. The wedding cake can be as simple or as ornate as you want it to be. It can be one tier or seven. It can be stacked upon its own layers, or it can incorporate architectural supports, and your choices of flavors, fillings, and icings are endless.

History

Wedding cakes have been around since ancient times. In Rome, a loaf of wheat bread (*farreus panis*) was broken over the bride's head to symbolize hope for a fertile and fulfilling life. The guests ate the crumbs, which were believed to be good luck. Later, a variation of the custom found its way to England, where guests brought small cakes to the ceremony. The cakes were put into a pile, and the bride and groom stood over the pile and kissed. Eventually, someone came up with the idea of stacking the cakes neatly and frosting them together, an early version of today's multitiered wedding cakes. Since then, the cake has lost most of its significance as a fertility symbol and is seen primarily as a decoration . . . and a tasty little treat.

Types of Cakes

Once upon a time, a wedding cake was white inside and out, but today there are countless options for decoration and consumption. The cake can be garnished with fresh flowers or greenery, and the icing or trimming can be made to match the wedding colors you've selected. The choices for cake flavors, frostings, decorations, and garnishes are plentiful—and tempting. Your cake can be designed any number of ways, including multiple tiers, stacked cakes, multiple sections . . . you might want to throw a bridge or a fountain into the mix, too.

Don't forget that your cake is edible; it's perfectly appropriate to serve it as dessert. Why spend tons of money and weeks of a baker's time to create the Mona Lisa of wedding cakes, only to have it sit uneaten in a corner of the room?

Flavors

Bakers have come a long way in a short time. Although many brides choose to have the traditional white or yellow cake, chances are you'll be presented with a long, long list of choices: chocolate, chocolate hazelnut, double chocolate, Italian rum, vanilla, lemon, orange, spice, carrot cake, cheesecake, citron chiffon, fruitcake, banana, Black Forest, cherry, and the list goes on.

Your baker may have also his or her own specialty that's out of this world. In addition, you can choose to have a different flavor for each tier of your cake, just to accommodate the different tastes and needs of your guests. You may have some guests whose stomachs just can't handle a heavy rum cake, for example, or who are allergic to carrot cake.

QUESTION?

What about the frosting?
The standard icing for most wedding cakes is butter cream. You can also get rolled fondant or a combination of butter cream with fondant artwork, but these will be more expensive options.

Fillings

Some people love cakes with a little something extra. Your baker will probably be able to offer you a wide variety of wedding cake fillings, which may include lemon, custard, raspberry, strawberry, almond crème, chocolate fudge, chocolate mocha, chocolate mousse, pineapple, or cherry-nut.

And then, you may have *another* opportunity to add a little extra oomph to the cake, with sauces or toppings such as ice cream/sorbet, fresh fruit or fruit sauce, or chocolate.

Cake Toppers

Time was, every wedding cake had a miniature newlywed couple on top of it. It didn't even matter if the couple on top of the cake bore the slightest resemblance to the real-life couple they were representing. They were there to stay.

Nowadays, of course, you have other options. You can still go with the bride and groom perched upon the top layer of your wedding cake, but they don't have to be a perky plastic couple. You can buy a keepsake china or porcelain cake-topper, which will look just lovely in your new home after the wedding.

Many brides choose to have fresh (or silk) flowers placed atop their cake, as well as in between any tiers. No doubt about it, this is a beautiful alternative to the traditional cake topper. Your baker can also add gum paste flowers to your cake.

Meeting the Baker

Depending on where you live, the availability of bakers there, and which season you're planning your wedding for, you may want to contact your baker up to a year in advance, or at least a few months before the big day. Bigger, full-service bakeries simply have more resources available and will be better staffed and equipped to handle a wedding on short notice. If you want that cute little bakery around the corner to make your wedding cake, get on the horn as soon as possible to them, and be prepared to fork over a big deposit for them to save the date for you. And though this phrase is getting very familiar at this point in your wedding planning, the best way to find a baker is through *word of mouth*. There's simply no better way of knowing whether a baker can make a delicious and beautiful cake than to talk to someone who has worked with this person.

If you're at a complete loss at to what style of cake you want, your baker will have photos available to help you pick out your cake design. Once you've found one you like, you can move on to questions of size and price.

The Interview

To get a baker's undivided attention (something you really want and need in order to discuss plans for your wedding cake), call the shop to make an appointment. You can't pop in during their busiest time and expect that someone will just drop everything to talk business with you. Also, by calling ahead, you're giving the bakery time to prepare batters and icings for your approval (or disapproval).

If you want your cake to include your wedding colors, bring a swatch of fabric with you. If there's a definite style of cake that you're after, bring a picture or sketch. You'll also need to bring along the names and numbers of your florist and photographer, as well as all the relevant information regarding your reception site (location, contact name and number, and directions).

ALERT!

You want to ensure the cake tastes as good as it's going to look. Your cake could be lovely to look at, but that won't count for much if 200 people can't quite manage to swallow it. And this brings you to one of the most fun parts of wedding planning— cake tastings! Be sure to taste a sample of any cake *before* you order it.

Here are some issues to address with the baker:

- **Size.** You'll have to know how many guests you're inviting in order to nail down what size cake you'll need.
- **Flavor, filling, icing.** You'll be given a list to choose from. If you want different flavors on different tiers, ask your baker if he or she can do this for you.
- **Specialty.** Does this baker have one? Can you taste it?
- **Backup plans.** If your cake should suffer an unforeseen tragedy on the morning of your wedding (a delivery van accident that totals your confection, for example), will this bakery have another cake ready to go?

Of course, the other big issue you'll want to discuss is price. Most bakeries will base their prices on a plain cake with buttercream frosting— *each slice* will cost you X number of dollars. (If you're having 200 guests and the cake is three dollars a slice, you're looking at a $600 cake.) From there, you'll add to the price of each slice with each upgrade. Fillings will cost you so much per slice, while rolled fondant frosting will cost you so much *more* per slice. And if you want any fancy design work on your cake, you're looking at paying even *more.* (You've always wondered how the cost of wedding cakes can spiral completely out of control?) If you decide to incorporate pillars, bridges, or fountains, you'll probably be charged a rental fee for these supports.

> How much cake will you need? Your baker is your best resource here. You don't want to have too little cake, after all. Your cake can be cut into three-inch or four-inch slices, with a corresponding change in yield. A sheet cake will yield about forty servings.

Delivery is usually included in the price of the cake. However, each bakery has its own specific delivery area (a radius of thirty miles from the bakery, for example). If your reception falls outside that area, an extra charge may be added. Also, some bakeries have minimum order amounts. If you fall short of that amount on your order, the bakery will make its money by charging you more for delivery.

You Take the Cake!

Make sure the baker arrives at the reception in time to set up the cake before the guests arrive. Multitiered cakes need to be transported in sections and assembled at the reception site. Unless you want this phenomenon to be part of the reception entertainment, make arrangements with the site coordinator to allow the baker plenty of time to get in early and do his or her thing. And remember to touch base with the coordinator about where the cake will be placed. Though traffic patterns and simple space restrictions may dictate where the cake goes, if the background will be unsightly for your pictures, your photographer may be able to bring a backdrop of his or her own.

Saving Cake

You may want to preserve the top layer of your cake for tradition's sake. There is a tradition of freezing the summit of your wedding cake so that you and your husband can thaw it out and enjoy it on your first anniversary. Your baker will probably address this issue with you. If he or she doesn't, and you're interested in saving the cake, make sure you bring it up. The smallest (top) layer is generally made of a special, freezer-friendly type of cake (regular wedding cake only lasts three months or so in the deep freeze); hence, your baker needs to know that you want the cake to make it through the long, cold winter in your freezer.

Cut It Down

Rest assured, there *are* ways to cut costs. Your decorated cake does not have to serve all the guests. Save money by ordering a smaller decorated cake, along with a supplemental sheet cake (which is kept in the kitchen, not on display) to feed your guests. On the other hand, if dessert is already included on your wedding menu, there's really no need for a wedding cake except for the traditional cake-cutting ceremony. If that's the case, you can cut costs by making it as small and simple as possible.

Placing the Cake

Now that you've spent a good deal of money on the perfect wedding cake, make sure it isn't ruined during its presentation. Wouldn't it just kill you to see that work of art destroyed by the elements, or by the atmosphere? You'll want to plan the presentation of your wedding cake wisely.

Eek! It's Melting!

If you're choosing a cake with shaved bits of chocolate on its icing, or with gum paste flowers, or if your cake has a mousse filling (or if you're having cheesecake, for that matter), make sure the weather isn't going to ruin your prized confection. These cakes require a chilled atmosphere, as heat and humidity can ruin them.

If you're getting married in July and your reception site is not air-conditioned, don't subject your guests to a cake that will droop, wilt, or sink because of the heat.

You're thinking, "It's never humid where I live, even in the summer!" Don't bet on it. Better to play it safe—you don't want to waste your money on a cake that won't stand up to the elements.

Consider the Background

A funny thing happens when you get your wedding pictures back from the photographer. You start seeing things that you didn't see on your wedding day. Make sure you know where your cake will be situated inside the reception hall. After all, the cake is the focal point for some of your wedding pictures. When you flip to the page in your wedding album that contains the pictures of your wedding cake, you don't want to see an exit sign, or a fire extinguisher, or a water fountain lurking in the background. This is something you need to address with your reception site coordinator well before the day of the wedding.

Baking Your Own Cake

You're confident that you can cut costs by making your own wedding cake. If you have loads of experience with baking and cake decorating, you may be up to the challenge. If you burn every batch of brownies you bake, though, you might want to reconsider taking on this particular culinary challenge.

Though your baker might make it look effortless, baking a moist, delicious cake is in itself not easy. Taking that cake and frosting and decorating and assembling it is something that is an actual *career* to many people—not just a hobby. The point is that if you have no experience in this field, you might not want to pick your own wedding cake to experiment with. You'll have a hundred other things going on, and balancing a cake on dowel rods may not be at the top of your priority list on your wedding day. Even if you're having a very small wedding, you'll probably want to leave the cake to the professionals.

If You Insist

Can't talk you out of this one, huh? Fair enough. If you're bound and determined to cut costs by making your own wedding cake, at the very least take some of that money and invest it in a good cake decorating class. If you don't know where to find one, ask a craft shop in your area. Many times, these stores host decorating classes. Some people have a real knack for figuring things out in the kitchen all by themselves, but other people need lots of guidance. No matter which camp you fall into, you don't want to leave any stone unturned on this project. If you're clueless, you'll definitely learn a lot, and if you're a natural at this, you might just pick up some techniques that will take your cake from being acceptable to being absolutely amazing.

The cake-decorating class will emphasize the appearance of your cake and will assume that the taste of the cake comes in a distant second on your list of cake priorities. Just remember, if the cake tastes like a shoe (or lard, for that matter), all your hard work will be for naught. Who wants to go around bragging that they made the cake that people are throwing in the trash can? Give both parts—baking and decorating—equal attention.

Ask for Help

Only the most disciplined and organized of brides would dream of tackling this task on her own. If you know someone who bakes (and decorates) a great cake, ask her for help. Your mom can help. Your friends can help. Lay out a plan, give everyone their parts, and get to work.

A few weeks before your wedding day, bake a tier every few days, until you have the three or four you need. Level each tier. Simply take a serrated knife and cut off any part of the cake that isn't completely flat on top; this will prevent the cake from cracking. Then wrap each one and store it in your freezer.

You can find simple but good recipes in standard cookbooks and on the Internet, with clear directions that explain every step of the process. For more references, troll the baking and cake-decorating section of your local library.

When you're ready, decorate very simply, with a few buttercream roses and swirls, or spun-sugar ornaments you can buy at cake-decorator supply houses. Simply adding edible silver shots will lend glamour, and leaves and fragrant blossoms, such as orange blossoms, violets, or tiny roses, will make it even more beautiful. If you haven't taken a decorating class, stick with a good white frosting.

Keep Investing

The right tools are essential to this job. You're probably been buried in a slide of pots and pans by this point. Use them. You need good, unblemished (read: not bent, not pitted, not misshapen) cake pans to turn out a good, unblemished (read: not crooked, not burned, not cracked) cake. If you haven't received anything that fits the bill, go buy some good pans. Now.

As far as decorating goes, buy the tools you need. Don't try to skimp and use something else, like a cotton swab or a swizzle stick. Yes, you're trying to save money, but a pastry bag isn't going to break your bank. And it will probably be a good part of the reason that your cake turns out looking like a professional did it.

The Groom's Cake

The groom's cake gives you another opportunity to work fruitcake into your wedding day. In the very old days, the groom's cake was referred to as the wedding cake, and what we now call the wedding cake was known as the bride's cake. The groom's cake was traditionally a dark fruitcake—a symbol of the sweet life that lay ahead for the newlyweds—and the slices were packaged in monogrammed boxes as a wedding favor for each guest. According to superstition, if a single woman sleeps with the cake box under her pillow that night, she'll dream of the man she is to marry.

FACT

Groom's cakes are more common in the southern regions of the United States than they are up north, but being a Yankee doesn't preclude you from offering your guests a crack at a second confection. Just be prepared to explain the purpose of the cake to your guests who have never heard of this tradition.

Of course, as with all wedding traditions, this one has evolved with time. Since very few people actually *like* fruitcake, you should choose a flavor that will please the masses.

The groom's cake is supposed to give the groom *his* moment in the spotlight, so it should reflect his interests. Get creative here. If he's a hockey player, order a cake in the shape of a hockey stick or a puck; if he's a tennis buff, order a racquet cake; if he's a couch potato, have the baker whip up a cake TV. The groom's cake is supposed to be a little more fun than the wedding cake, so nothing is off limits.

The groom's cake can be served at the reception, but you may want to serve it at the rehearsal. This way, he really gets his time to shine, and your wedding guests won't be bombarded with cake, cake, and more cake.

You can order a groom's cake from the same baker who is doing your wedding cake—and if you want to keep it a secret from the groom, that's all right, too.

The Cake Smoosh

Remember, a wedding cake is not just for eating. Before anybody gets to dig in, the cake performs a very important function. It's the centerpiece of the ever-popular cake-cutting ceremony, when the bride and groom together cut the first piece of cake and take turns feeding one another. Some couples (those who have extraordinarily good senses of humor) follow the *other* cake tradition—the one where they smash each other in the face with cake. Whether this is a good idea is up to you. Just remember that chances are, if you smear frosting all over your groom's face, he's going to return the favor—and *you're* the one who will have spent the better part of the morning (and a small fortune) at the hairdresser's.

If you absolutely do not want cake to be any part of your wedding-day wear, address the issue with your fiancé before the cake cutting. He might be egged on by his pals and by the other guests, and you might normally have a wacky sense of humor. In other words, he might very well think that you'd find the whole thing hysterical unless you make it clear that you won't. There's nothing that wedding guests want to see *less* than a bride who isn't speaking to her husband at their reception.

Let Them Eat Pastries!

You don't like six-foot-tall wedding cakes, and you don't care what anyone says, you're not spending good money on one. There are alternatives to the traditional wedding cake. You and your baker can put your heads together and come up with something. Here are a few ideas:

- **Individual decorated cakes.** Each guest gets his or her own mini-wedding cake.
- **Decorated cupcakes.** These can be served individually, or stacked to resemble one big cake.
- **Bride and groom cookies.** Your hair color and dress style can be copied onto a cookie!

And something that has always been part and parcel of the big Italian wedding, the pastry table, is becoming a staple at many other weddings these days. You may decide to offer your guests a variety of desserts immediately following dinner, or you may simply choose to set up a pastry table later in the evening, after your guests have worn themselves out boogying.

Whenever you decide to set the pastries out, they're sure to be a hit. (People just love their pastries!) Your baker can also provide this service for you, and he or she may suggest anything from coffeecake and Danish to éclairs and turnovers. And because cookies and caffeine go hand in hand, you'll also want to ask your reception site coordinator about setting up a coffee station near the pastries. Your guests will be wired for the evening, and you'll be sure to get your money's worth out of the band.

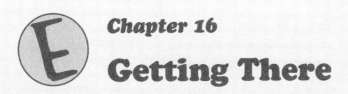

Chapter 16

Getting There

Most brides picture themselves arriving in style at the door of the church. If you're going to need a ride to the church, you'll need to start looking as soon as possible. And if you're thinking about ditching the limo in favor of a plane ride to a destination wedding site, you might be in a quandary as to how you're going to get your dress to the altar on time (not to mention your guests).

Whatever Moves You

Think about the entrance you want to make at your wedding ceremony. How do you picture it? Are you dropping from the sky in a hot-air balloon? Trotting to the church via horse-drawn carriage? Rolling by on a parade float? Or panting up to the door in your most comfortable sneakers after an invigorating run? Admittedly, some of these are less-than-great ideas. These days, though, very little is off-limits as far as wedding transportation goes. Innovative couples have been known to use helicopters, boats, hot rods, antique cars, Lear jets, Harley-Davidsons . . . as long as it can move you from here to there, it's okay for your wedding. (Unless it's a pair of sneakers. Or a bus pass.)

Limousine Luxury

Limousines are the most common mode of wedding transportation. Though it may not be as original or exciting as arriving in, say, a fighter plane, showing up in a well-kept limousine has its perks. You can seat ten (or more!) people comfortably, watch television, serve yourself from the bar, and have a chauffeur at your beck and call. Add a sunroof and a drunken best man, and you've got instant entertainment! A big shiny limousine is also impressive enough to instill awe in the occupants of those boring regular cars who are sitting next to it in traffic.

Must You Hire a Fleet?

If your transportation budget is on the smallish side, you might have to make some compromises. Some couples hire just one limousine. Usually this necessitates an intricate series of passenger exchanges on the wedding day. Here's how it works. The bride gets the first ride in the limo, which transports her and her parents to the ceremony site. It could then return to pick up the groom and deliver him to the site. After the ceremony, the bride returns to the limousine with her groom, and the two of them ride to the reception. (Alternate scenario: If the ceremony site is close enough to where the bride and bridesmaids are getting ready, the limousine can make its first trip to the ceremony site with the bridesmaids, then come back for the bride.) Depending upon the length of the limousine rental, the newlyweds might also be driven in style to their hotel after the reception—or perhaps to the airport to begin their honeymoon.

More Cars

If your budget is stretchable, you might want to rent one or two additional limousines to transport attendants and possibly another one for your parents—if you're feeling very generous. This not only saves you the hassle of coordinating other transportation for them but also leaves them thinking you're really swell.

Your attendants will pile into waiting limos after the ceremony. The picture-taking will go much more smoothly if everyone arrives at the site together, and you won't have to worry about any attendants getting lost on the way to the reception. Just make sure that no one gets left behind at the park where you've taken your photos. To avoid this possibility, it might be a good idea to assign attendants to limos by pairs (each bridesmaid and her groomsman)—particularly if your friends are prone to mishaps like this.

FACT

These days, you can also rent a super-sized SUV to carry you and your wedding party all around the town. These vehicles are luxury on wheels, and some can seat more than twenty people—yes, all at once. Think of the stares you'll get when people get a load of *all* of you packing into and piling out of this truck.

Logistics

If you're only hiring a car to take you to the church and the reception, how are you going to get to the hotel later? And how are your bridesmaids going to get home?

Your bridesmaids are really on their own, but you can always ask a friend or relative if they would be willing to take over the chauffeuring duties for any attendants who are going to be stuck for a ride home after the limo leaves for good.

You and your groom will have to make sure that someone is either going to drive you to your final destination for the evening, or that one of you has made arrangements to leave your own car in the parking lot at the reception. Oh, and make sure you bring the keys along, too. It would be a real bummer to be stuck in the parking lot after everyone else has left and the reception hall has locked its doors for the evening!

Finding the Right Limo

Picture this. It's your wedding day. You're all dressed and ready to go, and all you need now is the limousine to roll up and get you to the church on time. But it doesn't. Or it does come, but it's covered by a dusty haze and has mud caked on its three remaining hubcaps. Or it looks snazzy enough on the outside, but inside, the television and bar you requested are not to be found. You wouldn't mind any of that, would you?

Assuming you don't have the rare constitution that allows you to just grin and bear wedding-day nightmares, you'll want to do everything you can to prevent problems like this ahead of time. A recently married friend or relative may be able to recommend a reliable limousine service with good cars and thereby save you a lot of legwork. But if you're not that lucky, get yourself out there, look at the cars, and ask some questions.

Deal with the Owner

Try to find a company that owns its limousines. Owners are more likely to keep track of a car's maintenance and whereabouts. (You do not want to ride in a limo that has seen its share of unauthorized excursions.)

FACT

Some limo services rent cars out from another company, which means those cars are probably being shared by several other services, too. In addition to maintenance and overuse problems, it's harder for a company that doesn't own its own limos to ensure the availability of any given car, or to supply you with a car of the color and size you want.

Make sure you verify a service's license and insurance coverage. Get references. Verify that its chauffeurs show up on time, are courteous, don't break the speed limit, and don't have a habit of driving into trees.

Inspect all of the cars. Does the fleet look modern and up-to-date, or are the cars creaking and groaning and looking like they just might be on their last legs? Are there obvious scratches or dents on the cars? (There shouldn't be.) When you get in to inspect the vehicles, are the interior surfaces spotless? (They should be.) Are the windows clean? Do the cars smell like smoke? Is there enough room for your groom and his linebacker buddies to spread out without crushing any crinolines? Is there enough headroom for the gigantic hairdos your bridesmaids will be sporting?

Most importantly, does this company have the kind of limo you want? If you're looking at a pink limo and you won't accept anything but black, are there other cars available? Don't take a company's word that it can get you a black stretch limo with black leather interior. You need to see it with your own eyes—and don't sign anything until you have.

How Much?

Most limousine services charge by the hour. Unfortunately for you, the clock starts the second the driver leaves the base, not the moment he or she starts driving you around. (If you can find a service that's based near your home and the festivities, you'll save yourself some money.) Most companies have package deals with a specific number of hours included in the price—but you need to understand what's included. A three-hour deal might sound like more than enough time, since you know you're not going to be sitting in that limo for three hours. But if there's a delay between the ceremony and the reception—if you're getting married at one o'clock and your reception is at five, for example—you're going to need at least four and a half hours.

Find out the exact costs and exactly what you'll be getting for your money. Does the limo company provide champagne? Ice? Glasses? A red carpet? Some limo companies can add extras like balloons or flowers. Some also offer a "runner" service, which means that you can keep the driver "on call" to run home any guests who have had too much of the bubbly at the reception.

You might also want to have the limo take you and your hubby to the airport if you're leaving for your honeymoon after the reception. If you're interested in this, ask if it can be rolled into the package you're considering.

Sign Here

Once you decide on a limousine service, get all the details finalized in a written contract. It should specify the type of car, additional options and services you will need, the expected length of service, the date, and the time. If there's a specific limo you just have to have (it's the only one with two sunroofs, or it's the only one with a DVD player), ask the owner to specify it on the contract. Some limo companies have vanity plates on their cars for this very purpose. If the car you want has a plate that reads "Limo A-1", there will be very little chance of "Limo B-1"—a limo *without* a DVD player—showing up at your house on your wedding day, so long as everything's in writing.

Ask about contingencies. If you're choosing the company's top-of-the-line car and something happens to it, what then? Get this in writing, also.

Your Pal, the Driver

What's the appropriate way to treat your driver? A strange thing happens to brides, grooms, and their attendants. They sometimes feel as though they are the stars of some strange nighttime soap opera, one where the women are wearing bridesmaid dresses—or they're suddenly transported back to their prom night. Either way, they feel they are entitled to heap abuse upon the chauffeur.

Be kind to your driver. He is not your slave. He isn't being paid to be insulted or teased. He's just there to provide a service for you—namely, driving the car. If your attendants are giving the guy a hard time, step in. You never know when a chauffeur might snap and leave you stranded out in the middle of nowhere while your reception goes on without you.

The chauffeur's tip, usually 10 to 20 percent of the bill, is sometimes included in the fee, but read the fine print of your contract to find out for sure. You don't want to stiff someone who has provided you with good service and who has helped make your day run (or ride) smoothly. By the same token, if you are dissatisfied with the service your chauffeur provides, speak up—and don't be afraid to ask for your money back.

It's a good idea to arrange for the limo to arrive at least fifteen to thirty minutes before you're going to need it, just to be on the safe side. This way, if the driver gets caught in traffic, you won't be forced to hitchhike to the ceremony.

Other Vehicles

Limos aren't your thing, you say? Sure, they're fine for other brides, but you're looking for a something a little different—but not crazy-different? Fortunately for you, there are many other options. Some of the most popular—and easy-to-find—alternatives are included in this section.

Horse and Carriage

This is *romance* on wheels. No matter what the season, there's no sight more beautiful, and no sight that conjures up a more royal image, than a bride riding to church in a horse-drawn carriage—except for the sight of her leaving the church in the same carriage with her new husband.

If you're planning a winter wedding, obviously you will, at the very least, have to invest in a warm wrap. And in areas that are hit hard by winter storms, you may want to leave the carriage out of your planning altogether. There's no way you're going to get a horse to pull that carriage down the icy roads and through three feet of snow. (And if by some chance you manage to talk the horse into it, you'll be in a real pickle when he gets stuck somewhere.) Since the name on your driver's license isn't Mother Nature, you can't predict whether your January wedding will be in the midst of a mild winter or the fiercest one in forty years. Better to play it safe during this particular season and hire something with a motor—and snow tires. And a heater.

Shuttles and Trolleys

If you're not concerned with the aesthetics of your ride, an option that's gaining popularity is renting a shuttle bus for your wedding party. There are plenty of seats for everyone, plenty of room for purses, coats, and champagne bottles, and a fun, casual atmosphere on board.

To be fair, you can't expect this vehicle to be spit-shined, nor should you expect to feel as though you've stepped into anything resembling a limo. This is definitely a functional vehicle. Your entire wedding party fits inside, and that spells good times for you. Period.

Trolleys offer the same kind of space as a shuttle, but in a classier package. Many trolley rides are open-air affairs, but in colder climates, most offer some kind of protection from the winter elements.

Sleek Rides

If you want something less conventional, but you don't like the idea of flying, boating, or taking the subway, there are plenty of luxury and antique cars out there available for rental. Are you the white Rolls type? Perhaps a silver Bentley would suit you best. If you've got some extra cash on hand, go all out: Snag an Excalibur. It will make for a truly unforgettable shot in your wedding video.

Many limousine companies also have a few classic cars on their lots. You can also look in your phone book under "Livery." You don't have to squeeze your attendants into this car with you—you can hire a limo or SUV just for them.

FACT

Another option, for a summer (or warm climate) wedding is to rent a convertible for you and your groom to escape in. Is there a better picture of a fun-filled wedding than this? Of course, if you're paying an outrageous amount to have your hair done that morning, this may not be your best option.

Free Ride

If for some reason you are unable to rent wedding transportation, look around for family and friends who have nice big cars they'd be willing to lend you. (Years ago, this was actually how brides and grooms got around on their wedding days—*imagine*!) Some car buffs are likely to be horrified at the idea of someone else behind the wheel of their baby. If that's the case, you can always ask them to play the part of chauffeur for the day.

The only requirement here is that the cars have to be clean. You should pay for the pre-wedding car wash and detailing. And be sure to remember your generous friends with a little gift and a full tank of gas.

Advanced Reservations

Generally speaking, it's never too early to look into your transportation options. If you're getting married during the peak season (April through October), get on the ball right away. It's not uncommon for limos to be booked a year in advance; many companies will even take reservations up to a year and a half before an event. If you're unsure about your area (limos don't seem to be very popular, or there just aren't a lot of weddings), call some companies and ask for their recommendations.

Keep in mind that May and June are also big prom and graduation months and that limos will be in high demand for these events. As soon as you start *thinking* about your wedding-day transportation, get moving on booking your vehicles.

Getaway Car Décor

Of course, just because a friend is courteous enough to drive the car to the reception for you doesn't mean he'll refrain from enhancing its appearance a bit with some "decorations." Unfortunately, that's what friends—particularly male friends—are *really* for. Usually the ushers take the lead in this matter, but other friends and relatives of the groom may be so kind as to offer their services, too.

If you're really nervous about a bunch of men monkeying around with your vehicle, try to remind people beforehand that safety should come first. Attaching empty tin cans to the rear bumper is fine, but make sure nothing will impair the car's normal motion or in any way interfere with the drive train or motor. Another important consideration is the driver's field of vision. Be sure anything painted on, draped across, or attached to the windows leaves ample room for the driver to see in all directions.

Of course, your admonitions may only lead them to trash your car even worse than they would have in the first place. In the end, you really *can't* get angry at the men who re-invent the look of your car. They're just having a little fun and following tradition, which is what weddings are all about. Refrain from following a lesser-known tradition, the one in which the bride loses her cool and curses out the car decorators.

Transporting the Entire Wedding

If you're planning a wedding on a Caribbean island or somewhere overseas, you're going to be faced with much larger transportation issues. Getting yourself there is the easy part—but what about your dress?! If you're inviting guests, are you expected to pay for their transportation, too?

Destination Weddings Know-How

A wedding on a small island—or at a mountain resort, or on the shores of the Mediterranean—might be what you're after. The guest list for a destination wedding tends to be small, including only the people whom you are closest to. The ceremony is the focus of the trip. When all's said and done, you don't need to hop a flight to start your honeymoon.

Obviously, a lot of planning has to go into a wedding that you're taking on the road. Find yourself a good travel agent. He or she will know the ins and outs of all-inclusive resorts, as well as the requirements of any foreign country where you're thinking of saying your vows.

Many resorts that regularly host destination weddings have various reception packages for your consideration. If you're planning on saying your vows in a quiet country chapel in a distant land, your travel agent will once again be of invaluable assistance to you in this regard.

Of course, the Internet is also a great tool for researching your destination, but it should be used in conjunction with a travel agent. As good as the Internet is, you want to talk to someone who has either been to this place themselves, or who knows someone else who has. Word of mouth—you can't escape it.

Pack Your Wedding Bags!

Big, frilly wedding dresses don't like to be smushed into suitcases. They aren't really designed for the same kind of abuse that your weekend clothing or even your travel-friendly business suits can take. When transporting your wedding dress, you can't be careful enough. If you can arrange to have the dress packed and shipped, do it. Courier companies are much better equipped than your average airline to handle fragile items and to deliver them in one piece—and in a timely manner. If you're planning a wedding at a resort that specializes in destination weddings, there will probably be an on-site coordinator you will be able to work with who will know exactly how to steam those inevitable wrinkles out of the dress on your wedding day.

Of course, you may start to see the logic in forgoing the big dress when you're confronted with the reality of transporting it. For a beach wedding, you can absolutely go the less formal route and choose a gauze or cotton dress or sarong. (These fabrics make more fashion sense in a tropical climate than do satin or brocade, anyway.)

The Guests

You and your groom chose a destination wedding because you've always dreamed of walking down to the beach and saying "I do." Maybe you even thought that trading the big reception for your own travel expenses would just about even itself out. But you want your family and friends to come along. Are you expected to pay for *their* transportation—or for their lodging?

If you're including any attendants in the ceremony, their hotel bill is your responsibility. If you can afford their airfare, that's a nice touch. Everyone else is on their own, though that's not to say that you can't take everyone out for an island barbecue one evening.

ALERT!

When you extend your invitations, make the financial particulars of this trip *very* clear. If your aunt and uncle think you're paying for their trip—because you never said otherwise—there are going to be miscommunications worthy of a sitcom plot (minus the funny) somewhere on this trip.

So, to be fair, you can't expect that everyone that you want at your destination wedding will be able to make it. It *is* a costly proposition, and the folks on your guest list just might have other things that they'd like to do with their stash of cash.

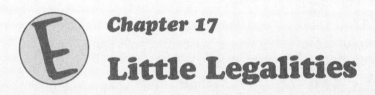

Chapter 17

Little Legalities

Legal details may not sound exciting, but they're necessary. Certain minor details—such as what your married name will be, such as the marriage license—will need to be addressed. There's also a bigger issue—a prenuptial agreement—that may warrant some attention in your relationship. These may not be *fun* tasks, but taking care of them will speed you on your way to the altar.

The Name Game

Have you ever really stopped to think about how much you like (or dislike) your own name? Maybe since you've accepted your fiancé's proposal, you've started thinking about how much you really love (*love!*) your name. This is the name you went through school with, the name you built your career with, the name everyone knows you by. How can you kiss it off? On the other hand, maybe your last name is ten syllables long, or no one ever pronounces or spells it right, and you can't wait to get rid of it. Your choice is an easy one.

If you're in a tizzy over what your married name should be, remember that these days that it isn't a societal issue when a women goes against the long-standing tradition of changing her name to her husband's. (Your business contacts aren't going to question your motives for keeping your own name if you decide to do so, in other words.) In fact, the only people who are likely to really care are your husband and perhaps your present and future family. (This is not to make light of the issue. These are the very people who will drive you over the edge on this matter if they happen to disagree with your decision. More on this later in the chapter.)

To Change or Not to Change?

So you're unsure about which name you prefer to have for all eternity—your name or your husband's. Though you may be advised by your friends to make this decision based on logic (think about how hard it will be to inform every business contact of your new name), and advised by your family to make the decision based on your level of commitment to the marriage (your mother might tell you that if you were intending to *stay* married, you'd take your husband's name), you have to decide what's appropriate for you.

Herewith, a little quiz to help you decide which side of the fence you fall on.

1. When you were a little girl, you dreamed of being a:
   a. Mrs.
   b. Flight attendant, cowgirl, astronaut, pop star . . .
   c. You lived in the moment—you still do, in fact.

   If you've been practicing your entire life to be Mrs. Someone (a), your decision about a name change is probably nonexistent—it's a done deal. If you never included a husband in your fantasies—in fact, you always planned on being exactly who you are, forever— (b) or (c)—you might have a little more soul-searching to do, now that a spouse has entered the picture.

2. In your opinion, married women who keep their maiden names are:
   a. Cutthroat business types.
   b. Women who dislike their in-laws.
   c. Normal women who like their names.

   Obviously, if you chose (a) or (b) as your answer, you don't have a high opinion of these women. These are unfortunate stereotypes. If you've bought into them, you may be overlooking (for the wrong reasons) the possibility of keeping your name.

3. If you were to keep your maiden name, your mother's reaction would be:
   a. Horror.
   b. Embarrassment.
   c. Acceptance.

   Ah-ha! Trick question! Your mother's reaction shouldn't matter here. No matter what she tells you, she's not the one who will be affected by your lack of a name change. (Keep in mind she's probably from a generation that looked unfavorably upon brides keeping their names.)

4. You've broached the subject with your fiancé of keeping your maiden name. His reaction was:
   a. "Whatever."
   b. *"What?!"*
   c. "No way, Babe."

   It's possible that your future husband will react negatively—(b) or (c)—to your proposal of not taking his name. He may feel as though your decision is a way of telling him that you don't truly value the relationship (or him). An in-depth discussion should clear up any misunderstandings.

5. True or false: You should address the issue of keeping your maiden name with your in-laws before the wedding.

   True. These people are about to become your family. How you get along with your family depends on the level of communication you establish with them. Keep in mind that these people are also from a past generation and may not approve of your decision. Acting as though this is an unimportant matter will make it a huge issue in their eyes.

6. You're keeping your maiden name because:
   a. Everyone else in your office has kept theirs.
   b. You don't want to be seen as "the little wife."
   c. You want to.

   The only good answer here is (c). No one else should influence your decision—whatever it is. If you're worried about looking like your husband's subordinate simply because you want to take his surname, but all of your friends have kept their own names, don't be. Being a strong woman means following your own instincts—not the crowd's.

7. When kids enter the picture, you plan on giving them:
   a. Your husband's last name.
   b. Your name or a hyphenated name.
   c. You're so stressed over this decision, you're not going to have kids.

   If you want the kids, have 'em. Keep in mind that society has changed a lot since you were in grade school, when it may have been unusual for a child to have a different last name from one or both parents. Nowadays, it's commonplace, and no cause for sleepless nights.

8. If anyone dares to call you by the wrong surname after you're married, you'll:
   a. Go up one side of them and down the other.
   b. Correct them politely.
   c. Ignore it—it'll be a harmless mistake.

   Wrong answer: (a). Whether you're taking your husband's name or not, keep in mind that there will always be someone who calls you by the other name. Flying off the handle at this innocent error will give you a name you weren't gunning for.

9. When you think about taking your husband's surname, you feel:
   a. Ecstatic.
   b. Sad.
   c. Relieved that you'll finally have a name that everyone can spell.

   If you have a particularly difficult-to-spell-and-pronounce maiden name, you might be jumping for joy at the thought of kissing it goodbye. If you're feeling blue losing your name, that's a normal reaction, too. You had some good times with your maiden name, after all. However, you shouldn't base your decision solely on sentimental feelings.

10. The husband of a woman who keeps her maiden name is:
    a. Wimpy.
    b. Progressive.
    c. Just a cog in the machine.

To make a sweeping generalization about the husband of a woman who keeps her name is as bad as—or even worse than—the stereotypes associated with the woman herself. All anyone needs to know is that he loves her and supports her decision. Period.

FACT

One point to consider when keeping your own name concerns taxes. If you file jointly with your husband, but you use your own name, the government may ask for proof of your marriage. On the other hand, if you use your husband's name on a government document when the name is not legally yours, you're courting trouble. Take care of the name issue before tax season.

The Name Remains the Same

If you decide to keep your name, you've made life easy for yourself in many regards. You won't have to change your business cards or your name on your bank accounts, for example. At the same time, there *are* a few situations that will inevitably pop up, and you'll want to be prepared for them.

His Family

If you decide to keep your maiden name, you should be sensitive to how your in-laws might react. Explain the reason for your decision (for example, that you've already established a career identity with your maiden name) and emphasize that your decision in no way reflects a lack of respect for their family. Ask your spouse to voice his support for your decision.

One thing that's been known to cause hard feelings with in-laws is a bride's decision to change her name *back* to her maiden name *after* she's already taken her husband's name. No matter what the reason, this can be interpreted as a slap in the face as far as the family is concerned, as though you've tried them on for size and decided that they just don't measure up. So if you *do* decide to take his name, make sure you're going to *keep* it. (You've been warned.)

FACT

When you submit your wedding announcement to your local newspaper, make it absolutely clear that you aren't taking your husband's name. Some papers have a small caption with the bride's name under her picture; others have a little blurb that reads something like this: "Mr. Miller and Ms. Andrews will reside in Philadelphia . . . " Your friends and relatives will be automatically informed of your decision.

The World

Until people are aware of your decision to keep your maiden name, you may find yourself in situations in which you are incorrectly addressed by your husband's surname. Realize you're always going to deal with people you barely know, like your husband's business associates, or your children's teachers. For that reason, this issue will never really be put to rest. You may well be dealing with correcting people for the rest of your life.

If someone should call you by your husband's surname, don't make him or her feel like a heel. It's a common assumption (yes, even in the new millennium). You can either let it pass or politely correct the person, depending on how important the issue is to you. If you're taking extreme offense to being addressed by your husband's surname, you're making a mountain out of a molehill and calling a lot of attention to the fact that you're *not* Mrs. So-and-so. Don't be surprised if the offending party starts regularly addressing you by the wrong name just to get a rise out of you.

As a way to avoid this awkwardness, you can simply take the initiative and introduce yourself to strangers first, where it's appropriate: "Hi, I'm Jennifer Andrews, Richard Miller's wife."

Don't read the riot act to someone who innocently addresses you as a Mrs. You'll be feeding into the misconception that women who keep their names are control freaks, and you're also just plain behaving badly. (If your sister-in-law introduces you by the wrong name for the twentieth time, however, you're allowed to make an issue of it.)

Kids

Some women who keep their maiden name will still choose to use their husband's surname for their children. If you're losing sleep worrying that your child will be ostracized in elementary school because of *your* decision to keep your maiden name, find something else to stress over. It's not an uncommon occurrence these days for kids to have different surnames from their parents, for a variety of reasons. Chances are, whatever decision you make about your surname and your kids' surname won't seem all that unusual when they enter school.

Little Changes

For many brides, the issue of the name change (or no change) is a game of eenie-meenie-minie-mo. They like their own name, but they also really want to take their husband's name, as a show of solidarity, or because they simply want to. In the past, of course, there was no discussion. There weren't any options—you took your husband's name, and that was it. Easy decision. Nowadays, it's very common for a bride to ask herself, "Hey—why should *I* completely change *my* name?" And fortunately, for these women, there are multiple options to accommodate just about any name combination or situation.

If you'd kind of like to take your husband's name, but you don't want to completely abandon your own, consider these options:

- **Use your maiden name as your middle name, and your husband's as your last.** (In this case Jennifer Andrews marrying Richard Miller becomes Jennifer Andrews Miller.)

- **Hyphenate the two last names**: Jennifer Andrews-Miller. That little dash means that the two separate last names are now joined to make one (like a marriage). Your husband can use this name, too.
- **Take your two last names and create an entirely *new* surname for both of you to use.** Andrews and Miller could be combined into Andler or Milland, for example.

Some women choose to take their husband's name legally but continue to use their maiden name for business. In everyday life and social situations, you'd use your married name, but in the office, you'd use the same name you have always used.

The Name *Has* Changed

So you're taking on a new name. Not quite as easy as it should be, but not quite the daunting task it sounds like it might be. Fortunately, changing your name when you get married is a lot easier than changing it for kicks. (An avid runner who wanted to be known as Ms. Speed Demon, for example, would have to go through a whole court proceeding in order to win the right to sign her checks with that name). Signing your name on the marriage license is proof of your new name. Now you just have to inform the appropriate people.

Wait until you've received a copy of your marriage license before you attempt to change your name on any accounts or documents. In many instances (when changing your name on bank accounts, for example), you'll need proof that you are who you say you are, and your marriage license is confirmation of your new title.

When booking your honeymoon plane tickets, use your maiden name. You will need a valid photo ID before you can board a plane—and the name on your ID *must match* the name on your ticket. If you can't produce an ID that matches the name on your ticket, you're not going anywhere, except to the airport coffee kiosk to cry your eyes out in your espresso.

Now you've got to inform relevant businesses that you no longer are who you used to be. Try to do all of this within a time frame of a week (two at the most), while you're still interested in informing everyone under the sun that you've gotten married.

Your first concerns should be these:

- Driver's license
- Social Security card
- Credit cards
- Bank accounts, loans, and so on

- Car registration
- Passport
- Insurance

These are the starting blocks. For more on who should be informed, see the worksheet on name changes in Appendix A.

Licensed to Marry

What do driving, fishing, hunting, boating, selling alcohol, and getting married have in common? Legally, you need a license for every one of them. Admittedly, you're not threatening the public safety by getting married (unless you're planning a particularly raucous reception), but that license binds you as a couple in the eyes of the law.

Give Me the License!

The criteria for obtaining a marriage license vary not only from state to state, but often from county to county within a single state. Before you head off to get your marriage license right away, find out how long the license is valid for. There's no rule of thumb here. In some regions, the license is valid for several weeks, while in others it never expires.

FACT

Most states no longer require a blood test for marriage, but some still do. The purpose of the test is to determine if you have any sexually transmitted diseases.

General Concerns

Regardless of where you get married, you should be aware of some guidelines for the marriage license. Every state addresses the following issues:

- **Paperwork.** You'll need some sort of valid identification (birth certificate, driver's license, proof of age, proof of citizenship). You must provide proof of divorce or annulment in the case of a previous marriage.
- **Fee.** Every state charges a fee. Most are not outrageous ($30 is about average). Be aware that many states will only accept cash as payment.
- **Minimum age.** If you're fourteen and looking to get married in most states, you're out of luck, unless your parents agree to it. In most areas, you need to be at least eighteen.
- **Waiting period.** Again, this varies by state. Some states require a waiting period of several days between obtaining the license and saying "I do." In other areas, you can get the license and get married on the same day.

Your best bet is to make a call to your county clerk's office. There's a lot of information on the Internet, but not all of it is accurate. Technology is a wonderful thing. In this case, however, it's best to talk to a human being who has the most up-to-date information on the matter.

License Limitations

Having a marriage license doesn't mean you are legally married. It means you have the state's permission to get married. To be valid and binding, the license has to be signed by a religious or civil official, so once you have the license in your possession, don't lose it.

When the ceremony rolls around, you'll leave the license with your officiant. Alas, there is no going off into a back room during the ceremony (à la Charles and Di and other members of the aristocracy) to have a grand signing ceremony. The officiant simply signs the license after the completion of the ceremony and sends it back to the proper state office. *Now* you're married. (Yay!)

When the time comes for you to sign the license—after the wedding ceremony—you should already have decided on your married name. The license is the first legal document containing your married name, so don't wait until the last minute to decide.

Prenups

The issue of prenuptial agreements is a hot-button topic among brides. Some feel that they are the most unromantic and depressing things ever. Other brides feel that they're worth the time and effort needed in order to ensure smooth sailing down the road. If you don't even want to acknowledge the existence of these contracts, that's understandable—go right on to the next chapter. If, on the other hand, you're really interested in this sort of thing . . . your information is here.

What Are They For?

Prenups aren't just for people with lots of money. They're also used to protect assets such as a family business from being attacked by lawyers if there is marital discord down the road. A common reason for having a prenuptial agreement is to protect the interests of any children from a previous marriage. Most mothers would want to make sure that their kids' inheritance was never an issue in the event of her death or divorce.

An interesting fact on prenups: The law in most states dictates that they have to be fair to both parties. Take a wife who is supporting her husband while he goes to med school, for example. The husband can't say that in the event of a divorce, he keeps every penny. In the prenup, the wife is protecting her future interests if the marriage dissolves (because, after all, she contributed to his success).

Whether or not the prenuptial agreement is fair is up to you and your attorney to decide before you sign anything. The recommendation is for each party to retain separate counsel for this purpose.

What's Addressed?

Prenups basically cover the assets, debts, and incomes of each spouse. They might also address any inheritances that either spouse receives during the marriage (who gets to spend it?); tax issues (will you file joint returns, or separate ones?); living arrangements; and children from a previous marriage (it's common for the kids—rather than the second or third husband or wife—to be named as benefactors of a will).

A prenup should include the following elements:

- Full, written disclosure of the assets and liabilities of each party.
- Reasonable terms.
- Adequate time for the parties to review the terms with their own lawyers.

Common Sense or Cynicism?

That's a judgment call on your part. If you've been married before and you went through a nasty divorce (or you walked away from everything because you didn't feel up to the fight), you might think it's a good idea to take care of this business before your next wedding. Likewise, if you're marrying someone who's been through the divorce-attorney wringer and he's pushing for a prenup, he probably thinks it's a practical move in an uncertain world. In other words, don't read too deeply into his motives. (E)

Chapter 18

Places, Please! The Rehearsal

If you're expecting your wedding rehearsal to go something like the final dress rehearsal for a Broadway play, it probably won't. You'll probably have jitters that echo an opening-night panic attack, but your rehearsal will be much less dramatic and nerve-wracking than you might think. The rehearsal is mainly a chance for the officiant to meet your wedding party and to acquaint everyone with the basics of the ceremony. And yes, it's *very* exciting.

Rehearsal Basics

The rehearsal is usually held the night before the wedding at the ceremony site itself. If that time is inconvenient for any of your key players, reschedule for another time, preferably during the week before the wedding. (If it's held too far in advance of the wedding, people may forget what they've learned.) Some brides are requesting—and being given—rehearsal dates several nights before the wedding, for the logical reason that on the eve of the wedding itself, the bride and groom are often on edge and/or incredibly busy.

Who (besides you and your groom) should attend the rehearsal? That one's easy: the officiant, every member of the wedding party, the father of the bride (to practice his suave look as he makes his way down the aisle, of course), Scripture readers and candle lighters, and any children taking part in the ceremony should all be included. Basically, you should invite anyone who is involved as more than just a guest. You want to make sure everyone knows what's happening when, and who's doing what where.

You can even invite the florist to discuss final issues of flower placement. You might also want to arrange for featured soloists or musicians to attend the rehearsal. Your readers should check with the officiant to make sure the version of Scripture they've been practicing in front of the mirror at home is in fact the one being used in the ceremony. (Sometimes the wording differs from Bible to Bible, depending on the version. The officiant will know for sure which version will be used in the ceremony.)

This section goes largely on the assumption that you'll be getting married in a church. Of course, you may be holding your ceremony in a gazebo in the park or on a rocky cliff. The procedure will be basically the same, in that case, and you can easily adapt it to fit your particular location and situation.

Remember, this is your chance to iron out last-minute details and resolve any remaining questions. Though it may not be enough to truly calm your nerves, get everything straight at the rehearsal. Make sure that everything is ready and that all of the participants know what's expected of them.

The big issue during the rehearsal is getting everyone comfortable with the setting and preparing them for the real thing. The location is secondary. If, for example, you're getting married in a country club that is booked solid with parties the entire week before your wedding, you may not be able to have a rehearsal at the site. And that's fine. Gather everyone together, and have a rehearsal anywhere space permits. It's important that your attendants and readers have some idea of what the actual ceremony will be like to ward off ceremony stage fright.

Seating the Guests

Though they're wearing the title of usher, your groomsmen may not know the first thing about escorting guests to their seats. Unless you address the issue with them at the rehearsal, one of these fine young men may seat your mother in the choir loft (it has the best view, after all) and your grandparents near the back door (because the speakers are back there).

Left, Right, Front, Back

The bride's family sits on the left side of the church for a Christian ceremony, while the groom's family sits on the right. The opposite is true for Reform and Conservative Jewish weddings. And in Orthodox Jewish ceremonies, men and women are usually segregated. If one side has many more guests than the other, you may dispense with this custom and just seat everyone together. This way, you won't end up seating some people way in the back when there are much closer seats on the other side. Your siblings should sit in the second row, behind your mother and father (who are, obviously, in the first row). Grandparents sit in the third row, and close friends and relatives sit in the fourth.

In some ceremonies, the first few rows of pews or chairs are sectioned off by ribbons to indicate that they are reserved for family and very special friends. No one else should be seated there. (You may choose to enclose pew cards or cards that read "In the ribbons" in the invitations sent to these guests.)

FACT

Guests are seated as they arrive, from front to back. The mothers of the bride and groom should be seated just before the ceremony begins. Late-arriving guests are not escorted to their seats by ushers. They should take seats near the back of the church, preferably via a side aisle.

Places of Honor

Typically, parents are seated in the first row (or in the second if the attendants will be seated during the ceremony). In the case of divorce, the bride's natural mother has the privilege of sitting in the first row and of selecting those who will sit with her, including her spouse, if she has remarried. If your divorced parents have remained amicable, your father may sit in the second row with his spouse or significant other. If there's some acrimony between the two parties, your father should be seated a few rows back. However, if you have been raised by your stepmother and prefer to give her the honor, she and your father may sit in the first row, while your *mother* sits farther back.

The Processional

After a brief overview of what's included in the ceremony, the officiant will talk everyone through a quick practice run-through, beginning with the processional, which is the very beginning of the ceremony, when the first bridesmaid takes her first step down that long aisle.

What's allowed in the processional in your particular church is anyone's guess—and part of the reason that you have the rehearsal in the first place. Some churches encourage the bridesmaids and groomsmen to traipse down the aisle together; others prefer to have the bridesmaids walk alone and have the ushers stand at the altar with the groom. Still others do a sort of hybrid of the two. The bridesmaids start out by themselves, and the ushers meet them halfway and escort them to the front of the church. Your officiant or the site coordinator will instruct your attendants on which is their preferred method.

So which bridesmaid leads the charge? That's up to you. While some churches may encourage you to line your maids up according to height, most brides like to keep their closest friends and/or family attendants close to them at the altar (which means your best friend would be one of the last maids to walk down the aisle). If you have a bridesmaid who is your fiancé's third cousin, for example, she probably won't be offended if you send her ahead of your three best friends from childhood.

But how do you decide which best friend goes where, when they're all equally important to you? Either pick names from a hat, or start sorting by height. For large weddings with many, many bridesmaids, you can send them to the altar in pairs. The honor attendant is the last maid to walk down the aisle, followed by the ring bearer and flower girl.

If your church has two side aisles instead of a single center aisle, your officiant will most likely advise you to use the left aisle for the processional and the right aisle for the recessional.

After the flower girl has left her station at the back of the church, it's all you, on the arm of the man who is giving you away (or by yourself, if you choose, or escorted by both parents), followed by pages (if you have them), who carry the bride's train.

Jewish Orthodox, Conservative, and Reform processions vary according to the families' preferences, devoutness, and local custom. A traditional religious Jewish processional may begin with the rabbi and cantor, with the cantor on the rabbi's right, followed by the ushers walking one by one, and then the best man. The groom then walks between his mother, on his right, and his father, on his left. The bridesmaids then walk one by one, followed by the maid of honor, the page, and the flower girl. The bride is the last to enter, with her mother on her right and her father on her left.

Giving the Bride Away

Traditionally, the father of the bride gives the bride away. But sometimes death or divorce changes people's circumstances. When faced with the loss of a father, many unmarried women wonder who will give them away at their wedding.

If your father has passed away, do whatever feels most comfortable to you. If your mother has remarried and you are close to your stepfather, he may be a good choice. Otherwise, a brother, a grandfather, a special uncle, or a close family friend can do the honors. Some brides walk down the aisle with their mothers or even with the groom. Others choose to walk without an escort. Keep in mind that whomever you choose will sit in the front pew with your mother during the ceremony (unless you choose your groom, of course).

If your parents are divorced and both parents are remarried, your decision will depend on your preference and family situation. To avoid risking civil war, take care to somehow include both men in the proceedings. If you've remained close to your father, you may prefer that he fulfill his traditional role, while your stepfather does a reading. Or perhaps you'll ask them both to escort you down the aisle. Often in Jewish ceremonies both parents, even when divorced, walk the bride down the aisle.

Many second-time brides walk down the aisle with their grooms, or with one of their children. However, it's also appropriate for the bride's father to escort her again, or for her to walk alone.

You may decide to do away with this tradition altogether. If so, there are options that you should discuss with your officiant. Instead of asking, "Who gives this woman . . . ?", he or she may ask, "Who blesses this union?" Your father may respond, "Her mother and I do," and take his seat next to your mother. It is also entirely appropriate for both parents to respond, "We do." In this case, your mother should also stand up when the officiant presents the question.

The Ceremony

You'll have a quick run-through of the ceremony, which probably will not include the music but probably will include your readers and gift presenters hitting their marks. You want everyone to know where the heck they're going, after all. (It would be a pity to watch your friend attempt to do a reading from the altar itself, instead of the pulpit, where she should be standing.)

Quick means *quick*. Your readers may not even present the readings during the rehearsal, and the gift bearers will obviously not be presenting any bread and wine. You and your groom will stand in your places, as well, as your officiant goes over the nuptials with you. He or she will remind you of the appropriate responses to his or her questions, and if you're going to be reciting your own vows, your officiant will let you know *when* you'll be expected to speak.

ALERT!

Your officiant may have special instructions, such as how to stand, whether you'll have your hands joined, how loudly you should speak, and so on. If this is the case, pay close attention. Remember, he or she is trying to help you.

Your officiant may seem nit-picky to you by telling you that you should be facing the groom more, or that you should enunciate, but he has performed countless ceremonies and knows the drill. He also knows the quirks of the acoustics of the place—and whether the people in the third row will have a hard time hearing the vows. *You*, on the other hand, are a novice at this. Follow the advice you're given.

In addition, your honor attendants will be instructed as to their special duties during the ceremony. For instance, your maid of honor will need to take your flowers at a certain point, and your best man will present the rings. And any child-attendant issues can be cleared up at this time, as well. (Is your two-year-old ring-bearer nephew going to stay for the entire ceremony, or will he be shuffled out the back door at some point?)

The Recessional

You've kissed, you've been pronounced husband and wife, now how do you get from the front of the church into your limousine? Arm in arm, you and your new husband (or, for purposes of the rehearsal, *almost-husband*) lead the recessional, followed by your child attendants. Your maid of honor and best man are next, followed by your bridesmaids, who are paired with ushers as they walk out. The order of the Jewish recession is as follows: bride and groom, bride's parents, groom's parents, child attendants, honor attendants, and bridesmaids paired with ushers. The cantor and rabbi walk at the end of the recession.

And that's that. On to dinner!

Your Last (Single) Supper

The majority of wedding rehearsals are merely warmups for the truly important event of the evening: the rehearsal dinner and ensuing party. This celebration gives everyone involved in the wedding a chance to eat, drink, be merry, and hopefully to relax and forget about the stresses of the big day to come. What this means is that your part in the planning is done. Once you leave the rehearsal site, you can't be giving orders to your bridesmaids concerning the upcoming ceremony. Leave the specifics of the wedding in the church. Everyone needs to let loose a little. Don't be a bossy bride and begrudge these people a nice evening.

FACT

Realize that there's only so much you can do to ensure that your wedding will run smoothly (and you've done most of it at this point). Try to really enjoy yourself tonight. Tomorrow will be staring you in the face before you know it. Save the anxiety for then.

Where Are We Eating?

The rehearsal dinner can be as formal or as informal as your host wants to make it. (However, it shouldn't be so formal as to run the risk of outdoing the wedding reception.) It can be held at someone's home, in a restaurant, in a park, on the beach—it can be anywhere. Dress accordingly.

Invitations can be extended by phone. There's no need to have special rehearsal dinner invitations printed up, unless you're just hankering to spend the money on them.

The Hosts and the Guests

Traditionally, the expense of the rehearsal party is borne by the groom's parents, but these days anyone who is up to the task can host the party. If you and your groom feel uncomfortable asking either set of parents to host this affair (and no one steps up to offer to play host in their places), go ahead and plan it yourselves.

Who should be invited? The absolute, bare-minimum guest list should include the following:

- All members of the wedding party, along with their spouses or significant others
- The parents of the bride and groom
- The ceremony officiant, along with his or her spouse
- Grandparents and godparents of the bride and groom

Of course, you can invite anyone else you want (with your hosts' okay), but try to keep the party on the intimate side. Remember, the goal of this party is to let everyone relax and to give you and your groom some additional time with loved ones who may only be in town for a few days.

Inviting out-of-town guests is a nice idea. You'll get to spend more time with people you probably don't see that often, and they'll feel that distance hasn't kept them from being a part of the festivities. They'll also appreciate a nice dinner and something to do instead of hanging out in their hotel rooms. Similarly, if you have any close friends that you couldn't manage to fit into the wedding party, you can invite them, too.

ALERT!

The parents of child attendants should also be invited to the rehearsal dinner. And unless you're counting on a temper tantrum from an overtired child to be part of the reception entertainment, make sure the dinner ends early enough for the parents to get the children home in time to get a good night's sleep.

One for You, and One for You . . .

The rehearsal dinner is usually when the bride and groom hand out their gifts to the attendants (and parents, if you've been feeling very generous). You might also choose to give your groom a wedding gift at this time, and he may have a little something wrapped up for you. However, if the two of you would rather hold off on giving each other your wedding gifts until the honeymoon, that's not a horrible idea, especially if one or both of you is just too exhausted or nervous to appreciate another gift at this point. After all, each of you has put a lot of thought into the gift you've chosen. You want your groom to be able to take the time to really take note of the significance of what you've given him, and you want to be able to do the same with the gift he's giving to you.

Speech! Speech!

If you follow tradition, toasts will be a part of the evening. If the groom's parents are hosting, the father of the groom offers up a toast to the bride and groom and to the bride's parents. The father of the bride responds with a toast to the hosts and to the almost-newlyweds. The groom then toasts the bride and her family, and the bride responds with a toast to the groom and his family.

Of course, you're not being watched by the etiquette police, so if someone *else* wants to make a toast (or someone on that list of toasters would rather not speak publicly), you're not bound to follow the traditional order. And if you prefer to skip the toasts altogether, that's fine, too. Remember, there'll be enough formality come the morning.

The Payoff

So you've made it through the rehearsal and you're laying your head on your pillow. What will the morning bring? Only time will tell, but this section might give you a pretty good idea.

Brrring! Alarm Clock!

You wake up. Or maybe you don't really wake up, since you never actually fell asleep the night before. You hop into the shower and stand in the spray long enough to feel clean, refreshed, and ready to face the day. You don't bother fussing with your hair or makeup too much because you have an appointment with your hairdresser, and you'll be wearing special makeup applied by a cosmetologist who's due to arrive later.

You jump into some jeans and a shirt that buttons down the front. You try to eat a light meal—maybe some tea, maybe some toast. You're looking for anything that will give you a little fuel and keep you from fainting as you walk down the aisle. Your maid of honor arrives, right on cue, to drive you to the appointment with your hairdresser. (Don't trust your own shaking hands behind the wheel.) After your hairdresser makes your hair (complete with headpiece if you brought it) look stunning, you jet back home.

Dress Up Time!

Your bridesmaids and maid of honor have started to assemble. Soon, the cosmetologist has arrived to put everyone's face on. Your gal pals are snacking away at the deli and cookie trays you picked up yesterday in an effort to prevent any bridesmaid temper tantrums fueled by low blood sugar. Your bouquet and the bridesmaids' flowers will have arrived during this time as well. The bridesmaids fight for a turn in the bathroom as they dress and primp, while your father sulks in his bedroom before changing into his tux. He's complaining about those darn rented shoes and how they pinch his toes, but you suspect that he's a little nervous himself.

Two hours before the ceremony, you start getting dressed. First, a good dousing of light powder, to make you feel fresh. Then you wrestle into your special undergarments, including your pantyhose, and call for help getting into your gown. Everyone else, including your mother, is almost done. You have plenty of hands to fasten any tricky buttons or zippers. You make sure you're equipped with something old, something new, something borrowed, and something blue.

ALERT!

Avoid ingesting an abundance of caffeinated beverages during the day. You'll already be nervous, and coffee or soda might just push you over the edge into bridal insanity (a bad move, really).

The photographer arrives at your house about an hour before the wedding to take shots of you alone, you with your family, and you with your attendants. The videographer catches some of the fun, too. Across town, your groom is stepping out of the shower and into his tux.

The limo pulls up and whisks your attendants to the ceremony site with plans to come back for you and your parents. Like clockwork, the limo comes for you. Outside, all of your neighbors are gathered to catch a glimpse of the lovely bride. You, of course, feel like a movie star. Wave to your adoring crowd. Pose for the photographer's last shot (for now), because he needs to hop into his car in order to beat you to the ceremony site. Your father helps you into the limo and you're off!

Your Grand Entrance

At the ceremony site, everyone is already seated. You gather in the vestibule with your bridesmaids. Maybe there's a little confusion in your mind as to why the girls are chatting away about a movie they've all seen—or maybe they're concerned about their own appearances—when they should be concentrating on *you*. ("Hello? Yoo-hoo! **Me**!", you gently remind them, and they snap to attention, as good bridesmaids should.) The on-site coordinator lines them up and ships them off as the processional begins, and there they go, walking, as ordered, *very slowly*.

Now it's your turn. As your groom steps out to the altar to greet you, you float down the aisle. The ceremony begins, and it goes without a glitch: Talking, reading, rings, giving, taking, kissing . . .

The Home Stretch

. . . And you're *married*!

You bounce back down the aisle together to that appropriately peppy recessional music you've chosen. If the weather is good, you have a brief receiving line outside in the courtyard. (Or you have it at the reception site. But you *do* have it.)

You and your new husband share some champagne in the limousine ride to the reception. At the reception site, you quickly have your formal photographs done and are back at the hors d'oeuvres table before everyone else has eaten all the stuffed mushrooms. You seat yourself at the head table with your groom and are immediately greeted with the sound of silverware clinking against glasses for the first time—and it just never stops, though at some point you feel forced to stop kissing, because darn it, you're *hungry*, and you can't eat with your lips connected to his.

Dinner is served. After everyone is satiated, you and your groom have your first dance. Then you cut the cake. Then you dance with your father. Then the groom dances with his mother. Then everybody pretty much dances with everybody. Toward the end of the reception, the groom removes your garter and tosses it away to all the eligible gents, and you toss your bouquet to the single ladies. Eventually, you say goodbye to everyone, and you leave for your wedding night and honeymoon.

Now, wasn't that *easy*?

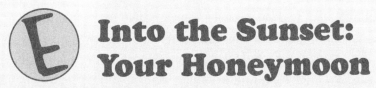

Chapter 19

Into the Sunset:
Your Honeymoon

You'll probably agree that, what with all the frenzied planning, coordinating, organizing, and worrying involved, getting yourself married can be a full-time job—and then some. When it's all over with, you'll need more than just an ordinary vacation to recuperate. Your honeymoon is the perfect occasion to plan the vacation of your dreams.

Planning the Getaway

On the surface, a honeymoon is no different from any other vacation. You pack your bags, make your reservations, and leave home for fun in the sun, snow, or wherever. But to a pair of newlyweds, a honeymoon is much more than that—it's your first getaway together as a married couple, and (you hope) the ultimate romantic experience. Ten years from now, you probably won't remember just when it was you spent that summer week in the mountains, or that long weekend skiing. But for better or for worse, the honeymoon tends to have more staying power in your memory. While you can't get a guarantee on perfection, you can eliminate a lot of potential problems by planning carefully—and early.

Where Are We Going?

You might have your honeymoon all planned out in your head right now (you know, the one you've been imagining since you were ten years old). However, your groom might have vastly different ideas. First, you'll need to pinpoint what each of you expects from this trip. Does he want to golf, or fish, or ski? Are you looking to see some shows, do some shopping, or sit by the pool? Each of you is allowed to insist on the inclusion of *one* activity (other than snuggling up to each other, that is). And if this doesn't help (he wants to sit in the sun, while you're planning on climbing Everest), you'll either have to plan a two-part honeymoon (where you'll spend the first part of the week on the beach and the second part of it in Nepal), or, more realistically, you'll have to find a happy compromise. Maybe you could forgo Everest in favor of hiking up a volcano.

ALERT!

Honeymoon or not, everyone has their limits. You don't want your honeymoon to be marred by an argument over who's calling all the shots. Make sure whatever you're planning is going to keep *both* of you entertained for the entire vacation.

Fair and Square

Keep in mind that the activities you're planning should be enjoyable to both of you. Many couples plan their honeymoon by saying to one another, "Whatever you want is fine with me," until one partner takes that ball and runs with it. The ensuing honeymoon turns out to be filled with activities that the planner finds interesting. And even though he or she may have genuinely thought that his or her spouse would enjoy the various outings, the non-planner ends up bored or annoyed instead.

It's fair to expect a certain amount of compromise on your honeymoon. For example, you might want to introduce your groom to waterskiing, a sport you mastered long ago. But you can't expect your spouse to spend the entire week giving in to your every demand. After all, this is his honeymoon, too. Likewise, if you really despise museums and your new husband loves to spend the day looking at abstract art, you might agree to accompany him for a day or two, but after that, chances are you'd be bored and a little miffed.

Money Talks

Ultimately, of course, your budget is likely to have at least as big an influence on your choice of destination as your dreams. Consult a travel agent or the Internet to find low-priced airfares, reduced-rate package deals, and other ways to save money. You may be pleasantly surprised. Perhaps you *can* afford a trip to Hawaii by staying at a less-than-four-star hotel, or travel Europe via hostels and bed and breakfasts. Remember, however, to confirm that "inexpensive" lodging does not mean "without running water," "dilapidated," or "situated in the red-light district" (though all of these situations, in their own way, may add some excitement to your trip).

Some couples choose to postpone the trip for several months, either for financial reasons or because one partner just can't get the vacation time from work right after the wedding. If you're still in the early stages of planning your wedding and you just know that you won't be able to afford any sort of honeymoon, your travel agent might be able to help you by setting up a honeymoon registry.

A honeymoon registry is similar to a gift registry, but instead of buying you pots and pans, your friends and family make monetary contributions to your vacation fund. Some agents can even set up a Web site for your registry, which makes things infinitely easier on everyone concerned.

Timing Is Everything

If you're lucky, you might have saved up enough vacation time (and enough moola) to take an extended honeymoon. If you're marrying a teacher and you're planning a wedding in September, however, chances are you're only going to have time for a quick getaway.

If you're on the fence—you could do either, in other words—take some time to consider what type of vacation each of you finds relaxing before you commit yourselves to anything. If your future husband can't stand to live out of a suitcase (or out of a backpack), a two-week whirlwind tour of Europe might not be the best plan. Likewise, if you don't even start feeling relaxed until you've had a day or two to get used to your vacation surroundings, a weekend fling may be out of the question.

If you have very limited time or funds available for your honeymoon, try to make things as special as possible within your limits. Book a room in the fanciest hotel you can find that's within driving distance, and *enjoy yourselves* for the weekend.

Honeymoon Hot Spots

Are you at a complete loss as far as picking a destination is concerned? Here are some of the most popular spots for newlyweds:

- **The Caribbean:** Aruba; Negril, Jamaica; Cayman Islands; Little Dix Bay, British Virgin Islands; Paradise Island, Bahamas; Montego Bay, Jamaica; St. Croix; Nassau, Bahamas; U.S. Virgin Islands

- **Mexico:** Baja California; Isla de Cozumel; Cancun; Puerto Vallarta; Guadalajara
- **South Pacific:** The Marquesas; Tahiti
- **Europe:** Greece; Spain; Switzerland; England; France; Italy; Monaco; Germany
- **United States:** Alaska; Hawaii; Grand Canyon National Park; Pennsylvania; Disneyland or Walt Disney World; Cape Cod; Martha's Vineyard; Nantucket

Of course, this list only scratches the surface. You have the entire globe to choose from, every state, (almost) every country, every region—and by definition, anywhere newlyweds choose to vacation is a honeymoon spot.

FACT

You shouldn't feel pressured into choosing a spot because everyone else goes there, nor should you shy away from a place because you don't want to follow the crowd. You want to go to St. Louis and see that big arch on your honeymoon? Go for it.

You and your groom need to decide what you'd like to do or see on your honeymoon and narrow down your choices from there. Obviously, some areas have more to offer than others. If you think you'd like to see a particular region on your honeymoon, but you aren't 100 percent sure about it, do some research on the region. This is something you should do anyway, no matter where you choose to go. Ask your travel agent for some brochures, or look online for the city's chamber of commerce Web site.

Once you and your fiancé agree on where you'd like to spend your honeymoon, you should start making your reservations, either through your travel agent or by scouting out the Internet travel sites. Some of the resorts in the more popular tourist and honeymoon spots can be booked solid up to a year in advance, so start as early as you can—especially if you've got your heart set on a particular location.

Book It!

Perhaps you're used to handling your vacation arrangements by yourself, without anyone's help. Or maybe you have a great travel agent and you'd never make a move without him or her. No matter which method you prefer, make sure you start early enough so that you can book the hotels, activities, and flights that you want.

Making Your Own Arrangements

If you're making your own travel arrangements and you're taking off soon after your wedding, don't forget that your plane tickets should be booked in your maiden name. You'll need a valid photo ID to board your flight, and the name on the ID must match the name on your ticket.

Also, if you're taking off immediately following the reception (or the morning after), try to arrange for smooth travel connections. As you're looking at tickets online, an eight-hour layover may seem like a bit of a hassle, but you may think you're willing to accept it for the sake of saving a few hundred bucks. But keep in mind that you're likely to be exhausted and anxious to get on with the honeymoonin'—and a long layover (or a series of them) on the day after your wedding might get your trip off on the wrong foot. Fatigue can breed irritability and forgetfulness. Add the stress of travel to that, and you have the recipe for potential disaster. Even if you get to your destination without mishap, you certainly don't want to risk bickering with your spouse your first full day as a married couple. Moods could swing, tears may be shed, and you'll lose almost an entire day to travel in the process.

ALERT!

If either of you is generally not a good traveler, you might want to keep things as close to home as possible. You could find a nice resort that's within driving distance, for example, instead of hopping flight after flight (which will only add to any travel-related misery).

If possible, try to get at least six hours of sleep the night before you take off. You may not wake up totally refreshed (given that weddings have a way of making you feel like you've run a marathon), but you'll be better off than if you only slept for two hours. Make some time for a long hot shower and a hearty breakfast, and you should have a good start to the first day of your honeymoon.

Using Travel Agents

Maybe you scoff at the very idea of travel agents, reasoning that you can do all of this yourself, no problemo! If you're going out of the country, however, you might benefit from working with an agent who can enlighten you as to the finer points of international travel. Because foreign vacations can get very complicated—with connecting flights that have to meet boats that have to meet trains—putting all the responsibility into the lap of a trained professional might be a good idea. After all, you've already got enough to think about with planning the wedding.

Your agent will be able to tell you which paperwork, identification, and other necessities you will need in order to travel abroad. With the exception of visits to Canada, Mexico, and some parts of the Caribbean, you'll need a passport, which takes at least six weeks (and sometimes longer) to obtain. (More on passports in the next section of this chapter.)

Documents you will need to track down if you're planning on leaving the country include these:

- Birth certificate
- Driver's license (or other picture ID)
- Proof of marriage
- Proof of citizenship

Travel agents are also on the ball as far as alerting you to potential troubles. You might not want to risk traveling to a spot during its rainy season. Or you might find out from your agent, who's in the know, that your four-star resort is planning on adding another entire wing during your stay, which will add up to lots of round-the-clock noise. This would be enough to make you want to stay across town. Nowadays, some foreign countries post travel alerts for Americans, which you'll obviously want to know about before you attempt to board a plane to a restricted or dangerous area.

Of course, you can find this information on your own, but it will take a considerable amount of time to research the things that your travel agent already knows. Just consider whether the time it will take is worth it, or if it could be better spent focusing on the wedding itself.

Passports

They sound so official, and so *intriguing*. Is it possible that you're going to have your very own passport soon? Yes, it is. And you can pretend you're an international spy if you want to.

Passports are relatively easy to obtain—as long as you're *not* an international spy. You'll need to give yourself a minimum of six weeks, but you should really start the process as soon as you can to avoid any last-minute problems. It is possible to pay extra (somewhere in the range of an arm and a leg) for expedited service, which generally takes about two weeks.

Your first step is to fill out an application, which can be found online at *www.state.gov/travel*. If you're applying for the first time, you'll have to take the application to a passport agency or a passport acceptance facility. This isn't as hard as it sounds—many of these facilities are located inside larger post offices, some libraries, and county offices. You'll bring proof of U.S. citizenship (your birth certificate or naturalization certificate will do); a photo ID (such as a valid driver's license or government ID); two passport photos (which can be taken at many one-hour photo shops); your Social Security number; and money (the fee currently totals $85).

Travel Tips

If you're leaving town, as most honeymooners do, you may be entering foreign territory—literally or not. Even if you're not leaving the country, if you're visiting a place you've never been to, it might feel as though you've been transported to another planet. Some advice on how to take care of yourself in strange surroundings follows.

Do Your Homework

Before you take off on any vacation, you should acquaint yourself with the area you're traveling to. If you're going to Chicago, for example, you won't need to rent a car, because public transportation is around every corner, and you'll never find a parking spot, anyway. If you're headed to New York City, you'd better start studying the subway system, unless you want to drop a fortune in cab fare. If you're going to land in a foreign airport, get yourself a map of its layout so that you'll know where to find the baggage claim and where you'll have to go to grab a taxi.

Do your research before you leave for your vacation. You can always buy maps in any city you visit, but if you *look* like a lost tourist— and you will if you're walking and reading that map—you're an easy mark for a pickpocket or a less-than-honest merchant. Avoid the additional stress, and buy maps before you go.

Know what kind of weather to expect. You're headed to the Caribbean, you say, and all you're going to need is a bikini and some sunscreen (you freckle so badly!). But if you're vacationing during hurricane season, you might want to bring a raincoat . . . *and* inquire as to your resort's money-back-guarantee.

If you're headed to an all-inclusive resort, find out what that means, *exactly*. Have you paid for your lodging and food only? Are water sports and entertainment included? What about gratuities? Do you have to shell out for transportation to and from the airport?

Educate Yourself *More*

If you're off to a foreign country, play the part of a diplomat. Learn some phrases in the native language. Don't expect everyone to speak

English, and don't balk at the customs. If the food turns your stomach, don't chastise the locals for eating it. If the entire region seems to be less-than-sanitary, deal with it without causing an international incident. Remember, *you're* the foreigner here. You're the fish out of water, the one with the strange ideas, the one who doesn't know the language. Act as you would if you were a guest in someone's home, and you should return to your home soil relatively unscathed.

You'll also want to research whether you'll need any vaccinations before traveling abroad, and you should try to work in a physical and dental checkup before you take off. Get yourself a good travel guide for any region you'll be traveling through. These books are updated constantly and offer some of the best, most realistic information on foreign travel.

Don't Forget . . .

There will be no lecture on the use of credit cards during the course of your honeymoon. It's actually safer to use your credit cards (or traveler's checks) than to carry around huge wads of cash. The regular stipulations apply. Don't go wild charging everything just because you're on vacation, and keep track of how much you're spending. Be aware that you will need some cash, however, if you're planning on hitting the smaller inns and restaurants in foreign countries, many of which operate on a cash-only basis. Have your groom wear a money belt for the safekeeping of your coin.

Confirm your hotel reservations the week before you leave. There's nothing quite like dragging all your heavy luggage into a hotel lobby in some exotic locale, dreaming of a nice, long nap—only to find that you don't have a room. And there's not a vacant room on the island. If the room you thought you booked isn't the room you're being given, speak up. Ask for the manager on duty, and don't take no for an answer.

Once you arrive at your hotel, don't be afraid to complain to the management if the service or accommodations are not to your satisfaction. And *don't* wait until you're leaving. Most reputable hotels will go out of their way to rectify any problems as soon as possible, whether that means having your room cleaned again (the right way), or moving you to another room if possible, one that's not right next to the vending machines.

FACT

Packing for your honeymoon will likely overlap with last-minute wedding stuff. Even if you're not the type of girl who packs a week before a trip, make an exception this time. That might mean buying things like brand-new toiletries specifically for the trip, instead of packing things you already have and will need during the week before your wedding—like lotion and shampoo.

The Fine Art of Tipping

It's raining tips! Or so you would think, especially if you've ever sat in the lobby of a grand hotel, watching the bellboy and the doorman collect their rewards, or gone to a fancy restaurant, where seemingly every employee has his or her hand out. Who gets tipped, why, and how much? In some situations you can ask your companions at the dining table in a hotel or on shipboard, or the management. However, it's *always* best to be armed with the knowledge before you're faced with a sticky situation and want to avoid any awkwardness.

On Cruises

Your cruise line will probably provide you with tipping guidelines, but you should know what you're in for. The room steward cleans your cabin, makes the bed, supplies towels, soap, ice, and room service. Tip $3.50 per day per person, in one lump sum at the end of the trip. Some also tip on the first day, "to insure perfect service"—a slogan said to be the origin of the word "tips."

Dining room waiters generally are tipped $3.50 per person per day; allow half that amount for the busboy. The maitre d' is the headwaiter in charge of the dining room. No tip is necessary unless he has handled special requests for you.

As for bartenders, wine stewards, pool and deck attendants, and so on, check the bar bill. On almost all ships, a service charge is automatically added, making a tip unnecessary. Other service personnel should be tipped when the service is given, at the same rate as for service ashore, usually 15 percent.

Some cruise lines advertise a "no tip" policy. People still tip for special service on such ships, but it is not necessary if you do not ask for anything "above and beyond."

At the airport, tip the porter $1 or $2 per bag when you check in at the curb or have bags taken to check in for you. If he goes way out of his way for you—like if you're cutting things close and he points out to you that you don't have to wait in that long line at the ticket counter, which you had every intention of doing—give him more.

At Hotels

Bellboys get $1 or $2 per bag, plus $1 or $2 for hospitable gestures (turning on lights, opening windows). If you send the poor boy on an errand, tip him $5. (This rate needs to be adjusted for the region you're in. In San Francisco or New York, you'll need to add a buck or two to the tip.) The doorman gets $1 to $2 for hailing a cab, and $2 to $5 for helping you out with your incredibly heavy suitcases or shopping bags.

Chambermaids are tipped $1 or $2 for each service, and you should try to leave the tip every day. You may not have the same maid for the entire week. Room service is pricey: you'll tip 15 to 20 percent of the bill in addition to a room service charge. But *check the bill* to make sure that the gratuity hasn't already been added in.

Valets get $2 to $3 for retrieving your vehicle. The concierge is tipped $5 to $10 if he provides you with special service (for instance, books tickets for a show or makes dinner reservations).

In Restaurants

The headwaiter (or maitre d') is a tricky little character. While he basically plays the role of host, he's in full control of the dining room.

How much you tip him depends on how badly you want to eat in this particular restaurant, where you want to sit, and how long you want to wait. It's not unusual for headwaiters to receive $50 tips at the best restaurants in the biggest cities. For guidance as to the particular area you're staying in, ask your hotel concierge.

Wine stewards are tipped 15 to 20 percent of the wine bill. Your waiter or waitress is tipped 15 to 20 percent of the food bill (as long as the gratuity hasn't already been included). Buffet servers are tipped a buck or two per person as long as the service (clean plates, drinks, etc.) was decent.

Note that in a foreign country, the amount of the tip should be calculated in the local currency. It may be less or more than you would tip in dollars, depending on the exchange rate. And in many foreign countries, the gratuity is added into the bill.

ALERT!

Remember, these are only guidelines for good service. Keep in mind that people in the service industry are sometimes paid less than minimum wage and depend on tips. However, if you get lousy service *anywhere,* you're not obligated to reward the person who provided it.

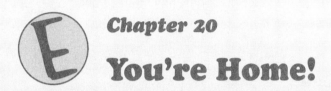

Chapter 20

You're Home!

The idea of moving in together sounds so romantic, and you probably can't wait. But there are a lot of things to take into consideration when you start planning this part of your future. You'll need to have a sound financial plan (and a knack for compromise) in order to make a smooth transition.

Before You Begin Packing . . .

Like the decisions you make concerning your wedding, you might want to discuss any pre-wedding cohabitation plans you and your fiancé are making with both sets of parents. Plan to talk with them well before you start putting your possessions into boxes. You want to have plenty of time to work out any glitches, such as a parent's stern refusal to accept your decision and subsequent refusal to attend the wedding if you don't change your mind.

Parental Problems?

If the reactions you receive are negative, you'll feel like you're in a real pickle. You *are* an adult, after all, and you might not really care if your parents (or your groom's parents) approve of your decision to move in with your man prior to saying "I do."

ALERT!

Remember that what seems natural (and necessary) to you as far as your living arrangements are concerned may seem just plain *wrong* to a person from another generation or cultural background. Try to anticipate reactions before broaching the subject, and most importantly, be sensitive to the responses.

Of course, you don't want to back down from your position, but the months before your wedding should be happy times. They shouldn't be filled with family squabbles and various threats (of your parents disinheriting you and your responsive threat to put yourself up for adoption). So what should you do?

If you're really interested in keeping the peace, look for a compromise. Perhaps your fiancé can move into the new apartment you'll pick out together a month before your wedding, while you stay where you are until after the honeymoon. You can still get the place in shape during that month; you just won't be living there.

Those Left Behind

There may be another person or people who need to know about your future living arrangements: roommates. While your roommates are undoubtedly happy for your triumph in finding the perfect man, they may also be concerned that when you move out they're going to be left holding the bag full of bills. They might also be worrying about getting stuck finding another roommate to take your place (though everyone knows no one will really *ever* take your place).

Try to give your roommate at least a month's notice before you move. Offer to help find a replacement by asking friends if they know of anyone in need of a place, by putting (and paying for) an ad in the newspaper, or by listing the opening in a roommate locator service.

Keep your space tidy, knowing that your roommate will be showing the place to prospective new inhabitants. Transfer any bills that are currently in your name to your roommate's name to avoid future confusion or tension. A few days before you move, settle up unpaid bills. If you are owed a security deposit refund, be sure your roommate knows you've contacted the rental agent for its return. Let your roommate know the date and time you plan to move your belongings. Finally, leave your room in pristine condition for the next occupant, and make sure your roommate knows your forwarding address and how to reach you in case anything comes up.

The Financial Picture

Moving into a new home is a huge expense, whether you're renting or buying. Buying is usually technically a bigger expense, but if you're having trouble coming up with the rent for a dirt-cheap apartment, it feels the same either way. To make things easier on yourselves in the long run, make sure you know what you can afford. Lay out your budget *before* you go house-hunting, and don't expect to find the perfect place on your first day. Finding the right place can be an emotionally draining and time-consuming process.

Setting Up Your Budget

You'll be combining your income with someone else's in a joint budget, which may be the first time you've ever shared your income and spending. What this means, in plain English, is that you need to know how much money your fiancé is earning. Maybe the subject has never come up. Or maybe you've been afraid to ask—whatever the reason, if you don't have a clear idea of what this man's net pay is at the end of each week, now's the time to find out.

If you're like most women, though, you probably already have a good idea of how much your fiancé brings home each paycheck. But do you know how he *budgets* his money? That may be the trickier part of the picture. And on the flip side, does he know how you spend your earnings each month? Make a date to sit down with your fiancé and talk frankly about how you might go about setting up a budget you both can live with.

You'll also want to discuss the use of credit cards. There's nothing scarier than assuming you're in the black, only to see a lot of numbers (and a few commas) in the "balance due" box on your credit card statement.

When setting up the budget, you'll add your paycheck to his, plus any other regular source of income, and then subtract the following expenses:

- Rent/mortgage
- Utilities (electric, heat, phone, cable, water, and so on)
- Food
- Debts (student loans, car payments, credit cards, and so on)
- Insurance (car and/or homeowners')
- Other expenses, such as child support, commuting expenses, home business expenses, and so on

The balance you end up with should not have a minus sign in front of it. If it does, you're paying out too much, and you need to find someplace to cut back. What this means for you in terms of housing is that you should not take on a bigger rent or mortgage payment—or one that will increase the cost of your living expenses—if you can't pay the bills you have now.

Dealing with the Budget

If you're moving into your groom's place, or he's moving into yours, you'll already know how much the utilities cost each month. If you're moving into a new place, you'll want to ask if any utilities are included in the rent, and take it from there. If you're moving into an apartment in an old house, you might want to ask the other tenants what they typically pay for heat (the insulation might not be up to par) and/or air conditioning (and don't be surprised to learn that there isn't any central air). You'll be able to get some idea of what a new apartment is really going to cost you in the end. To be on the safe side, consider padding the amounts by $20 or so.

QUESTION?

How much should you be spending on the rent or on a mortgage?
As a rule of thumb, the amount you spend monthly for rent or mortgage should not exceed 33 percent of your total income (totaling both paychecks). Some estimates go as high as 36 percent—any more than that is too much.

Spending more than a third of your income on housing is risky, in that you'll likely find yourselves "house poor." Sure, you'll have a beautiful home, but if you can't afford to furnish it (or eat, for that matter), it will lose its luster in your eyes very quickly. The danger of buying more house than you can reasonably afford intensifies if one partner loses his or her job. This is exactly the way in which many people find themselves dealing with foreclosures.

If you're shopping around for a mortgage, run the numbers yourself and figure out what you can afford (and what you can't). Unfortunately, many lending companies are only too eager to give you a bigger mortgage than you should have, because in the end, they're making more money from you. And your real estate agent will be only too happy to sell you a house that's above your *real* price range, because she gets a percentage of the selling price—the more it costs, the bigger her commission. How do you think she bought that luxury car she's driving?

Finding a Place

If you're lucky, you or your fiancé already lives in a place that's large enough for two and that both of you love. That certainly makes your life a lot easier, at least until the two of you decide that you need more room, or that you'd like to be in a different neighborhood, or until some other reason for moving creeps into the picture. But if you're like many couples, you'll want to (or have to) start fresh. One of the first decisions facing you will be where you want to live.

Your vision of married bliss may be a cozy little house in the country, hours from the bustling city. But what if your job means commuting back into the bustle five days a week? Chances are, you'd rather spend time with your new husband than on the road between your office and your home. Likewise, if it's your husband who's doing the commuting, you don't want to be stuck at home drumming your fingers on the table as you wait for him to finally walk through the door. Unless you simply can't live without that country house, you'll be better off searching for a place that's more convenient to both your workplaces—and saving that dream home for a time in your life when commuting isn't as big an issue (or when kids suddenly *are*).

Research the Area

When choosing a place to live, you'll want to be sure it has at least some of the amenities that are important to your and your husband's daily life. If you like a good game of tennis on the weekends, make sure there are public tennis courts available. Maybe you're a gourmet cook who needs ingredients found only in specialty markets. If so, then the typical supermarket chain probably won't suit you. Do you need a place where you can easily launch your boat? Make sure there's water nearby.

Once you've decided what your town or neighborhood must have, drive through a few possibilities to check them out more thoroughly. Park the car in the downtown area and take a stroll to get a feel for the place. Strike up a conversation with the person who serves your coffee. Pick up a copy of the local paper. Time the commute from the town center to your office.

If you know someone who lives in a town you're considering, pump him or her for information. Do they like what the town has to offer? What are the pluses and minuses? How long have they lived there? Does the community have several housing options to choose from?

The Dwelling

Determining the type of housing you should be looking at usually comes down to two factors: money and time. Generally speaking, apartments are the least expensive option and the easiest to find. You go through the apartment listings in the paper and make some calls to set up appointments to check them out. First and last month's rent plus a security deposit are the standard up-front financial requirements. You hand over a check, sign some papers, and move in. Unless you choose the most luxurious apartment in the ritziest part of town, chances are your monthly rental costs will be less than any mortgage you would pay for a house or condo.

Condominiums and houses are more expensive for several reasons. First, in order to purchase one you need to come up with a down payment (usually twenty percent of the total cost). On top of that, there are other fees to pay when the final paperwork is processed, at the closing—fees that will likely run into the thousands of dollars. (You'll need to hire a lawyer, for one thing, who will pretty much sit back during the closing and tell you to write all sorts of checks to people and agencies you've never heard of, and will never hear *from*, and then you'll write *him or her* a check to top it all off.) Finally, monthly mortgage payments are generally higher than rent. For newlyweds, these costs can be prohibitive, often making a nice apartment more attractive than a house or a condo in the early years of marriage.

FACT

Since condos and houses are more permanent residences than apartments, you'll want to spend time finding the perfect place. That can take as little as a week (if you're extremely lucky) or as long as a year, depending on what's available on the market and on your personal preferences.

Prioritize

Once you've decided what fits your budget, you'll have a narrowed-down list of possible homes to choose from. You'll be faced with some decisions, which may mean that you'll have to make some big concessions. How many rooms do you need? Must you have cathedral ceilings? Do you or your husband need an at-home office? What about a gourmet kitchen? A first-floor laundry room?

If you're on a tight budget, you may ultimately have to decide on the *one* most important feature of prospective homes, whether it's space, style, or convenience. It's best to have relatively meager expectations of your first home or apartment when you're pinching pennies.

If you have a slightly larger budget to work with, your house needs will be determined more by your lifestyles and personalities. If you like to entertain, for example, you'll be on the lookout for a home with a spacious kitchen and dining room. You might opt for a place with a spare bedroom if you hope to have frequent overnight guests or need a separate office space. And everyone has heard stories of how fights for closet and bathroom-counter space have ruined relationships. If you're concerned you and your husband will fall into this category, go for the place with the walk-in closets and the bath and a half.

In the end, you might have to give up a few wish-list items in order to find a good place to start your future together. But if you're armed with a solid idea of what both of you really must have, you can save yourself time and aggravation as you search.

Don't forget to include your outdoor expectations in the list. If you love to barbecue, you'll want to be sure you have a place to do it. Two cars might not need a garage, but they will need parking. And a yen for gardening probably won't be satisfied with just a window box or two.

The Timing

If parental reaction isn't an issue for you, the time that the two of you choose to move in together depends on what's most practical. The most logical time to move is when your current living arrangement changes. For instance, if your lease is up, and it makes more sense to move than to renew it; your roommate is leaving, and you don't want to look for a new one; or you just have to move out of your parents' house now because they're driving you crazy.

Unless you and your fiancé are both faced with these decisions at the same time, you'll need to coordinate your move carefully. It would be expensive and wasteful to be paying for your new apartment together if you still have to pay rent on an old place where you couldn't get out of the lease. If that's what you're faced with, ask your current rental agent if he or she would consider letting you sublet your apartment. It will be up to you to find a suitable tenant, and any problems that tenant causes become *your* problems. Or, if your lease is up, see if you can remain in your apartment on a month-to-month basis until you're ready to move.

You Already Live Together

It may be that you and your fiancé have been living together, or will be living together for some time before the wedding. This can make certain aspects of the wedding planning a lot less complicated.

If you're coordinating the bulk of the wedding yourself, you can have RSVPs mailed to you instead of your parents. Your gifts will be transported from your shower(s) directly into your home, and you won't have to worry about having to pack and move right after the honeymoon.

You and your partner will also have a clear picture of what you should register for. If you see your fiancé using the same ratty towel day after day, you know for a fact that a new set of bath linens will be more than welcome. Likewise, if your fiancé has listened to you complain about your broken hand mixer and the food processor that really smushes vegetables more than it slices them, he won't balk (or ask you, "What do you need that for? Can't we get those cool beer mugs instead?") when you check off those goodies on the registry.

Living at the same address for a period of time before the wedding means you and your partner have a better understanding of each other's finances. You won't have to set up billing procedures for your utilities or cable or figure out a system for paying those bills. With the potential tension surrounding the planning of a wedding, *not* having to deal with the mundane tasks of everyday life can be really nice.

Distance Makes the Heart Grow Fonder

While living together before the wedding does have its practical side, many couples prefer to stick with tradition. They don't want to experience what it's like to be married before they've taken their vows. For these couples, the excitement and romance of the first night in their new home (and starting the budgeting, and buying furniture) is a continuation of the excitement and romance of the pre-wedding season.

FACT

Give yourself plenty of time to prepare yourself and your belongings for the big move. You don't want to end up leaving your apartment in a huge rush because you waited until after the wedding to start packing. You'll never find anything in those boxes if they aren't labeled accurately and packed carefully.

Waiting until you're officially husband and wife can be a wonderfully romantic way to go. If this is your decision, you'll just be on a time-delay behind the couples who have chosen to set up house before the wedding. Getting yourselves organized is key here. You'll be moving (presumably) right after the honeymoon, which means that you'll likely be packing as you're preparing for your wedding day and your vacation.

Home Sweet Home

Whether you're moving in together before the wedding or waiting until the ink is dry on the marriage license, learning to live with someone else can be a rocky transition. If you're finding, suddenly, that your fiancé (or new husband) has some questionable hygiene rituals or that he is obsessive-compulsive about where the condiments can be placed in the refrigerator (*they go on the door, not on the big shelves*!), you might be wondering what the heck you've gotten yourself into. How could you have agreed to spend all of eternity with this person?

This is one thing that many newlyweds (or new roommates) don't talk about. To admit that the bloom is off the rose, so to speak, would be lessening your relationship in the eyes of others. You definitely don't want anyone to think that what you and your guy have is anything less than perfect, right?

You'd probably be surprised at how many of your friends feel the same way. One day, someone will admit to a little something (that her husband hogs the entire bed every night, for example, and that she doesn't find it the least bit endearing), and the floodgates will be opened. In the meantime, though . . .

Be Honest with Each Other

The worst thing you can do, if your partner has a habit that really, truly irritates you, is to pretend that you love it. Chances are a hundred to one that by suppressing your true feelings, you're setting yourself up for a big blowout one day down the road, when his whiskers in the sink will be given equal weight with some felonious act. If you want him to pick up his own socks and put them into the laundry basket, ask him to do it. If you don't want to come home to an apartment that looks as though a bomb filled with chips and beer bottles has exploded on the coffee table, tell him. (And when he asks *you* not to leave your long hair in the bathroom sink, respect his feelings and make the effort to accommodate his wishes.)

Division of Domestic Duties

Another thing that often happens in new cohabitation situations is that the woman will somehow feel as though she's been stuck with the bulk of household chores—in addition to her own full-time job outside of the home. Though this same woman has lived on her own for years and has learned to tackle big cleaning jobs and small repair issues, it's unfair for her partner to expect her to take on twice the responsibilities after marriage (or after the move-in).

If you find that you've been landed unfairly with responsibilities for doing everything—all the laundry, all the cleaning, most of the repairs—you may need to hold a summit to address the household chores. After all, this man loves you. Unless you tell him, he may not have the slightest idea how overwhelmed you're feeling by all of the work.

Things you'll be faced with include the following:

- Maintenance (anything from clogged sinks to painting to cleaning the gutters)
- Everyday cleaning
- Laundry
- Cooking
- Grocery shopping
- Child care (if and when the kiddies arrive)

Ask anyone who runs a household on their own if it's possible for one person to successfully tackle all of these items without help. It isn't. Nor should one spouse be expected to make the attempt to do everything on his or her own. You're *partners* now, for better or for worse, for home repairs or for grocery shopping.

Wives sometimes get a reputation for being nags, and usually, it's an unfair assessment. Still, in an effort to avoid being labeled as such, many new wives look the other way on issues that drive them up the wall. How can you find a middle ground *and* ask for the things you want without somehow crossing the line into nagging territory? Just remember this. There's a right way to ask for something, and a wrong way. You don't need to address your mate as though he's a six-year-old, even if he's acting like one. Treat him with the same respect you'd expect from him, and you'll avoid the "n-a-g" labeling process.

There's no right way to divide chores. Play to each other's strengths. You're particularly good at waterproofing the deck, while he makes a mean casserole? Whatever works in your house is the right way to do it. You can also make tradeoffs on the really undesirable chores. Your hubby's been painting woodwork for the past three weekends? Let him do the dusting while you make a dent in the job this weekend. Above all, realize that this is an ever-evolving process. You'll be working on these issues for a long, long time. Don't expect the perfect solutions to pop up the day after you've moved in together.

Congratulations on your new life together as a married couple!

Planning

Planning Checklist

Six to twelve months before the wedding:

- [ ] Announce engagement
- [ ] Decide on type of wedding
- [ ] Decide on time of day
- [ ] Choose the location
- [ ] Set a date
- [ ] Set a budget
- [ ] Select bridal party
- [ ] Plan color scheme
- [ ] Select and order bridal gown
- [ ] Select and order headpiece
- [ ] Select and order shoes
- [ ] Select and order attendants' gowns
- [ ] Start honeymoon planning
- [ ] Go to bridal gift registry
- [ ] Start compiling the guest list
- [ ] Select caterer
- [ ] Select musicians
- [ ] Select florist
- [ ] Select photographer
- [ ] Start planning reception
- [ ] Reserve hall, hotel, etc., for reception
- [ ] Plan to attend premarital counseling at your church, if applicable
- [ ] Select and order wedding rings

Planning Checklist (continued)

Three months before the wedding:

☐ Complete guest list

☐ Make doctor's appointments

☐ Plan to have mothers select attire

☐ Select and order invitations

☐ Order personal stationery

☐ Start compiling trousseau

☐ Finalize reception arrangements (rent items now)

☐ Make reservations for honeymoon

☐ Confirm dress delivery

☐ Confirm time and date with florist

☐ Confirm time and date with caterer

☐ Confirm time and date with photographer

☐ Confirm time and date with musicians

☐ Confirm time and date with church

☐ Discuss transportation to ceremony and reception

☐ Order cake

☐ Select and order attire for groomsmen

☐ Schedule bridesmaids' dress and shoe fittings

Two months before the wedding:

☐ Mail all invitations to allow time for RSVPs

☐ Arrange for appointment to get marriage license

☐ Finalize honeymoon arrangements

Planning Checklist (continued)

One month before the wedding:

- ☐ Schedule bridal portrait
- ☐ Reserve accommodations for guests
- ☐ Begin to record gifts received and send thank-you notes
- ☐ Plan rehearsal and rehearsal dinner
- ☐ Purchase gifts for bridal party
- ☐ Purchase gift for fiancé if gifts are being exchanged
- ☐ Schedule final fittings, including accessories and shoes
- ☐ Schedule appointments at beauty salon for attendants
- ☐ Schedule bridesmaids' luncheon or party
- ☐ Arrange for placement of guest book
- ☐ Obtain wedding props, e.g., pillow for ringbearer, candles, etc.
- ☐ Get marriage license

Two weeks before the wedding:

- ☐ Mail bridal portrait with announcement to newspaper
- ☐ Finalize wedding day transportation
- ☐ Arrange to change name on license, Social Security card, etc.
- ☐ Confirm accommodations for guests
- ☐ Prepare wedding announcements to be mailed after the wedding

Planning Checklist (continued)

One week before the wedding:

- [ ] Start packing for honeymoon
- [ ] Finalize number of guests with caterer
- [ ] Double-check all details with those providing professional services (photographer, videographer, florist, etc.)
- [ ] Plan seating arrangements
- [ ] Confirm desired pictures with photographer
- [ ] Style your hair with headpiece
- [ ] Practice applying cosmetics in proper light
- [ ] Arrange for one last fitting of all wedding attire
- [ ] Make sure rings are picked up and fit properly
- [ ] Confirm receipt of marriage license
- [ ] Have rehearsal/rehearsal dinner (one or two days before wedding)
- [ ] Arrange to have the photographer and attendants arrive two hours before ceremony if there are to be pre-wedding pictures
- [ ] Arrange for music to start one half hour prior to ceremony
- [ ] Arrange to have the mother of the groom seated five minutes before ceremony
- [ ] Arrange to have the mother of the bride seated immediately before the processional
- [ ] Arrange for the aisle runner to be rolled out by the ushers immediately before the processional

On your wedding day:

- [ ] Try to relax and pamper yourself; take a long bath, have a manicure, etc.
- [ ] Eat at least one small meal; drink plenty of water
- [ ] Have your hair and makeup done a few hours before ceremony
- [ ] Start dressing one to two hours before ceremony

Wedding Budget Worksheet

Item	Projected Cost*	Deposit Paid	Balance Due	Who Pays?
Wedding Consultant				
Fee				
Tip (usually 15–20%)				
Pre-wedding Parties				
Engagement**				
Site rental				
Equipment rental				
Invitations				
Food				
Beverages				
Decorations				
Flowers				
Party favors				
Bridesmaids' party/luncheon				
Rehearsal dinner**				
Site rental				
Equipment rental				
Invitations				
Food				
Beverages				
Decorations				
Flowers				
Party favors				
Weekend wedding parties				

*(including tax, if applicable) **(if hosted by bride and groom)

Wedding Budget Worksheet (continued)

Item	Projected Cost*	Deposit Paid	Balance Due	Who Pays?
Ceremony				
Location fee				
Officiant's fee				
Donation to church (optional, amount varies)				
Organist Tip (amount varies)				
Other musicians Tip (amount varies)				
Program				
Aisle runner				
Business and Legal Matters				
Marriage license				
Blood test (if applicable)				
Wedding Jewelry				
Engagement ring				
Bride's wedding band				
Groom's wedding band				
Bride's Formalwear				
Wedding gown				
Alterations				
Undergarments (slip, bustier, hosiery, etc.)				
Headpiece				
Shoes				
Jewelry (excluding engagement and wedding rings)				

Wedding Budget Worksheet (continued)

Item	Projected Cost*	Deposit Paid	Balance Due	Who Pays?
Purse (optional)				
Cosmetics, or makeup stylist				
Hair stylist				
Going-away outfit				
Going-away accessories				
Honeymoon clothes				
Groom's Formalwear				
Tuxedo				
Shoes				
Going-away outfit				
Honeymoon clothes				
Gifts				
Bride's Attendants				
Groom's Attendants				
Bride (optional)				
Groom (optional)				
Reception				
Site rental				
Equipment rental (chairs, tent, etc.)				
Decorations				
Servers, bartenders				
Wine service for cocktail hour				
Hors d'oeuvres				
Entrees				
Meals for hired help				

Wedding Budget Worksheet (continued)

Item	Projected Cost*	Deposit Paid	Balance Due	Who Pays?
Nonalcoholic beverages				
Wine				
Champagne				
Liquor				
Dessert				
Toasting glasses				
Guest book and pen				
Place cards				
Printed napkins				
Party favors (matches, chocolates, etc.)				
Box or pouch for envelope gifts				
Tip for caterer or banquet manager (usually 15–20%)				
Tip for servers, bartenders (usually 15–20% total)				
Photography and Videography				
Engagement portrait				
Wedding portrait				
Wedding proofs				
Photographer's fee				
Wedding prints				
Album				
Mothers' albums				
Extra prints				
Videographer's fee				
Videotape				

Wedding Budget Worksheet (continued)

Item	Projected Cost*	Deposit Paid	Balance Due	Who Pays?
Reception Music				
Musicians for cocktail hour				
Tip (optional, up to 15%)				
Live band				
Tip (optional, usually $25 per band member)				
Disc jockey				
Tip (optional, usually 15–20%)				
Flowers and Decorations				
Flowers for wedding site				
Decorations for wedding site				
Bride's bouquet				
Bridesmaids' flowers				
Boutonnieres				
Corsages				
Flowers for reception site				
Potted plants				
Table centerpieces				
Head table				
Cake table				
Decorations for reception				
Wedding Invitations and Stationery				
Invitations				
Announcements				
Thank-you notes				
Calligrapher				
Postage				

Wedding Budget Worksheet (continued)

Item	Projected Cost*	Deposit Paid	Balance Due	Who Pays?
Wedding Cake				
Groom's cake				
Cake top and decorations				
Flowers for cake				
Cake serving set				
Cake boxes				
Wedding Transportation				
Limousines or rented cars				
Parking				
Tip for drivers (usually 15–20%)				
Guest Accommodations				
Guest Transportation				
Honeymoon				
Transportation				
Accommodations				
Meals				
Spending money				
Additional Expenses (list below)				
Total of All Expenses				

Newspaper Engagement Announcement Worksheet

To appear in _____ newspaper on_____.
(name of newspaper)   (date)

Names of the bride's parents:

Address: _____

Telephone number with area code: _____

Mr. and Mrs. _____ of _____
(bride's parents' names)   (their city, if out of town)

announce the engagement of their daughter, _____, to
(bride's first and middle name)

_____, the son of Mr. and Mrs. _____,
(groom's first and last name)   (groom's parents' names)

of _____. A _____ wedding is planned. (Or, No date has
(groom's parents' city)   (month/season)

been set for the wedding.)

Newspaper Wedding
Announcement Worksheet

To appear in _____ newspaper on_____.
(name of newspaper)   (date)

Name(s) of sender:

Address: _____

Telephone number with area code: _____

_____ and _____ were married at
(bride's first, middle, and maiden names)   (groom's first, middle, and last name)

_____ in _____.
(name of church or synagogue)   (town)

The bride, _____,
(optional: name change information, for example, "will continue to use her surname")

is the daughter of Mr. and Mrs. _____ of _____.
(bride's parents' names)   (their city, if out of town)

She graduated from _____ and is a/an _____
(optional: name of college or university)   (job title)

at _____. The bridegroom, son of Mr. and
(name of employer)

Mrs. _____ of _____, graduated
(groom's parents' names)   (their city, if out of town)

from _____ and is a/an _____ at
(optional: name of college or university)   (job title)

_____. The couple will live in _____ after
(name of employer)   (city or town)

a trip to _____.
(honeymoon vacation)

Bridal Attire Worksheet

Bridal Salon:

Address: | Telephone:

Salesperson: | Store hours:

Directions: | Notes:

Wedding Gown: | Description:

Manufacturer: | Style number:

Color: | Cost:

Order date: | Deposit paid: | Date:

Balance due: | Date: | Delivery date and time:

Delivery instructions/Pick-up date: | Notes:

Headpiece and veil: | Description:

Manufacturer: | Style number:

Color: | Cost:

Order date: | Deposit paid: | Date:

Balance due: | Date: | Delivery date and time:

Delivery instructions/Pick-up date: | Notes:

Accessory	Size	Color	Cost	Where Purchased (if different from above)	Picked Up?
Slip					
Bra					
Hosiery					
Garter					
Gloves					
Shoes					
Jewelry					
Other					

Bride's Attendants List

Maid/Matron of Honor:

Name: Address:

Telephone: Special duties:

Bridesmaids:

Name: Address:

Telephone: Special duties:

Name: Address:

Telephone: Special duties:

Name: Address:

Telephone: Special duties:

Name: Address:

Telephone: Special duties:

Flower Girl:

Name: Address:

Telephone: Special duties:

Other Honor Attendants:

Name: Address:

Telephone: Special duties:

Name: Address:

Telephone: Special duties:

Name: Address:

Telephone: Special duties:

Name: Address:

Telephone: Special duties:

Name: Address:

Telephone: Special duties:

Groom's Attendants List

Best Man:

Name: Address:

Telephone: Special duties:

Ushers:

Name: Address:

Telephone: Special duties:

Name: Address:

Telephone: Special duties:

Name: Address:

Telephone: Special duties:

Name: Address:

Telephone: Special duties:

Ring Bearer:

Name: Address:

Telephone: Special duties:

Other Honor Attendants:

Name: Address:

Telephone: Special duties:

Name: Address:

Telephone: Special duties:

Name: Address:

Telephone: Special duties:

Name: Address:

Telephone: Special duties:

Name: Address:

Telephone: Special duties:

Attendants' Attire Worksheet

Place of Purchase: Name:

Address: Telephone:

Salesperson: Store hours:

Directions: Notes:

Attendants' Attire:

Description of dress: Manufacturer:

Style number: Color:

Cost per dress: Number ordered:

Total cost of dresses: Order date:

Sizes ordered:

Deposit paid: Date:

Balance due: Date:

Delivery date and time:

Delivery instructions/Pick-up date:

Description of alterations: Alterations fee (**total**):

Description of accessories   Cost of accessories:
(hosiery, shoes, jewelry, etc.):

Cost of dyeing shoes (if applicable):   Color:

Notes:

Maid/Matron of Honor:

Name: Dress size:

Shoe size: Other sizes:

Fitting date #1:   Time:

Fitting date #2:   Time:

Fitting date #3:   Time:

Notes:

Attendants' Attire Worksheet (continued)

Bridesmaids:

Name:	Dress size:
Shoe size:	Other sizes:
Fitting date #1:	Time:
Fitting date #2:	Time:
Fitting date #3:	Time:
Notes:	

Name:	Dress size:
Shoe size:	Other sizes:
Fitting date #1:	Time:
Fitting date #2:	Time:
Fitting date #3:	Time:
Notes:	

Name:	Dress size:
Shoe size:	Other sizes:
Fitting date #1:	Time:
Fitting date #2:	Time:
Fitting date #3:	Time:
Notes:	

Name:	Dress size:
Shoe size:	Other sizes:
Fitting date #1:	Time:
Fitting date #2:	Time:
Fitting date #3:	Time:
Notes:	

Attendants' Attire Worksheet (continued)

Flower Girl's Attire:

Description of dress:

Manufacturer:

Style number:

Color:

Cost per dress:

Number ordered:

Total cost of dresses:

Order date:

Sizes ordered:

Deposit paid:

Date:

Balance due:

Date:

Delivery date and time:

Delivery instructions/Pick-up date:

Alterations fee (**total**):

Description of alterations:

Description of accessories (hosiery, shoes, jewelry, etc.):

Cost of accessories:

Cost of dyeing shoes (if applicable):

Color:

Notes:

Bridal Shower Guest List

Name: _____   Address: _____

Telephone: _____   RSVP Number in Party: _____

Name: _____   Address: _____

Telephone: _____   RSVP Number in Party: _____

Name: _____   Address: _____

Telephone: _____   RSVP Number in Party: _____

Name: _____   Address: _____

Telephone: _____   RSVP Number in Party: _____

Name: _____   Address: _____

Telephone: _____   RSVP Number in Party: _____

Name: _____   Address: _____

Telephone: _____   RSVP Number in Party: _____

Name: _____   Address: _____

Telephone: _____   RSVP Number in Party: _____

Name: _____   Address: _____

Telephone: _____   RSVP Number in Party: _____

Name: _____   Address: _____

Telephone: _____   RSVP Number in Party: _____

Name: _____   Address: _____

Telephone: _____   RSVP Number in Party: _____

Name: _____   Address: _____

Telephone: _____   RSVP Number in Party: _____

Name: _____   Address: _____

Telephone: _____   RSVP Number in Party: _____

Name: _____   Address: _____

Telephone: _____   RSVP Number in Party: _____

Name: _____   Address: _____

Telephone: _____   RSVP Number in Party: _____

Name: _____   Address: _____

Telephone: _____   RSVP Number in Party: _____

Bridal Shower Guest List (continued)

Name: _____   Address: _____

Telephone: _____   RSVP Number in Party: _____

Name: _____   Address: _____

Telephone: _____   RSVP Number in Party: _____

Name: _____   Address: _____

Telephone: _____   RSVP Number in Party: _____

Name: _____   Address: _____

Telephone: _____   RSVP Number in Party: _____

Name: _____   Address: _____

Telephone: _____   RSVP Number in Party: _____

Name: _____   Address: _____

Telephone: _____   RSVP Number in Party: _____

Name: _____   Address: _____

Telephone: _____   RSVP Number in Party: _____

Name: _____   Address: _____

Telephone: _____   RSVP Number in Party: _____

Name: _____   Address: _____

Telephone: _____   RSVP Number in Party: _____

Name: _____   Address: _____

Telephone: _____   RSVP Number in Party: _____

Name: _____   Address: _____

Telephone: _____   RSVP Number in Party: _____

Name: _____   Address: _____

Telephone: _____   RSVP Number in Party: _____

Name: _____   Address: _____

Telephone: _____   RSVP Number in Party: _____

Gift Registry Checklist

	Desired Quantity:	Quantity Received:	Manufacturer:	Pattern/Model:
FORMAL DINNERWARE				
Dinner plates				
Sandwich/lunch plates				
Salad/dessert plates				
Bread and butter plates				
Cups and saucers				
Rimmed soup bowls				
Soup/cereal bowls				
Fruit bowls				
Open vegetable dishes				
Covered vegetable dishes				
Gravy boat				
Sugar bowl				
Creamer				
Small platter				
Medium platter				
Large platter				
Salt and pepper shakers				
Coffeepot				
Teapot				
Butter dish				
Other:				
CASUAL DINNERWARE				
Dinner plates				
Sandwich/lunch plates				
Salad/dessert plates				

Gift Registry Checklist (continued)

	Desired Quantity:	Quantity Received:	Manufacturer:	Pattern/Model:
CASUAL DINNERWARE (cont.)				
Bread and butter plates				
Cups and saucers				
Rimmed soup bowls				
Soup/cereal bowls				
Fruit bowls				
Open vegetable dishes				
Covered vegetable dishes				
Gravy boat				
Sugar bowl				
Creamer				
Small platter				
Medium platter				
Large platter				
Salt and pepper shakers				
Coffeepot				
Butter dish				
Mugs				
Other:				
FORMAL FLATWARE				
Five-piece place setting				
Four-piece place setting				
Dinner forks				
Dinner knives				
Teaspoons				
Salad forks				

Gift Registry Checklist *(continued)*

	Desired Quantity:	Quantity Received:	Manufacturer:	Pattern/Model:
FORMAL FLATWARE (cont.)				
Soup spoons				
Butter spreader				
Butter knives				
Cold meat fork				
Sugar spoon				
Serving spoon				
Pierced spoon				
Gravy ladle				
Pie/cake server				
Hostess set				
Serve set				
Silver chest				
Other:				
CASUAL FLATWARE				
Five-piece setting				
Dinner forks				
Dinner knives				
Teaspoons				
Salad forks				
Soup spoons				
Hostess set				
Serve set				
Gravy ladle				
Cake/pie server				
Other:				

Gift Registry Checklist (continued)

	Desired Quantity:	Quantity Received:	Manufacturer:	Pattern/Model:
CRYSTAL				
Wine glasses				
Champagne flutes				
Water goblets				
Cordials				
Brandy snifters				
Decanters				
Pitchers				
Other:				
CASUAL GLASS/BARWARE				
Water glasses				
Juice glasses				
Beer mugs				
Pilsners				
Highball glasses				
Decanter				
Pitcher				
Punch bowl set				
Cocktail shaker				
Ice bucket				
Champagne cooler				
Irish coffee set				
Whiskey set				
Martini set				
Wine rack				
Bar utensils				
Other:				

Gift Registry Checklist (continued)

	Desired Quantity:	Quantity Received:	Manufacturer:	Pattern/Model:
ADDT'L SERVING PIECES				
Sugar/creamer				
Coffee service				
Serving tray				
Relish tray				
Canapé tray				
Chip and dip server				
Cheese board				
Cake plate				
Large salad bowl				
Salad bowl set				
Salad tongs				
Gravy boat				
Butter dish				
Salt and pepper shakers				
Round baker				
Rectangular baker				
Demitasse set				
Other:				
HOME DÉCOR				
Vase				
Bud vase				
Bowl				
Candlesticks				
Picture frame				
Figurine				
Clock				

Gift Registry Checklist (continued)

	Desired Quantity:	Quantity Received:	Manufacturer:	Pattern/Model:
HOME DÉCOR (cont.)				
Lamp				
Framed art				
Brass accessories				
Picnic basket				
Other:				
SMALL APPLIANCES				
Coffee maker				
Coffee grinder				
Espresso/cappuccino maker				
Food processor				
Mini processor				
Mini chopper				
Blender				
Hand mixer				
Stand mixer				
Bread baker				
Pasta machine				
Citrus juicer				
Juice extractor				
Toaster (two-slice or four-slice)				
Toaster oven				
Convection oven				
Microwave				
Electric fry pan				
Electric wok				
Electric griddle				

Gift Registry Checklist (continued)

	Desired Quantity:	Quantity Received:	Manufacturer:	Pattern/Model:
SMALL APPLIANCES (cont.)				
Sandwich maker				
Waffle maker				
Hot tray				
Indoor grill				
Crock-Pot				
Rice cooker				
Can opener				
Food slicer				
Electric knife				
Iron				
Vacuum cleaner				
Fan				
Humidifier				
Dehumidifier				
Space heater				
Other:				
CUTLERY				
Carving set				
Cutlery set				
Knife set				
Knife block				
Steel sharpener				
Boning knife (specify size)				
Paring knife (specify size)				
Chef knife (specify size)				
Bread knife (specify size)				

Gift Registry Checklist (continued)

	Desired Quantity:	Quantity Received:	Manufacturer:	Pattern/Model:
CUTLERY (cont.)				
Slicing knife (specify size)				
Carving fork				
Utility knife (specify size)				
Kitchen shears				
Cleaver				
Other:				
BAKEWARE				
Cake pan				
Cookie sheet				
Bread pan				
Muffin tin				
Cooling rack				
Bundt pan				
Springform cake pan				
Pie plate				
Roasting pan				
Pizza pan				
Covered casserole				
Soufflé dish				
Rectangular baker				
Lasagna pan				
Pizza pan				
Pizza stone				
Other:				

Gift Registry Checklist (continued)

	Desired Quantity:	Quantity Received:	Manufacturer:	Pattern/Model:
KITCHEN BASICS				
Kitchen tool set				
Canister set				
Spice rack				
Cutting board				
Salad bowl set				
Salt and pepper mill				
Kitchen towels				
Pot holders				
Apron				
Mixing bowl set				
Measuring cup set				
Rolling pin				
Cookie jar				
Tea kettle				
Coffee mugs				
Other:				
COOKWARE				
Saucepan (small)				
Saucepan (medium)				
Saucepan (large)				
Sauté pan (small)				
Sauté pan (large)				
Frying pan (small)				
Frying pan (medium)				
Frying pan (large)				

Gift Registry Checklist (continued)

	Desired Quantity:	Quantity Received:	Manufacturer:	Pattern/Model:
COOKWARE (cont.)				
Stockpot (small)				
Stockpot (large)				
Roasting pan				
Omelet pan (small)				
Omelet pan (large)				
Skillet				
Double boiler				
Steamer insert				
Wok				
Griddle				
Stir-fry pan				
Microwave cookware set				
Tea kettle				
Dutch oven				
Other:				
LUGGAGE				
Duffel bag				
Beauty case				
Carry-on tote				
Suitcases (specify quantity and sizes)				
Garment bag				
Luggage cart				
Other:				

Gift Registry Checklist (continued)

	Desired Quantity:	Quantity Received:	Manufacturer:	Pattern/Model:
HOME ELECTRONICS				
Stereo				
CD player				
Television				
VCR				
Camcorder				
Telephone				
Answering machine				
Portable stereo				
Camera				
Other:				
TABLE LINENS				
Tablecloth				
Place mats				
Napkins				
Napkin rings				
Other:				
BED LINENS				
Flat sheets (specify full, queen, or king)				
Fitted sheets (specify full, queen, or king)				
Pillowcases (specify standard or king)				
Sets of sheets (specify full, queen, or king)				

Gift Registry Checklist (continued)

	Desired Quantity:	Quantity Received:	Manufacturer:	Pattern/Model:
BED LINENS (cont.)				
Comforter				
Comforter set				
Dust ruffle				
Pillow shams				
Window treatment				
Down comforter				
Duvet cover				
Bedspread				
Quilt				
Blanket				
Electric blanket				
Cotton blanket				
Decorative pillows				
Down pillows (standard, queen, or king)				
Pillows (standard, queen, or king)				
Mattress pad				
Other:				
BATH TOWELS AND ACCESSORIES				
Bath towels				
Bath sheets				
Hand towels				
Washcloths				

Gift Registry Checklist (continued)

	Desired Quantity:	Quantity Received:	Manufacturer:	Pattern/Model:
BATH TOWELS AND ACCESSORIES (cont.)				
Fingertip towels				
Shower curtain				
Bath mat				
Bath rug				
Lid cover				
Hamper				
Scale				
Wastebasket				
Other:				
OTHER				

Shower Gift Recorder

Name	Description of Gift	Thank-you note sent?
		☐
		☐
		☐
		☐
		☐
		☐
		☐
		☐
		☐
		☐
		☐
		☐
		☐
		☐
		☐
		☐
		☐
		☐
		☐
		☐
		☐
		☐
		☐
		☐

Bride's Name and Address Change Worksheet

	Name of Institution	Notified of		
		Name Change?	Address?	Marital Status?
401k accounts				
Automotive insurance				
Bank accounts				
Billing accounts				
Car registration				
Club memberships				
Credit cards				
Dentist				
Doctors				
Driver's license				
Employment records				
Homeowner's/Renter's insurance				
IRA accounts				
Leases				
Life insurance				
Loans				
Medical insurance				
Other insurance accounts				
Passport				
Pension plan records				
Post office				
Property titles				
Safety deposit box				
School records				
Social Security				
Stocks and bonds				
Subscriptions				
Telephone listing				
Voter registration records				
Wills/Trusts				
Other (list below)				

Groom's Name and Address Change Worksheet

| | Name of Institution | Notified of | | |
		Name Change?	Address?	Marital Status?
401k accounts				
Automotive insurance				
Bank accounts				
Billing accounts				
Car registration				
Club memberships				
Credit cards				
Dentist				
Doctors				
Driver's license				
Employment records				
Homeowner's/Renter's insurance				
IRA accounts				
Leases				
Life insurance				
Loans				
Medical insurance				
Other insurance accounts				
Passport				
Pension plan records				
Post office				
Property titles				
Safety deposit box				
School records				
Social Security				
Stocks and bonds				
Subscriptions				
Telephone listing				
Voter registration records				
Wills/Trusts				
Other (list below)				

Appendix B

Vendors

Wedding Consultant Worksheet

Name:

Address:

Phone:

Contact:

Hours:

Appointments:

Date: Time:

Date: Time:

Date: Time:

Date: Time:

Service:

Number of hours:

Overtime cost:

Provides the following services:

Cost:

Fee: ☐ Flat   ☐ Hourly percentage: _____   ☐ Per guest

Total amount due: Date:

Amount of deposit: Date:

Amount due: Date:

Gratuities included?   ☐ Yes   ☐ No

Sales tax included?   ☐ Yes   ☐ No

Date contract signed:

Terms of cancellation:

Notes:

Ceremony Worksheet

Location of ceremony: .... Address: ....

Date of ceremony: .... Time of ceremony: ....

Officiant's name: .... Location fee: ....

Officiant's fee: .... Recommended church donation: ....

Wedding program available? .... Fee: ....

Part of Ceremony	Description	Notes
Processional		
Opening words		
Giving away or blessing		
Reading		
Prayers		
Marriage vows		
Exchange of rings		
Pronouncement of marriage		
Lighting of unity candle		
Benediction		
Closing words		
Recessional		
Other		

Ceremony Music Worksheet

Organist's name:

Address:

Telephone: Fee:

Soloist's name:

Address:

Telephone: Fee:

Name of other musician, if applicable:

Address:

Telephone: Fee:

Part of Ceremony	Musical Selection	Performed By
Prelude		
Processional		
During the ceremony (list specific part below)		
Recessional		
Other		

Reception Site Worksheet

Reception site: ....

Address: ....

Telephone: ....

Contact: .... Hours: ....

Appointments: ....

Date: .... Time: ....

Date: .... Time: ....

Date: .... Time: ....

Date: .... Time: ....

Total amount due: .... Date: ....

Amount of deposit: .... Date: ....

Balance due: .... Date: ....

Sales tax included? ☐ Yes ☐ No ....

Room reserved: ....

Date: .... Time: .... Number of hours: ....

Overtime cost: ....

Occupancy: ....

Final head count due date: ....

Reception location includes the following services: ....

....

Reception location includes the following equipment: ....

....

....

Terms of cancellation: ....

Other: ....

....

....

....

....

Reception Site Worksheet (continued)

Item	Description	Cost	Notes
Reception Site			
Site rental			
Overtime fee			
Other			
Equipment			
Tent			
Chairs			
Tables			
Linens			
Other			
Service			
Servers			
Bartenders			
Valet parking attendants			
Coat checkers			
Other (list below)			
Total of All Expenses:			

Reception Events Worksheet

Give a copy of this checklist to your reception site coordinator and band leader or disc jockey.

Introduce entire bridal party? ☐ Yes ☐ No Music:

Introduce only bride and groom? ☐ Yes ☐ No Music:

Parent(s) of bride:

Parent(s) of groom:

Grandparent(s) of bride:

Grandparent(s) of groom:

Flower girl(s):

Ring bearer(s):

Bridesmaids: Ushers:

Maid of honor: Best man:

Matron of honor:

Bride's first name: Groom's first name:

Bride and groom as they are to be introduced:

Receiving line at reception? ☐ Yes ☐ No When:

Music:

Blessing? ☐ Yes ☐ No By whom:

First toast? ☐ Yes ☐ No By whom:

Other toasts? ☐ Yes ☐ No By whom:

By whom:

By whom:

Reception Events Worksheet (continued)

First dance: ☐ Yes ☐ No When:

Music:

To join in first dance:
  Maid of honor and best man? ☐ Yes ☐ No
  Parents of bride and groom? ☐ Yes ☐ No
  Bridesmaids and ushers? ☐ Yes ☐ No
  Guests? ☐ Yes ☐ No

Father-daughter dance? ☐ Yes ☐ No Music:

Mother-son dance? ☐ Yes ☐ No Music:

Open dance floor for guests after first dance? ☐ Yes ☐ No

Cake-cutting? ☐ Yes ☐ No Music:

Bouquet toss? ☐ Yes ☐ No

Garter toss? ☐ Yes ☐ No

Last dance? ☐ Yes ☐ No Music:

Other event:

When: Music:

Other event:

When: Music:

Special requests and dedications:

Notes:

Caterer Worksheet

Name (if different from reception site):

Address:

Telephone:

Contact: Hours:

Appointments:

Date: Time:

Date: Time:

Date: Time:

Date of hired services:

Number of hours: Cocktail hour:

Overtime cost: Final head count due date:

Menu:

Sit down or buffet?

Includes the following services:

Includes the following equipment:

Cost:

Total amount due: Date:

Amount of deposit: Date:

Balance due: Date:

Gratuities included? ☐ Yes ☐ No   Sales tax included? ☐ Yes ☐ No

Terms of cancellation:

Notes:

Caterer Worksheet (continued)

Item	Description	Cost	Notes
Food			
Appetizers			
Entrees			
Dessert			
Other food			
Beverages			
Nonalcoholic			
Champagne			
Wine			
Liquor			
Equipment			
Tent			
Chairs			
Tables			
Linens			
Dinnerware			
Flatware			
Glassware			
Serving pieces			
Other			
Service			
Servers			
Bartenders			
Valet parking attendants			
Coat checkers			
Overtime cost			
Other			
Gratuities			
Sales tax			
Total of All Expenses:			

Menu and Beverage Worksheet

Item	Description	Cost	Notes
Appetizers			
Entrees			
Desserts (if any)			
Beverages (nonalcoholic)			
Wine			
Champagne			
Open bar			
Other			
Gratuities			
Sales tax			
Total of All Expenses:			

Equipment Rental Worksheet

Name of rental company: .... Address: ....

Telephone: .... Contact: ....

Hours: .... Order date: ....

Date: .... Time: .... ☐ Delivery? ☐ Pick up?

Special instructions: ....

Total amount due: .... Date: ....

Amount of deposit: .... Date: ....

Balance due: .... Date: ....

Cancellation policy: ....

Damaged goods policy: ....

Notes: ....

Item	Description	Quantity	Cost	Total Cost (Quantity x Cost)
Ceremony Equipment:				
Aisle runner				
Candelabra				
Canopy/Chuppah				
Lattice arch				
Microphone				
Other				
Tents:				
Size				
Size				
Flooring/Carpeting				
Lighting				
Decoration				
Other				

Equipment Rental Worksheet (continued)

Item	Description	Quantity	Cost	Total Cost (Quantity x Cost)
Chairs:				
Style				
Style				
Style				
Other				
Tables:				
Size				
Size				
Size				
Other				
Linens:				
Table				
Chair covers				
Napkins				
Other				
Dinnerware:				
Dinner plates				
Salad plates				
Bread plates				
Dessert plates				
Cake plates				
Soup bowls				
Fruit bowls				
Cups and saucers				
Other				

Equipment Rental Worksheet (continued)

Item	Description	Quantity	Cost	Total Cost (Quantity x Cost)
Flatware:				
Dinner forks				
Salad forks				
Dinner knives				
Steak knives				
Butter knives				
Spoons				
Soup spoons				
Serving spoons				
Meat forks				
Carving knives				
Cake serving set				
Other				
Glassware:				
Wine glasses				
Champagne glasses				
Water goblets				
Highball glasses				
Double rocks glasses				
Snifters				
16 oz. glasses				
8 oz. glasses				
Punch cups				
Other				

Equipment Rental Worksheet (continued)

Item	Description	Quantity	Cost	Total Cost (Quantity x Cost)
Bar Equipment:				
Ice buckets				
Ice tubs				
Bottle/can openers				
Corkscrews				
Cocktail shakers				
Stirring sticks				
Electric blenders				
Strainers				
Cocktail napkins				
Other				
Serving pieces:				
Serving trays				
Platters				
Serving bowls				
Punch bowls				
Water pitchers				
Salt and pepper sets				
Butter dishes				
Creamer/sugar sets				
Bread baskets				
Condiment trays				
Other				

Equipment Rental Worksheet (continued)

Item	Description	Quantity	Cost	Total Cost (Quantity x Cost)
Miscellaneous:				
Coffeemaker				
Insulated coffee pitchers				
Hot plates				
Microwaves				
Grill				
Coolers				
Coat racks				
Hangers				
Ashtrays				
Trash cans				
Other				
Total of All Expenses:				

Photographer Worksheet

Name of photographer/studio: ....

Address: ....

Telephone: ....

Contact: ....

Hours they can be reached: ....

Directions: ....

Appointments:

Date: .... Time: ....

Date: .... Time: ....

Date: .... Time: ....

Date: .... Time: ....

Name of package (if applicable): ....

Date of hired services: .... Time: ....

Number of hours: .... Overtime cost: ....

Travel fee: .... Fee for custom pages: ....

Fee for black and white prints: .... Fee for sepia prints: ....

Fee for album inscription: .... Additional fees (if any): ....

Engagement session included? ☐ Yes ☐ No Additional cost, if any: ....

Will attend rehearsal? ☐ Yes ☐ No Additional cost, if any: ....

Cost of film, proofing, and processing included? ☐ Yes ☐ No Additional cost, if any: ....

Type of wedding album included: .... Date proofs will be ready: ....

Date order will be ready: ....

Additional services included:

.... Cost: ....

.... Cost: ....

Total amount due: .... Date: ....

Amount of deposit: .... Date: ....

Balance due: .... Date: ....

Sales tax included? ☐ Yes ☐ No

Terms of cancellation: ....

Notes: ....

Photographer Worksheet (continued)

Included in Package:

Item	Number Included	Cost of Each Additional	Notes
8" x 10" engagement portraits			
5" x 7" engagement prints			
4" x 5" engagement prints			
Wallet-size engagement prints			
Wedding proofs			
Wallet-size prints			
3" x 5" prints			
4" x 5" prints			
5" x 7" prints			
8" x 10" prints			
11" x 14" portraits			
Other prints (list below)			
Preview album			
Wedding album			
Wedding album pages			
Parent albums			
Other (list below)			

Photographer Checklist

Give a copy of this completed form to your wedding photographer.

Name of bride and groom: Address:

Telephone: Wedding date:

Ceremony location: Reception location:

Special instructions:

Portraits:

- [ ] You and the groom during the ceremony (if possible)
- [ ] An official wedding portrait of you and your groom
- [ ] The entire wedding party
- [ ] You, your groom, and family members
- [ ] You and your mother
- [ ] You and your father
- [ ] You with both parents
- [ ] You with your groom's parents (your new in-laws)
- [ ] The groom with his mother
- [ ] The groom with his father
- [ ] The groom with both parents
- [ ] The groom with your parents (his new in-laws)
- [ ] Combination photos of the attendants
- [ ] You and your groom with any special people in your lives, such as grandparents or godparents
- [ ] Other:

Photographer Checklist (continued)

Photos from the ceremony (if possible):

- [ ] Each member of the wedding party as he or she comes down the aisle
- [ ] The mother of the bride as she is ushered down the aisle
- [ ] The groom's parents
- [ ] You and your father coming down the aisle
- [ ] Your father leaving you at the altar
- [ ] The wedding party at the altar
- [ ] The ring exchange
- [ ] The vows
- [ ] The lighting of any candles or special ceremony features
- [ ] Any relatives or friends who participate in the ceremony by doing a reading or lighting a candle
- [ ] The kiss
- [ ] The walk from the altar
- [ ] Other:

Candids:

- [ ] Getting ready for the ceremony; putting on the veil, the garter
- [ ] The bridesmaids, and you with them before the wedding
- [ ] You and your father leaving
- [ ] You and your father arriving at the ceremony
- [ ] Getting out of the limousine/car
- [ ] You and your groom getting in the car
- [ ] Toasting one another in the car
- [ ] Reception arrival
- [ ] The first dance
- [ ] The cutting of the cake
- [ ] Tossing the bouquet
- [ ] Removing/tossing the garter
- [ ] Going-away dance
- [ ] Leaving for the honeymoon (possibly with a "just married" sign on the car)
- [ ] Other:

Videographer Worksheet

Name of videographer/studio: .... Address: ....

Telephone: .... Contact: ....

Hours they can be reached: .... Directions: ....

Appointments: ....

Date: .... Time: ....

Date: .... Time: ....

Date: .... Time: ....

Date: .... Time: ....

Name of package (if applicable): ....

Date of hired services: .... Time: ....

Number of hours: .... Number of cameras: ....

Overtime cost: .... Travel fee: ....

Additional fees (if any): ....

Will attend rehearsal? ☐ Yes ☐ No   Additional cost, if any: ....

Length of videotape: ....

Date tape will be ready: ....

Videotape will include:

Pre-wedding preparations: ☐ Yes ☐ No   Notes: ....

Individual interviews with bride and groom prior to ceremony: ☐ Yes ☐ No

Notes: ....

....

Ceremony: ☐ Yes ☐ No   Notes: ....

Reception: ☐ Yes ☐ No   Notes: ....

Photo montage: ☐ Yes ☐ No   Notes: ....

Other: ....

....

....

Videographer Worksheet (continued)

Package includes:

Sound: ☐ Yes ☐ No Notes:

Music: ☐ Yes ☐ No Notes:

Unedited version of wedding events: ☐ Yes ☐ No Notes:

Edited version of wedding events: ☐ Yes ☐ No Notes:

Price of additional copies of videotape:

Other:

Additional services included:

Cost:

Cost:

Cost:

Cost:

Total amount due: Date:

Amount of deposit: Date:

Balance due: Date:

Sales tax included? ☐ Yes ☐ No

Terms of cancellation:

Notes:

Florist Worksheet

Name of florist: ....

Address: ....

Telephone: ....

Contact: ....

Hours: ....

Directions: ....

Appointments: ....

Date: ....

Time: ....

Date: ....

Time: ....

Date: ....

Time: ....

Services provided: ....

....

....

....

Date of delivery: ....

Time: ....

Location of bridal party: ....

Travel fee: ....

Additional fees (if any): ....

Cost: ....

Total amount due: ....

Date: ....

Amount of deposit: ....

Date: ....

Balance due: ....

Date: ....

Sales tax included? ☐ Yes ☐ No

Terms of cancellation: ....

Notes: ....

....

....

....

....

....

....

....

....

....

Reception Music Worksheet

Name of band/DJ: .... Address: ....

Telephone: .... Manager/contact: ....

Hours he or she can be reached: .... Number of performers: ....

Description of act: ....

Demo tape available? .... ☐ Yes ☐ No

Notes: ....

View live performance? .... ☐ Yes ☐ No

Date: .... Time: .... Location: ....

Appointments: ....

Date: .... Time: ....

Date: .... Time: ....

Date: .... Time: ....

Date of hired services: .... Time: ....

Number of hours: .... Cocktail hour: ....

Overtime cost: ....

Includes the following services: ....

Equipment provided: .... Equipment rented: ....

Rental costs: ....

Total amount due: .... Date: ....

Amount of deposit: .... Date: ....

Balance due: .... Date: ....

Sales tax included? ☐ Yes ☐ No

Terms of cancellation: ....

Notes: ....

....

....

....

....

Wedding Party Flowers Worksheet

Person/Item	Description	Quantity	Cost
Bride:			
Bouquet			
Headpiece			
Toss-away bouquet			
Going-away corsage			
Maid/Matron of honor:			
Bouquet			
Headpiece			
Bridesmaids:			
Bouquet			
Headpiece			
Flower Girl(s):			
Flowers			
Basket			
Headpiece			
Mothers of the bride and groom:			
Corsage			
Grandmothers of the bride and groom:			
Corsage			
Groom:			
Boutonniere			
Best man:			
Boutonniere			

Wedding Party Flowers Worksheet (continued)

Person/Item	Description	Quantity	Cost
Ushers:			
Boutonniere			
Ring bearer:			
Boutonniere			
Pillow			
Fathers of the bride and groom:			
Boutonniere			
Grandfathers (bride and groom):			
Boutonniere			
Readers:			
Corsage			
Boutonniere			
Other (list below)			
Total of All Expenses:			

Ceremony Flowers and Decorations Worksheet

Item	Description	Quantity	Cost
Aisle runner			
Altar flowers			
Garland			
Potted flowers			
Potted plants			
Pews/chair flowers			
Pews/chair bows			
Candelabra			
Candle holders			
Candles			
Unity candle			
Wedding arch			
Columns			
Trellis			
Wreaths for church doors			
Other (list below)			
Total:			

Reception Flowers and Decorations Worksheet

Item	Description	Quantity	Cost
Guest tables:			
Centerpieces			
Garland			
Candles			
Head table:			
Centerpieces			
Garland			
Candles			
Buffet table:			
Flowers			
Garland			
Decorations			
Cake table:			
Cake top			
Flowers			
Garland			
Decorations			
Guest book table:			
Flowers			
Decorations			

Reception Flowers and Decorations Worksheet (continued)

Item	Description	Quantity	Cost
Envelope table:			
Flowers			
Decorations			
Candelabra			
Candle holders			
Candles			
Archway:			
Columns			
Trellis			
Wreaths			
Garlands			
Potted flowers			
Potted plants			
Hanging plants			
Other (list below)			
Total:			

Baker Worksheet

Name of bakery: Address:

Telephone: Contact:

Hours: Directions:

Appointments:

Date: Time:

Date: Time:

Date: Time:

Order date:

Delivery/Pick-up date: Time:

Delivery/Pick-up instructions: Cost:

Total amount due: Date:

Amount of deposit: Date:

Balance due: Date:

Sales tax included?   ☐ Yes   ☐ No

Terms of cancellation:

Notes:

Wedding Cake Worksheet

Item	Description	Cost
Wedding cake:		
Size		
Shape		
Number of tiers		
Number cake will serve		
Flavor of cake		
Flavor of filling		
Flavor of icing		
Icing decorations		
Cake top		
Cake decorations		
Other		
Groom's cake:		
Size		
Shape		
Number cake will serve		
Flavor		
Icing		
Cake top		
Cake decorations		
Other		
Cake serving set		
Cake boxes		
Delivery charge		
Other		
Total:		

Transportation Worksheet

Name of company: .... Address: ....

Telephone: .... Contact: ....

Hours: .... Directions: ....

Services provided: ....

....

....

....

....

....

....

....

....

....

....

....

Number of vehicles rented: ....

Description: .... Cost per hour: ....

Minimum number of hours: .... Overtime cost: ....

Hours of rental: .... Name of driver(s): ....

Cost: ....

Total amount due: .... Date: ....

Amount of deposit: .... Date: ....

Balance due: .... Date: ....

Sales tax included? ☐ Yes ☐ No

Terms of cancellation: ....

Stationery Worksheet

Name of Stationer: Address:

Telephone: Contact:

Hours: Directions:

Appointments:

Time: Date:

Time: Date:

Time: Date:

Wedding Invitations:

Description: Manufacturer:

Style: Paper:

Paper color: Typeface:

Ink color: Printing process:

Tissue paper inserts: Printed outer envelopes:

Inner envelopes: Envelope liner:

Number ordered: Cost:

Reception Cards:

Description: Number ordered:

Cost:

Response Cards:

Description: Printed envelopes:

Envelope liner: Number ordered:

Cost:

Stationery Worksheet (continued)

Ceremony Cards:

Description: Number ordered:

Cost:

Pew Cards:

Description: Number ordered:

Cost:

Rain Cards:

Description: Number ordered:

Cost:

Travel Cards/Maps:

Description: Number ordered:

Cost:

Wedding Announcements:

Description: Printed envelopes:

Envelope liner: Number ordered:

Cost:

At-home Cards:

Description: Printed envelopes:

Envelope liner: Number ordered:

Cost:

Thank-you Notes:

Description: Printed envelopes:

Envelope liner: Number ordered:

Cost:

Stationery Worksheet (continued)

Ceremony Programs:

Description: _____ Number ordered: _____

Cost: _____

Party Favors:

Description: _____ Number ordered: _____

Cost: _____

Other:

Description: _____ Number ordered: _____

Cost: _____

Order date: _____ Ready date: _____ Time: _____

Delivery/Pick-up instructions: _____

Description: _____ Number ordered: _____

Cost: _____

Order date: _____ Ready date: _____ Time: _____

Delivery/Pick-up instructions: _____

Description: _____ Number ordered: _____

Cost: _____

Order date: _____ Ready date: _____ Time: _____

Delivery/Pick-up instructions: _____

Cost

Total amount due: _____ Date: _____

Amount of deposit: _____ Date: _____

Balance due: _____ Date: _____

Sales tax included? ☐ Yes ☐ No

Terms of cancellation: _____

Rehearsal Dinner Worksheet

Wedding Rehearsal:

Location:

Telephone:

Contact:

Date:

Time:

Directions:

Notes:

Dinner:

Location:

Telephone:

Contact:

Date:

Time:

Directions:

Number of Guests:

Menu:

Beverages:

Notes:

Guest Accommodations Worksheet

Be sure to give a copy of this to your mother, maid/matron of honor, and anyone else guests may contact for information about accommodations.

Blocks of Rooms Reserved for Wedding at:

Hotel:

Address:

Directions:

Approximate distance from ceremony site: Reception site:

Telephone:

Toll-free reservations number:

Fax number:

Contact:

Number of single rooms reserved in block: Daily rate:

Number of double rooms reserved in block: Daily rate:

Total number of rooms reserved in block:

Date(s) reserved:

Cut-off/Last-day reservations accepted:

Terms of agreement:

Payment procedure:

Notes:

Hotel:

Address:

Directions:

Approximate distance from ceremony site: Reception site:

Telephone:

Toll-free reservations number:

Fax number:

Contact:

Honeymoon Budget Worksheet

Item	Description	Projected Cost	Actual Cost	Balance Due
Transportation				
Airfare				
Car rental				
Moped rental				
Bike rental				
Train pass				
Taxi				
Parking fees				
Other				
Accommodations				
Wedding night				
Honeymoon destination				
Other				
Food				
Meal plan				
Meals				
Drinks				
Entertainment				
Souvenirs				
Spending money				
Tips				
Other				
Total:				

Travel Services Worksheet

Travel Agency:

Address: Telephone:

Fax number: Contact:

Hours: Directions:

Notes:

Car Rental Agency:

Address: Telephone:

Fax number: Contact:

Hours:

Description of reserved vehicle (make/model):

Terms:

Notes:

Transportation:

Destination:	Destination:
Carrier:	Carrier:
Flight/Route:	Flight/Route:
Departure date:	Departure date:
Time:	Time:
Arrival date:	Arrival date:
Time:	Time:
Confirmation number:	Confirmation number:
Date:	Date:
Notes:	Notes:

Travel Services Worksheet (continued)

Accommodations:

Hotel:	Address:
Telephone:	Fax number:
Check-in date:	Time:
Check-out date:	Time:
Type of room:	Daily rate:
Total cost:	Confirmation number:
Date:	
Notes:	

Hotel:	Address:
Telephone:	Fax number:
Check-in date:	Time:
Check-out date:	Time:
Type of room:	Daily rate:
Total cost:	Confirmation number:
Date:	
Notes:	

Hotel:	Address:
Telephone:	Fax number:
Check-in date:	Time:
Check-out date:	Time:
Type of room:	Daily rate:
Total cost:	Confirmation number:
Date:	
Notes:	

Index

THE **EVERYTHING** SERIES!

BUSINESS & PERSONAL FINANCE

Everything® Budgeting Book
Everything® Business Planning Book
Everything® Coaching and Mentoring Book
Everything® Fundraising Book
Everything® Get Out of Debt Book
Everything® Grant Writing Book
Everything® Homebuying Book, 2nd Ed.
Everything® Homeselling Book
Everything® Home-Based Business Book
Everything® Investing Book
Everything® Landlording Book
Everything® Leadership Book
Everything® Managing People Book
Everything® Negotiating Book
Everything® Online Business Book
Everything® Personal Finance Book
Everything® Personal Finance in Your
    20s & 30s Book
Everything® Project Management Book
Everything® Real Estate Investing Book
Everything® Robert's Rules Book, $7.95
Everything® Selling Book
Everything® Start Your Own Business Book
Everything® Time Management Book
Everything® Wills & Estate Planning Book

COOKING

Everything® Barbecue Cookbook
Everything® Bartender's Book, $9.95
Everything® Chinese Cookbook
Everything® Chocolate Cookbook
Everything® College Cookbook
Everything® Cookbook
Everything® Dessert Cookbook
Everything® Diabetes Cookbook
Everything® Easy Gourmet Cookbook
Everything® Fondue Cookbook
Everything® Grilling Cookbook

Everything® Healthy Meals in Minutes
    Cookbook
Everything® Holiday Cookbook
Everything® Indian Cookbook
Everything® Low-Carb Cookbook
Everything® Low-Fat High-Flavor Cookbook
Everything® Low-Salt Cookbook
Everything® Meals for a Month Cookbook
Everything® Mediterranean Cookbook
Everything® Mexican Cookbook
Everything® One-Pot Cookbook
Everything® Pasta Cookbook
Everything® Quick Meals Cookbook
Everything® Slow Cooker Cookbook
Everything® Soup Cookbook
Everything® Thai Cookbook
Everything® Vegetarian Cookbook
Everything® Wine Book

HEALTH

Everything® Alzheimer's Book
Everything® Anti-Aging Book
Everything® Diabetes Book
Everything® Hypnosis Book
Everything® Low Cholesterol Book
Everything® Massage Book
Everything® Menopause Book
Everything® Nutrition Book
Everything® Reflexology Book
Everything® Stress Management Book

HISTORY

Everything® American Government Book
Everything® American History Book
Everything® Civil War Book
Everything® Irish History & Heritage Book
Everything® Middle East Book

HOBBIES & GAMES

Everything® Blackjack Strategy Book
Everything® Brain Strain Book, $9.95
Everything® Bridge Book
Everything® Candlemaking Book
Everything® Card Games Book
Everything® Cartooning Book
Everything® Casino Gambling Book, 2nd Ed.
Everything® Chess Basics Book
Everything® Crossword and Puzzle Book
Everything® Crossword Challenge Book
Everything® Cryptograms Book, $9.95
Everything® Digital Photography Book
Everything® Drawing Book
Everything® Easy Crosswords Book
Everything® Family Tree Book
Everything® Games Book, 2nd Ed.
Everything® Knitting Book
Everything® Knots Book
Everything® Motorcycle Book
Everything® Online Genealogy Book
Everything® Photography Book
Everything® Poker Strategy Book
Everything® Pool & Billiards Book
Everything® Quilting Book
Everything® Scrapbooking Book
Everything® Sewing Book
Everything® Woodworking Book
Everything® Word Games Challenge Book

HOME IMPROVEMENT

Everything® Feng Shui Book
Everything® Feng Shui Decluttering Book, $9.95
Everything® Fix-It Book
Everything® Homebuilding Book
Everything® Landscaping Book
Everything® Lawn Care Book
Everything® Organize Your Home Book

All Everything® books are priced at $12.95 or $14.95, unless otherwise stated. Prices subject to change without notice.

EVERYTHING® KIDS' BOOKS

All titles are $6.95

Everything® Kids' Animal Puzzle & Activity Book
Everything® Kids' Baseball Book, 3rd Ed.
Everything® Kids' Bible Trivia Book
Everything® Kids' Bugs Book
Everything® Kids' Christmas Puzzle & Activity Book
Everything® Kids' Cookbook
Everything® Kids' Halloween Puzzle & Activity Book
Everything® Kids' Hidden Pictures Book
Everything® Kids' Joke Book
Everything® Kids' Knock Knock Book
Everything® Kids' Math Puzzles Book
Everything® Kids' Mazes Book
Everything® Kids' Money Book
Everything® Kids' Monsters Book
Everything® Kids' Nature Book
Everything® Kids' Puzzle Book
Everything® Kids' Riddles & Brain Teasers Book
Everything® Kids' Science Experiments Book
Everything® Kids' Sharks Book
Everything® Kids' Soccer Book
Everything® Kids' Travel Activity Book

KIDS' STORY BOOKS

Everything® Bedtime Story Book
Everything® Bible Stories Book
Everything® Fairy Tales Book

LANGUAGE

Everything® Conversational Japanese Book (with CD), $19.95
Everything® French Phrase Book, $9.95
Everything® French Verb Book, $9.95
Everything® Inglés Book
Everything® Learning French Book
Everything® Learning German Book
Everything® Learning Italian Book
Everything® Learning Latin Book
Everything® Learning Spanish Book
Everything® Sign Language Book
Everything® Spanish Grammar Book
Everything® Spanish Phrase Book, $9.95
Everything® Spanish Verb Book, $9.95

MUSIC

Everything® Drums Book (with CD), $19.95
Everything® Guitar Book
Everything® Home Recording Book
Everything® Playing Piano and Keyboards Book
Everything® Reading Music Book (with CD), $19.95
Everything® Rock & Blues Guitar Book (with CD), $19.95
Everything® Songwriting Book

NEW AGE

Everything® Astrology Book
Everything® Dreams Book, 2nd Ed.
Everything® Ghost Book
Everything® Love Signs Book, $9.95
Everything® Meditation Book
Everything® Numerology Book
Everything® Paganism Book
Everything® Palmistry Book
Everything® Psychic Book
Everything® Reiki Book
Everything® Spells & Charms Book
Everything® Tarot Book
Everything® Wicca and Witchcraft Book

PARENTING

Everything® Baby Names Book
Everything® Baby Shower Book
Everything® Baby's First Food Book
Everything® Baby's First Year Book
Everything® Birthing Book
Everything® Breastfeeding Book
Everything® Father-to-Be Book
Everything® Father's First Year Book
Everything® Get Ready for Baby Book
Everything® Getting Pregnant Book
Everything® Homeschooling Book
Everything® Parent's Guide to Children with ADD/ADHD
Everything® Parent's Guide to Children with Asperger's Syndrome
Everything® Parent's Guide to Children with Autism
Everything® Parent's Guide to Children with Dyslexia
Everything® Parent's Guide to Positive Discipline

Everything® Parent's Guide to Raising a Successful Child
Everything® Parent's Guide to Tantrums
Everything® Parent's Guide to the Overweight Child
Everything® Parenting a Teenager Book
Everything® Potty Training Book, $9.95
Everything® Pregnancy Book, 2nd Ed.
Everything® Pregnancy Fitness Book
Everything® Pregnancy Nutrition Book
Everything® Pregnancy Organizer, $15.00
Everything® Toddler Book
Everything® Tween Book
Everything® Twins, Triplets, and More Book

PETS

Everything® Cat Book
Everything® Dachshund Book, $12.95
Everything® Dog Book
Everything® Dog Health Book
Everything® Dog Training and Tricks Book
Everything® Golden Retriever Book, $12.95
Everything® Horse Book
Everything® Labrador Retriever Book, $12.95
Everything® Poodle Book, $12.95
Everything® Pug Book, $12.95
Everything® Puppy Book
Everything® Rottweiler Book, $12.95
Everything® Tropical Fish Book

REFERENCE

Everything® Car Care Book
Everything® Classical Mythology Book
Everything® Computer Book
Everything® Divorce Book
Everything® Einstein Book
Everything® Etiquette Book
Everything® Great Thinkers Book
Everything® Mafia Book
Everything® Philosophy Book
Everything® Psychology Book
Everything® Shakespeare Book

RELIGION

Everything® Angels Book
Everything® Bible Book
Everything® Buddhism Book
Everything® Catholicism Book

All Everything® books are priced at $12.95 or $14.95, unless otherwise stated. Prices subject to change without notice.

Everything® Christianity Book
Everything® Jewish History & Heritage Book
Everything® Judaism Book
Everything® Koran Book
Everything® Prayer Book
Everything® Saints Book
Everything® Torah Book
Everything® Understanding Islam Book
Everything® World's Religions Book
Everything® Zen Book

SCHOOL & CAREERS

Everything® After College Book
Everything® Alternative Careers Book
Everything® College Survival Book, 2nd Ed.
Everything® Cover Letter Book, 2nd Ed.
Everything® Get-a-Job Book
Everything® Job Interview Book
Everything® New Teacher Book
Everything® Online Job Search Book
Everything® Paying for College Book
Everything® Practice Interview Book
Everything® Resume Book, 2nd Ed.
Everything® Study Book

SELF-HELP

Everything® Dating Book
Everything® Great Sex Book
Everything® Kama Sutra Book
Everything® Self-Esteem Book

SPORTS & FITNESS

Everything® Fishing Book
Everything® Fly-Fishing Book
Everything® Golf Instruction Book
Everything® Pilates Book
Everything® Running Book
Everything® Total Fitness Book
Everything® Weight Training Book
Everything® Yoga Book

TRAVEL

Everything® Family Guide to Hawaii
Everything® Family Guide to New York City, 2nd Ed.
Everything® Family Guide to RV Travel & Campgrounds
Everything® Family Guide to the Walt Disney World Resort®, Universal Studios®, and Greater Orlando, 4th Ed.
Everything® Family Guide to Washington D.C., 2nd Ed.
Everything® Guide to Las Vegas
Everything® Guide to New England
Everything® Travel Guide to the Disneyland Resort®, California Adventure®, Universal Studios®, and the Anaheim Area

WEDDINGS

Everything® Bachelorette Party Book, $9.95
Everything® Bridesmaid Book, $9.95
Everything® Creative Wedding Ideas Book
Everything® Elopement Book, $9.95
Everything® Father of the Bride Book, $9.95
Everything® Groom Book, $9.95
Everything® Mother of the Bride Book, $9.95
Everything® Wedding Book, 3rd Ed.
Everything® Wedding Checklist, $9.95
Everything® Wedding Etiquette Book, $7.95
Everything® Wedding Organizer, $15.00
Everything® Wedding Shower Book, $7.95
Everything® Wedding Vows Book, $9.95
Everything® Weddings on a Budget Book, $9.95

WRITING

Everything® Creative Writing Book
Everything® Get Published Book
Everything® Grammar and Style Book
Everything® Guide to Writing a Book Proposal
Everything® Guide to Writing a Novel
Everything® Guide to Writing Children's Books
Everything® Screenwriting Book
Everything® Writing Poetry Book
Everything® Writing Well Book

· ·

We have Everything® for the beginning crafter!
All titles are $14.95.

Everything® Crafts—Baby Scrapbooking
1-59337-225-6

Everything® Crafts—Bead Your Own Jewelry
1-59337-142-X

Everything® Crafts—Create Your Own Greeting Cards
1-59337-226-4

Everything® Crafts—Easy Projects
1-59337-298-1

Everything® Crafts—Making Cards with Rubber Stamps
1-59337-299-X

Everything® Crafts—Polymer Clay for Beginners
1-59337-230-2

Everything® Crafts—Rubber Stamping Made Easy
1-59337-229-9

Everything® Crafts—Wedding Decorations and Keepsakes
1-59337-227-2

Available wherever books are sold!
To order, call 800-872-5627, or visit us at *www.everything.com*.
Everything® and everything.com® are registered trademarks of F+W Publications, Inc.